The Orphan Country

The Orphan Country

Children of Scotland's Broken Homes from 1845 to the Present Day

LYNN ABRAMS

JOHN DONALD PUBLISHERS LTD
EDINBURGH

ISBN 0 85976 497 4

British Library Cataloguing in Publication Data.

A catalogue record for this book is available
from the British Library.

Typesetting & origination by Brinnoven, Livingston.
Printed & bound in Great Britain by Bell & Bain Ltd, Glasgow.

VII; 3; 9-10 _-20 ; 26-9; 40

204

CONTENTS

PREFACE

This book is about the consequences of family crisis and breakdown. It focuses on the most vulnerable victims of that crisis, children, and the means by which Scottish society has sought to protect and care for them for more than 150 years. In the late twentieth century the child welfare system is something of which few of us have any direct experience. Although there are around 12,000 children in Scotland today officially in the care of local authorities, only a minority of these are living apart from their natural families and a tiny proportion stay in children's homes. This is a modern phenomenon. From the mid-nineteenth century through to the Second World War the child care services played a significant and active role in Scottish family life. Families battered and sometimes torn apart by death, illness, poverty and cruelty were no strangers to the parish inspector, 'the cruelty' and the local children's home. Such was the scale of urban and rural deprivation that the child care services were used as a temporary prop by families unable to cope. And the Scottish preference for boarding out meant that rural communities all over the country were populated by children sent away from the slums to start a fresh life with a new family. Undoubtedly then, a high proportion of Scots before World War Two had first hand experience of the child care system and during the war, as a result of evacuation, many more came face to face with children separated from their parents on a mass scale.

At the end of the twentieth century child welfare is back on the agenda for a different reason. Although a much smaller proportion of children today end up 'in care', the fact that hardly a week passes without a new child abuse scandal hitting the headlines has pushed the issue of how our society cares for its children to the forefront of public debate. Children are news. As a result, the stigma of care is lifting and individuals who experienced the system are beginning to talk more openly about their childhood. This book has undoubtedly benefited from that openness.

In the 1930s my father, his twin brother and another younger brother were placed in a children's home in the south of England while their mother was confined during one of her nine pregnancies. The family lived on a farm some distance from social amenities and there was no-one to look after the young boys. Their stay was short — around six months — the home was strict but they were well treated and the three boys returned home seemingly no worse for the experience. This kind of respite care in a children's home was common at that time. While writing this book I have often thought about my father's brief experience 'in care' and throughout I have attempted to adopt what might be called a child-centred perspective, both respectful of and sympathetic to the child's point of view. At the heart of this book, therefore, are the memories of those who spent part or all of their childhood in care. Special thanks go to all the people who gave up their time to talk to me and to write to me about years spent in foster care and children's homes across Scotland. The emotions evoked by these reminiscences were predictably varied. Painful and unhappy memories sat side by side with recollections of kindness and affection. I am indebted to all of those who shared with me their very personal memories and I trust I have reproduced their accounts with sensitivity and integrity.

When I moved to Scotland in 1995 I had no immediate plans to 'go native'. However, having almost by chance embarked upon this journey into a neglected area of Scottish social history, I have been grateful for the unselfish assistance provided by numerous people who are better versed in the history of this country. George Dixon of Stirling Archive Services introduced me to a treasure trove of documents relating to the local children's home and pointed me in the direction of more. At Quarrier's Homes, Bill Dunbar generously permitted me open access to the rich records of the Orphan Homes of Scotland and Zoe White did the same at Aberlour Child Care Trust in Stirling. At Speyside High School in Aberlour, built close to the site of the former orphanage, Ian Morrison kindly allowed me to trawl the materials gathered by a school project. Eric Mackenzie, formerly an inspector with Glasgow Corporation, shared his memories with me and put me in touch with a number of former 'boarded-outs'. John Powles at Glasgow Caledonian University guided me through the rich archive of the RSSPCC and at the Heatherbank Museum of Social Work Alan helped me to find many of the photographs which enliven this book. I would also like to thank Glasgow City Council

Department of Social Work and Children 1st for permission to consult sensitive archival materials, and BBC Scotland for permission to reproduce broadcast materials.

I have also incurred numerous personal debts along the way. Friends at the Universities of Lancaster and Glasgow have remained interested in and supportive of this foray into the social history of Scotland. Sarah Barber, Chris Black, Stephen Pumfrey and Mike Winstanley offered ideas and moral support in equal measure. Callum Brown, Steve Constantin and Frank Savage commented on parts or all of the manuscript and helped to make this a better book. The project would not have been started, let alone finished, without Callum. In his unofficial capacity as my advisor on Scottish history and geography his assistance has been invaluable. I have benefited greatly from his frank and constructive criticism of the text, not to mention his number-crunching skills. This book is dedicated to my 'families' north and south of the border.

L.A.

ABBREVIATIONS

BPP	British Parliamentary Papers
GCA	Glasgow City Archives
GCU	Glasgow Caledonian University
OHS	Orphan Homes of Scotland
RSSPCC	Royal Scottish Society for the Prevention of Cruelty to Children
SAS	Stirling Archive Services
SNSPCC	Scottish National Society for the Prevention of Cruelty to Children
SRO	Scottish Register Office

CHAPTER 1
THE HOMELESS CHILD

Annie is an orphan, her mother died three years last March and her father 6 weeks ago. He was a decent man, a french polisher by trade but ill health reduced the family very low. The step mother is a decent woman but having four other children to keep besides being out working all day she could not attend or manage Annie who was fond of having her own way. An aunt in Govan kept the girl for a time but could not manage her either as she ran away several times.

— Case of Annie Campbell:
Quarrier's Homes, 1875.

Social Crisis — Family Breakdown?

The case of orphan Annie Campbell, who was admitted to Quarrier's Homes near Glasgow in 1875 at the age of 10, is typical of the child who was placed in care in the nineteenth century. Her story was replicated over and over again throughout Scotland as families cracked under the strain of poverty, illness and death. This book is about children like orphan Annie who were the innocent victims of family crisis. It traces their journey into care, their separation from cultural roots and their experiences with substitute families. It is a book about children like twins Aleck and Peter McIntosh who were admitted to the Whinwell Children's Home in Stirling in the summer of 1902. They were the youngest in the family and had been removed from their house in the Castlehill district of the town upon the recommendation of a Stirling parish council inspector who observed:

The house is in a filthy condition and pervaded by a horrible stench. The floor is covered in filth of all kinds including the excreta of animals and human beings. The house consists of one room about 14 by 12 feet and 6 feet high. The inhabitants are — the mother, five children and an old man lodger. The children are illfed, illclad and in a filthy condition. I consider it not fit for human habitation and that the mother is not giving proper attention to the children.[1]

The mother of the boys had clearly been left alone to provide for the family and was unable to cope. The boys remained at the Whinwell Home until September 1905 when they were removed to their mother's parish of settlement in Inverness and, in line with the usual practice of poor law authorities, they were boarded out with foster parents. However, this was to be just another temporary home. Six years later Aleck and Peter, now almost 14 years of age, left Inverness for Liverpool. The Scottish National Society for the Prevention of Cruelty to Children (SNSPCC) had arranged for them to join a child emigration party to Canada, a fate shared by thousands of other homeless boys and girls. Nothing more is known about their fate.

Children were the most vulnerable victims of family breakdown. In the absence of material or emotional sustenance, shelter or adequate supervision arising from a variety of circumstances including unemployment, poverty, poor housing, death of a parent as well as neglect, cruelty and desertion, the care and protection of children passed from the responsibility of the immediate family to a variety of agencies: the parish which administered poor relief, charitable and philanthropic bodies and institutions which provided residential care and facilitated adoption and emigration, and individuals who opted to foster boarded-out children. Although poverty and destitution were common enough in urban Britain and Europe for much of the nineteenth century, these children's experiences — both before their homeless status and during their care — are probably distinctive to Scotland, especially in the period before the First World War. As we shall see, the Scottish family suffered more than most. Scotland was a country in which the social consequences of industrialisation, urbanisation, rural depopulation and poverty were of unparalleled intensity. The stability and survival of the lower-class family on the croft, in the village, in the fast-growing towns as well as the cities of Glasgow, Edinburgh, Aberdeen and Dundee were challenged by working conditions amongst the most brutal and dangerous in the British Isles, a low-wage and seasonal economy, high mortality rates, and intense overcrowding. In the absence of a comprehensive welfare safety-net many families could not survive intact. In urban and rural parts of the country the family could frequently be described as broken, dysfunctional and fractured. Families expanded and contracted according to the

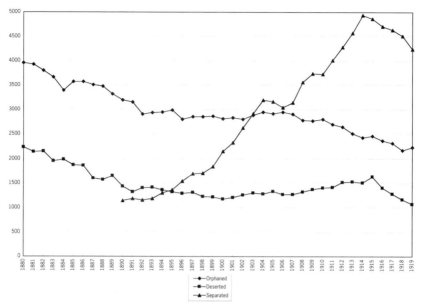

Figure 1.1. Number of Orphaned, Deserted and Separated Children under Poor Law Care, Scotland 1890–1914.

Note: the category 'separated from parents' was not counted separately until 1890.

Source: Annual Reports of the Board of Supervision for Scotland and the Local Government Board for Scotland.

availability of employment, the quality of housing and the health of parents and kin. And it was the children who were frequently the innocent victims of family crisis; boarded out with relatives, neighbours or employers when parents were no longer able to cope; placed in institutions for short periods at times of intense pressure; removed from their parents by the state or, in the event of the death of one or both parents, desertion or alleged neglect and cruelty, found more permanent homes, often far away from their place of birth. In the decades prior to the First World War at any one time the number of children in the care of one of the child welfare providers in Scotland probably exceeded 10,000.[2] Since children in voluntary homes, shelters and those privately fostered and adopted went unrecorded the true figure is impossible to estimate. By far the largest number, as Figure 1.1 shows, were those children in receipt of parish relief — pauper children — and between 1890 and 1914 the number of this group increased so that by 1914 almost 9,000 were supported in this way.

Moreover, the profile of child paupers changed over time; on the eve of the First World War the largest proportion were no longer orphans or even deserted children but those who had been separated — by the poor law authorities — from their natural family.[3]

The economic, social and structural crisis wrought by the Industrial Revolution in Scotland should not be underestimated. There is no doubt that the material conditions in which the family struggled for survival, both in the towns and rural areas, were qualitatively worse than the situation prevailing in England. By the 1840s the speed of urban expansion and the failure to provide the most basic of civic amenities combined to herald an unprecedented social crisis in Scottish towns and cities. By 1850 almost one third of Scots lived in towns with 10,000 inhabitants or more and by 1911 the four cities of Glasgow, Edinburgh, Dundee and Aberdeen contained 30 per cent of the Scottish population. 'Town expansion was...altogether more abrupt and swift [than in England] and was therefore more likely to inflict much greater strain and pressure on urban social relationships...'[4] Contemporary descriptions of urban squalor presented a disturbing picture of an environment in which children were the most likely to suffer. In 1878 Robert Louis Stevenson penned his famous essay on Edinburgh which highlighted the extremes of poverty and wealth in that fair city. 'In one house, perhaps, two-score families herd together', he wrote of the High Street:

> and perhaps, not one of them is wholly out of the reach of want. The great hotel is given over to discomfort from the foundation to the chimney-tops: everywhere a pinching, narrow habit, scanty meals, and an air of sluttishness and dirt...High words are audible from dwelling to dwelling and children have a strange experience from the first: only a robust soul, you would think, could grow up in such conditions without hurt.[5]

In turn, the demands of towns and cities had a profound impact on the social structure of rural communities in the Highlands and Lowlands. Rural overpopulation and the Clearances had already led to mass migration of the displaced peoples to new communities, often along the coasts, or to Scotland's industrialising areas or overseas, and this movement of people continued throughout the nineteenth century. In-migration of Irish also influenced the social milieu in Glasgow and Paisley and the Clyde towns such as

Group of boys playing in sewage, Molindinar burn, Glasgow, c. 1916.
Courtesy of Glasgow City Archives (Libraries and Archives).

Greenock, with the numbers increasing after the potato famine of
1846. In 1851 8.2 per cent of Glasgow's population had been born
in Ireland and it was well documented that this group,
concentrated in the poorest part of the city, endured more severe
social conditions than natives of Scotland.[6] Poor material
circumstances undoubtedly affected the ability of families to
provide for and protect their children and although the precise
nature of the relationship between poverty and child neglect is
still debated, overcrowding and insanitary conditions combined
with unstable employment and low wages for men and women
certainly meant working-class parents were frequently unable to
guarantee the material and moral welfare of their children for short
periods. Such was the opinion expressed in Edwin Chadwick's
1842 report which highlighted the inability of the weakest in
society — women and children — to fend for themselves. In
Greenock, described as 'notoriously the dirtiest town in the west
of Scotland', the local doctor described how when:

> I was passing one of the poorest districts not long ago, a little girl
> ran after me and requested me to come and see her mother as she
> could not keep her in bed; I found the mother lying in a miserable

straw bed with a piece of carpet for covering, delirious from fever; the husband, who was a drunkard, had died in the hospital of the same disease. There was no fire in the grate, some of the children were out begging, and the two youngest were crawling on the wet floor...None of the neighbours would enter the house; the children were actually starving, and the mother was dying without any attendance whatever.[7]

One of the most distinctive features of Scotland's transition to an industrial economy was the level of overcrowding experienced by the urban working-class population. In 1901 around half of Scots were housed in dwellings of one or two rooms and 11 per cent lived in one-roomed homes; the notorious 'single-end' — one small room in a four-storey tenement containing kitchen and sleeping accommodation — was roundly condemned but continued to house a large proportion of Glasgow families. In 1880 25 per cent of them were living in one-apartment accommodation and many of these also housed a lodger to help pay the rent. Twenty per cent of these single-ends were occupied by five or more persons in 1911 and the vast majority of their inhabitants shared sanitary facilities.[8] Immigrants from Ireland, the Highlands and other parts of Scotland, often unable to find work and ineligible for poor relief, congregated in Glasgow's slum housing making these parts of the city centres of destitution. On the eve of the First World War more than 50 per cent of Scottish housing was still of the one or two roomed variety, comparing unfavourably with the English figure of 7.1 per cent.[9] In Scotland as a whole 45 per cent of the population lived in overcrowded housing which was five times the proportion of English — nine per cent — who suffered similar conditions.[10] Tenement living typically provided less space than the standard English terraced house, especially for activities such as washing, drying, working and playing.[11] Tenements facilitated close communities and neighbourliness but they were crowded, dark and unhealthy.

Such low standards of housing in Scotland inevitably had a deleterious effect on child health and development. Overcrowded accommodation with deficient lighting, ventilation and sanitation produced children more prone to ear, nose and throat defects, respiratory diseases, visual impairments and specific urban conditions such as rickets; indeed a whole series of acquired as opposed to congenital deformities were ascribed to poor housing

Children gathered on the steps at Wood Street, Port Dundas, Glasgow, 1910. The deprivation of the children is indicated by their bare feet and assorted clothing. Courtesy of Glasgow City Archives (Libraries and Archives).

quality.[12] As one would expect the infant mortality rate was also highest in overcrowded housing conditions. Thirty-two per cent of all infant deaths in Glasgow in 1905 were of babies in 'single-ends'.[13] An infant contracting measles was twice as likely to die in a one-roomed dwelling in a house with two rooms.[14] Even as late as 1935 in Glasgow the wards with the highest concentration of overcrowded housing — such as Hutchesontown, Gorbals, Parkhead and Dalmarnock — had correspondingly high infant-mortality rates which saw little improvement until after World War Two.[15] The worst general mortality rates in Scotland were to be found in Glasgow too with deaths from cholera and typhus, for instance, far higher than in comparable English cities. And all the attendant ills of the industrial city — drunkenness, violence and crime — affected not only Glasgow, Edinburgh and Dundee but many of the smaller 'frontier' towns such as the steel centres of Airdrie and Coatbridge, Greenock and Port Glasgow on the Clyde, and colliery towns such as Methil in Fife. By the 1870s and 1880s such urban 'vices' were being explicitly linked to family disintegration, indigence and inevitably child neglect, and headline cases of individuals prosecuted in the courts simply highlighted the alleged connection between urban conditions, moral decline and the fate of children.

Overcrowding and atrocious social conditions were not only to be found in urban areas however. In 1861 the worst housing conditions were found in Shetland, and they were almost as bad in Orkney, the Outer Hebrides and most of the Highlands as they were in Lanarkshire.[16] Highland inhabitants were frequently accommodated in so-called 'black houses' constructed of stone and peat and thatched with heather and straw, consisting of one long room subdivided for humans and animals with few windows. Basic facilities were limited and in many Highland dwellings well into the twentieth century most cooking and water heating was carried out over an open fire. Social commentators regarded these traditional and functional dwellings as a health risk, with the dirt, the lack of fresh air, the proximity to animals and the risk of tuburculosis especially hazardous for children.

> Look, for instance, at the black house [on Lewis] where two children — perhaps over two years, but under five — are looking out from the gloom at the strangers passing…But note the steady flow of smoke coming through the door. To these children that is the normal condition of the house, day or night…it irritates the children's eyes and perhaps, by excess of dry dust and irritating vapours, spoils the resistance of their lungs…the discomfort alone, not to speak of the possible ultimate danger, is a heavy price to pay…[17]

Of course overcrowding and poor housing conditions do not necessarily, have a direct impact on the quality of material or emotional care received by children. Numerous autobiographies recounting the realities of Scottish working-class life, whilst not shying away from the very real hardship, tell stories of survival in the face of appalling living conditions and debilitating poverty.[18] Social investigators, though, clearly believed decrepit housing to have an immoral effect on inhabitants — children as well as adults. Measured against the middle-class ideology of domesticity which emphasised the safety of the hearth, the sight of working-class children of both sexes sleeping several to a bed and roaming out of doors in the courts, wynds and closes because there was no room for them indoors appeared 'demoralising' and corrupting. 'I did not believe, until I visited the wynds of Glasgow' remarked one observer in 1840, 'that so large an amount of filth, crime, misery and disease existed on one spot in any civilised country.'[19] And there seemed to be no shortage of evidence to support this judgement. Prosecutions of parents who failed to provide for their children appeared to confirm the extent to which children were the victims of family breakdown in the urban environment. In 1915 Govan Combination prosecuted a widower father of seven children, only three of whom were still at home, on the grounds that he was failing to support the children whilst receiving relief:

> A visit saw Martha who keeps house and Lizzie. Both children are pale and thin, not very well clothed, hair nitty and verminous, house fairly tidy but not very clean, bedding sufficient but very dirty. Martha states that her father drinks a great deal, has pawned any clothes they had and the children are evidently insufficiently fed...[20]

In its first Annual Report for the year 1884–1885 the Glasgow Society for the Prevention of Cruelty to Children identified 595 cases it had investigated involving over 1,000 children. The majority were victims of neglect but more than 200 had been 'rescued' from the streets of Glasgow begging or selling at all hours of the day and night.[21] By 1910, after 15 years of investigative experience, the SNSPCC in Glasgow had seen almost 20,000 cases of neglect, 1,000 cases of children being brought up in 'immoral surroundings', and more than 10,000 begging and singing on the streets of the city.[22]

Of course the urban working class lived in housing it could afford, and it could afford very little with wages estimated at some five per cent lower in Scotland compared with England, and stable, permanent employment only a dream for many.[23] Scotland was a low-wage economy especially in respect of unskilled industrial workers and farm workers, at least until the 1850s, and certainly in Glasgow for much of the nineteenth century industrial work for unskilled men was often of a casual and seasonal nature. Large numbers of casual labourers were employed in the Clyde docks and shipyards and the construction industry preferred to employ casual workers to enable it to react swiftly to peaks and troughs in building activity. Rarely was a working man able to earn sufficient to provide for a family — the elusive family wage — necessitating both female and child labour to supplement income. A lone parent, then, was especially vulnerable, men as well as women. It is noticeable that widowers were prominent amongst those who placed their children in an orphanage. Not only was it difficult for a man of the urban or rural lower classes to provide for a family without the income of his wife and her housekeeping skills, but almost invariably he was unable to find a substitute mother for his children. John Gibb, a 'widower in very humble circumstances', placed his youngest daughter Agnes in Stirling's Whinwell Children's Home shortly after his wife had died of cancer. 'This is a case of a respectable man whose wife after a lingering illness dies on 30 July 1913 leaving him with 5 children aged 11, 9, 6, 2 years and 8 months respectively to provide and care on 21/- per week' commented the orphanage director. 'There are no grandparents or other relatives.'[24] Fortunately, John Gibb was able to remove his daughter a few months later after he had remarried.

The lives of the urban and rural working class were dominated by poverty. Until the implementation of the 1845 Poor Law (Scotland) Act which obliged Scottish parishes to raise money to relieve the poor, there was little in the way of welfare to support those in need and distress. In practice, before 1845, the unemployed had to rely on the support of family and neighbours and the inadequate funds raised by the kirk-sessions. After this date a safety-net was put in place — poor relief was raised from a parish rate and the poorhouse, which already existed in some parishes, was more widely used — but still in Scotland the able-bodied had no entitlement to relief unless they were unfit for work. This meant that a pauper in Scotland was treated less generously than his or her English counterpart. The poorhouse became the refuge of the helpless which included not only the sick, the elderly and the disabled but also mothers of illegitimate children, widows, and deserted wives although, as we shall see later, the Scottish authorities were reluctant to keep children in this environment. Pauper children were usually boarded out with a foster family and were thus separated, often permanently, from their natural parents.

Poverty was most severe in the Highlands and yet rural paupers were amongst those least likely to receive adequate poor relief as rural inhabitants were too poor to contribute to the poor rates. In some areas only the old and the sick were left behind in depopulated communities as the young and the able-bodied migrated, either overseas or to the towns in search of work. This may have eased the situation in the countryside — and ironically may have opened the way for poor law authorities to use rural areas for the boarding out of pauper children in the homes of widows and those whose children had flown the nest — but it placed greater pressure on the towns and cities. The urban centres had to deal with the largest number of paupers particularly as a result of low wages, seasonal employment and high rates of immigration. Migrants to the towns, especially those from the Highlands and Ireland, were required to fulfil a five year residence qualification before they became eligible for poor relief and individuals could be sent 'home' to claim relief in their place of birth. In these circumstances the proximity of kin to provide support was crucial. Those who were separated from family were vulnerable, none more so than deserted wives and widows and lone mothers of illegitimate children.

Illegitimate children constituted a significant proportion of the poor in urban and rural Scotland and were, in most respects, the most vulnerable group requiring care. Illegitimacy rates varied from county to county. In 1861 in Glasgow 8.8 per cent of live births were recorded as illegitimate compared with around 13 per cent in Aberdeenshire and 15 per cent in the south west.[25] Andrew Blaikie has demonstrated for rural Rothiemay in Banffshire that high numbers of illegitimate births were incorporated into the local community with the children commonly brought up within the grandparents' household while the mother returned to service. In urban areas, by contrast, such women and their children were often less fortunate.[26] The support system which tolerated illegitimacy in Banffshire could be absent in the cities. The urban mother of an illegitimate child was more likely to find herself abandoned and unable to care for the child alone than her rural sister.[27] In 1857 more than 60 per cent of children on the nurses roll of Glasgow Parochial Board were 'supposed illegitimate'.[28] Deserted mothers were unlikely to be able to trace the fathers of their children, according to a parish council report of 1909; a number of fathers simply assumed a new identity and disappeared into the streets and lanes of Glasgow, 'about 70 per cent of the deserters were apprehended in Glasgow, residing in models, not one in fifty using his own name…[this] enables married men to come in and hide themselves, and leave their wives and families to be supported by the rates.'[29] Such was the fate of the family of Glasgow man John Lafferty. His wife, it was alleged, had been driven on to the streets owing to her husband's drinking habit. Of the twelve children born to the couple, only three had survived. In March 1910 their five year old son became chargeable to the parish having been deserted by both parents. 'The mother was living in cohabitation with another man and the father was residing in the Models under an assumed name...The wife had recently given birth to an illegitimate child and was unable to take the child.'[30] An attempt by the parish to persuade John Lafferty to pay maintenance for the upkeep of his own son had been unsuccessful. The dilemma of the deserted mother was a persistent one. In the 1930s Glasgow Corporation doggedly pursued men who were guilty of failing to support their dependants, forcing women and children to rely on public assistance. One man who deserted his wife and six children 'absconded with the unemployment benefit', gambled it away, stayed in a model lodging house thus forcing his family to live on 26s 6d assistance weekly.[31]

Before 1845 a large number of Scottish parishes did not grant unconditional poor relief — monies raised and administered by the church — to the mothers of illegitimate children. Indeed such women were still being disciplined by the kirk sessions in rural districts until the mid-nineteenth century. These women and their children were most vulnerable in the Highlands and Islands and in agricultural crofting parishes, and most likely to receive help on the east coast and in urban industrial centres.[32] Undoubtedly the moral dimension of illegitimacy influenced parishes' assessment of the deservedness of this category of poor but the moral repugnance directed at the mother had to be tempered by concern for the 'innocent' child who would be the chief victim if relief was denied. 'Were the sum withdrawn', stated the Haddington Parochial Board in 1873, 'their mothers would be compelled probably to leave their service to keep their children depending on daily and precarious employment, a position of much greater peril than that which they now occupy.'[33] This is a dilemma facing welfare systems to this day. Nevertheless, many mothers of illegitimate children were only given the option of the poorhouse and understandably many refused the offer which still left parishes with the problem of how to deal with the children if the father could not be traced. By 1884 parishes were permitted to forcibly separate illegitimate children from their mothers and place them in foster care — a policy which had the advantage, according to the authorities, of removing the child from a pauper's environment and freeing the mother of the responsibility for a child thus facilitating her search for stable employment.[34] The alternative for a mother who rejected admission to the poorhouse — and most did reject it — was to manage on low wages or to make alternative provision for her child. This ranged from temporary child minders to permanent care in a children's home.

Women's work in industrial areas, and especially on the west coast which was dominated by heavy industry, was to be found mainly in the textile and clothing trades and domestic service. Indeed, these three sectors accounted for almost 60 per cent of women's paid employment in 1911 in Scotland as a whole.[35] Wages were universally lower than those earned by men and domestic service offered the lowest wages, the longest hours and the most restrictive working conditions. It was extremely difficult for a woman to continue working outside the home while supporting a young child or children. Those who did would often pay relatives or neighbours to mind children during the daytime.[36] Thousands of women resorted to working from home in the sweated trades for a pittance and supplementing their income with poor relief. But even if a woman did secure some kind of work she still found it difficult to care for a young child. Employment outside the home and child care were incompatible for a lone working-class mother. Little Dora Jones, just three months old and illegitimate, was placed in Aberlour Orphanage on Speyside in 1898 by her widowed mother. The orphanage was asked:

> Would you receive a baby of 10 days old from Edinburgh? The child is illegitimate, the mother was a chambermaid in a hotel and could go there again if the baby could be kept for her…but this baby no-one will have (poor mite) and if she keeps it she can't go out to work.[37]

Nellie Galloway was in a similar predicament when she replied to an advertisement in a newspaper placed by the Whinwell Children's Home in Stirling on behalf of a couple looking for 'a wee girlie to adopt'. 'I have a very nice wee girl' wrote Nellie, 'but she is 5 next June. I would gladly give her over to you as I have had to keep her out at the nursing all these years and pay out of my earnings.' Her daughter Sonya was illegitimate but Nellie was keen to emphasise that 'I am come of a very decent family, though only working class.'[38] Little had changed by the 1930s. Mothers of illegitimate children were still subjected to moral judgement. Frances, the illegitimate daughter of a Glasgow Jewish woman and an unemployed Scotsman, was boarded out to Aberdeenshire when her mother's parents seemingly disowned their pregnant daughter. Her baby was born in a hospital and shortly after Frances had been removed her mother was admitted to a psychiatric institution.[39]

Less fortunate were those babies, often illegitimate, whose mothers were forced to hand them over to individuals who offered to unofficially 'adopt' them. 'Baby-farming', as this trade or service came to be known, was essentially the continuation in an urban setting of the common practice of wet-nursing which had been widespread across Europe since the early modern period. Mothers who were unable or did not wish to breast-feed their babies would employ a wet-nurse, usually a woman who already had children of her own and who earned much needed extra income by undertaking to care for the babies of others in her own home. In some countries wet-nurses were regulated and inspected and were recognised as providing a genuine service.[40] Whilst the mortality rate amongst wet-nursed babies was certainly very high, this was probably due more to the impoverishment of the wet-nurses than to deliberate neglect. However, in the 1870s wet-nursing was transformed in the public imagination into the 'murderous trade' of baby-farming, stoked by the highly publicised trial of two sisters in London and the subsequent hanging of one of them, Margaret Waters, for the manslaughter and murder of five of the eleven babies found in their care.[41] Although the employment of a wet-nurse continued to be a short-term strategy used by working-class mothers who were in need of child-care while they worked, the Scottish newspapers were full of emotive stories describing the shady business of baby-farming. This appeared to be no less prevalent in Glasgow and Edinburgh than in London. Descriptions of babies wallowing in squalor, drugged with opium and starved to death by unfeeling 'mothers' who were motivated by the insurance benefit they would receive on the child's death prompted a public furore which culminated in the 1872 Infant Life

Protection Act.[42] This legislation provided for stricter regulation of privately run child-care establishments, particularly those which took in more than two infants for lengthy periods. Yet, as a correspondent in the *Glasgow Herald* in 1910 pointed out, legislation did nothing to alleviate the condition of lone mothers or their infants and indeed left loopholes exploited by those lying-in establishments

> in which unhappy women are received until they give birth to their illegitimate children...The women, already so cruelly victimised, are pitilessly despoiled, all the money they may possess being exacted in payment of 'services rendered'...The desire to hide their shame must be powerfully operative in the victims, and many, if not most, of them will submit to be bled rather than lose their 'character' and their situation.[43]

A woman expecting an illegitimate child who entered one of these homes would be unlikely to see her child again after the birth as most were given up for adoption.

By the turn of the century a more humane alternative for a small number of unmarried mothers was provided by voluntary organisations such as the Salvation Army Hostels and the Church of Scotland Maternity Home in Glasgow. The latter, established in 1915, claimed to 'provide a home for respectable girls who have been led astray' and aimed to prevent the separation of mother and child. Other homes were more akin to the so-called magdalene institutions, created from the 1810s, as homes professing to rescue girls from prostitution. In these establishments the provision of a temporary shelter for destitute mothers and their children came at a price — the moral rescue of the mother. The Glasgow Home for Deserted Mothers, for instance, only accepted first time mothers, thus entertaining 'the hope that the Home will...prove instrumental in preventing vice and crime...'[44]

Before the First World War there was little help for lone mothers and indeed lone fathers with babies and young children. The focus of most of those involved in child welfare was the removal of children from the care of indigent parents rather than helping parents to help themselves. Isolated examples of the latter approach include the day nursery established in 1886 by the Edinburgh branch of the SNSPCC 'on the good old principle of "helping those who help themselves" — women struggling for a livelihood, who have no-one with whom to leave their children while they are out at work for them.'[45] Similar day nurseries were set up in Glasgow and Paisley. In 1902 Glasgow Parish Council attempted to ameliorate the condition of widows with young children by introducing a Special Roll to allow such deserving women to stay at home and care for their children; however, deserted women who constituted almost 20 per cent of first time female applicants for poor relief in Glasgow parish would not have fallen into the category of the 'deserving' poor, many being tainted with the label 'immoral'.[46] Lone mothers, then, faced an impossible dilemma. With so few sources of support for mother *and* child, women may have chosen voluntarily to place an infant in care, believing that they maintained at least some control over the fate of their child. Mary Hingley from Dundee was desperate to find a good home for her four year old illegitimate son in 1914 as she explained to her local minister:

> I am in trouble and write to you. You will know that my aunt...is very weak and her sister Mary is also very ill. The doctor says the children must go away but I have nowhere to take them to. My stepmother was not kind to them when she had them for a time. Besides Mr Hodson, I cannot keep them myself. My wage is £18 and I feel I can hold out no longer. What I want you to do then, if you would be so kind, is to try and get Tommy at the least sent to Aberlour Orphanage in Banffshire. There is a description of it in 'The Standard Bearer'...as the home was founded by our church and I was confirmed into it, one would suppose they would consider the matter...I have thoroughly repented the wrong I have done now I am older I see it all so clearly...[47]

In such circumstances some women took desperate measures. The observation that 'the practice of mothers going off and leaving their illegitimate children is becoming far too common in Glasgow' can only be ascribed to the limited options open to lone mothers. Child abandonment has always been used as a last resort by desperate women. Annie McGinlay had left her illegitimate child in Glasgow to be nursed for payment of £1 per month but when the money was not forthcoming the nurse placed the child in Stobhill hospital. Annie was traced working as a kitchenmaid in Grantown-on-Spey and only then did her story emerge. The 'putative father' of the child was said to be a Spanish waiter who had worked with Annie in Dundee; when she became pregnant he promised to marry her. However, when preparations for the wedding were already underway, he deserted her, running off with her savings. Since leaving her child with the nurse, clearly a desperate act, it was said 'not once...has she made any enquiries about the child, and it is clear that she has been giving Glasgow a wide berth, simply to get rid of it altogether.' Furthermore, noted the parish criminal officer, 'She is very fond of dress and gaudy show and I am informed she spends most of her earnings in this fashion.'[48] A penchant for nice clothes was clearly deemed incompatible with motherly virtues.

Greater attention was paid to initiatives to reduce the appalling infant mortality rate than to alleviating the problems of lone mothers. In Scotland as a whole deaths of infants under one year peaked at 138 per 1,000 registered live births in 1897, but in industrial areas the rate was significantly higher.[49] In Glasgow an infant mortality rate of 153 in 1900 compared unfavourably with a declining Scottish rate of 122.[50] Moreover, although rates in rural Scotland were improving at the end of the nineteenth century, in industrial areas they were to get temporarily worse before any significant improvement was realised and this only really occurred after 1945.[51] The mortality rate for illegitimate infants was consistently higher still. Indeed, in the city of Glasgow in 1874, 55 per cent of unregistered illegitimate babies died before their first birthday — a statistic which prompted Glasgow's Medical Officer of Health, J.B.Russell to note:

> ...the more dependent and helpless of itself the life is, the less attention it receives from those on whom it depends. When we refine still further, and distinguish between the unwished-for life, which is to those who begot it, while it exists, a badge of disgrace, and the life which springs up in the home where it is expected and in some degree cherished, we can understand in what a hopeless struggle for existence the illegitimate child is entered at its birth.[52]

Russell's frankly unsympathetic and misguided interpretation of the high infant mortality rate for illegitimate children in Glasgow is indicative of a more widespread attitude which regarded the illegitimate mother as worthless and unfit. The structural problems which underpinned the difficulties encountered by these women and their babies were conveniently ignored. Voluntary and official initiatives to improve the health of mother and child concentrated on keeping babies alive and healthy rather than keeping mothers and babies together. For instance, in 1904 milk depots providing sterilised milk for infants were established in Glasgow and Dundee, voluntary health visitor associations formed in 1908 in Glasgow and Edinburgh began to visit all new born babies, and the provision of ante-natal care was pioneered in Edinburgh in 1915. These measures may have had some impact on the infant mortality rate which declined to 113 per 1,000 live births on the eve of the First World War, but women and children had to wait until the post-war era for maternity and welfare schemes that provided practical support. Infant and Child Welfare Clinics and day nurseries, and material help such as meals for expectant mothers and milk and cod liver oil for needy children were a help but they were no substitute for better housing and secure and well paid jobs.[53]

If conditions were difficult for urban mothers and children, rural women fared little better. Agricultural work was still employing large numbers of women in the nineteenth century. In the 1871 census 26 per cent of agricultural employees were counted as women and this was a serious underestimate of the numbers involved as seasonal labourers, of whom a high proportion were women, were excluded.[54] However, although women made up a far higher proportion of the agricultural labour force in Scotland than they did in England and Wales, after the First World War female employment experienced a steady decline; in 1913 58,000 female regular and casual workers were employed on farms, declining to 33,500 in 1921 as alternative forms of employment such as domestic service and the textile industry competed for women workers.[55] In Lowland Scotland the decline continued through the inter-war period; by 1939 female workers were only 14.3 per cent of the regular labour force compared with 20.2 per cent in 1921.[56] Moreover, all agricultural labour undertaken by women was poorly paid. In 1870 the Royal Commission on Employment of Women in Agriculture noted: 'It is no doubt owing to the comparatively lower wages at which female labour can be obtained that Scotch farming in an economical point of view owes a considerable portion of its success.'[57] In the Border counties of the south-east the bondage system continued to operate until well into the twentieth century whereby male farm-servants were required to provide a woman worker who might be his wife, his daughter or a hired farm servant, to carry out duties to be paid by the farmer.[58] Some argued that this system maintained family ties by permitting, in effect, the hiring of the whole family, but countering this was the length of contract service, commonly six months or one year, after which men and women were obliged to seek new employment, necessitating high degrees of mobility. However, by the 1930s the bondager system had all but collapsed in the south-east. In the Highlands where crofting was still the predominant form of agriculture it might be suggested that families were more firmly knitted into the reciprocal web of the community and thus less likely to crack under the pressure of poverty; as Lynn Jamieson and Claire Toynbee suggest of this area, 'economic reciprocity was paralleled socially.'[59] With so little research on the family in the crofting counties it is only possible to speculate that the persistence of the extended family was something of a guarantor of family survival. As we shall see, crofting communities were net importers (by means of the boarding-out system) rather than exporters of children, and the absence of child care institutions in the more isolated parts of the country — notably Orkney and Shetland, the Western Isles and much of the Highlands — demanded that the care of homeless children be undertaken by the community.

Survival Strategies

It is not at all surprising then, that the family in rural and urban Scotland before the First World War was under serious duress. Across much of the country the family was placed under such economic and social strain that it had to adapt to circumstances or face being pulled apart. In addition to the strains placed upon family relationships and stability by the consequences of industrialisation and urbanisation, individual families were also adversely affected by explicit crises. Amongst these were: the serious illness or death of one or both parents; long term unemployment, especially affecting the male earner; temporary or long-term physical incapacity of one or both parents; drunkenness or mental instability; and desertion by the husband or wife. Against the background of a distinctive matrix of conditions in Scotland it was necessary for the family to be permeable; families had to adopt temporary or permanent strategies to deal with the care of children. Thus families in Scotland adopted flexible and open living arrangements in order to accommodate children who otherwise might have been left homeless. There is no doubt that working-class families endured additional privation and made sacrifices in order to avoid the permanent break up of the family or to prevent children being admitted to an institution. Relatives did their best to help out. When the mother of five year old Peter Hepburn from Alloa died in 1899 and his father, described as 'dissipated and reckless', deserted him he was taken in by his aunt. However, she already had nine children of her own and an aged mother to support but she was willing to take the five year old boy to prevent him being admitted to Stirling's Whinwell Home.[60]

In London's East End where housing conditions were, in some parishes, broadly comparable with those in the larger Scottish towns, it has been shown that difficult family circumstances often necessitated community care of children with relatives and neighbours willingly stepping in to take children at times of crisis, thus avoiding the workhouse or an institution.[61] 'There was a general sense that institutional care was a last resort and that responsibility for children extended beyond the family and concerned neighbours as well as parents.'[62] Anna Davin suggests that for many working-class London children '"home" and "family" were less fixed than in middle-class thinking' and the statement clearly applies to Scottish cities too.[63] Jessie Kesson's autobiographical novel *The White Bird Passes* which tells the story of a young girl growing up in a Scottish city in the 1920s encapsulates the notion of the community as family, where the other inhabitants of the Lane were on hand to take responsibility for children until the 'Cruelty Man' (the local SNSPCC inspector) authorised Janie's removal to the orphanage.[64] There is little danger of romanticising the life of large families forced to stay in one and two roomed tenements but the sense of community survival engendered in the closes and back courts, the almost forced reciprocity coming from living in such close proximity to neighbours, may have lessened the impact of deprivation somewhat. In rural parts of Scotland too, where poorhouses or children's homes could be hundreds of miles away, few children would be removed from the immediate community.

Yet some distinctive characteristics of the Scottish urban

Glasgow Corporation property at 5 King Street, Calton, c. 1916. This model housing was an improvement on the traditional tenement and housed the more affluent members of the working classes. Glasgow City Archives.

experience may suggest that although neighbours would look out for children playing in the tenement closes or take in a child while a mother was in hospital, community care of vulnerable children was not always forthcoming at times such as the death or long-term incapacity of a parent or long-term unemployment. This is not to portray Scottish working-class communities as uncaring but simply to recognise the constraints on unselfish support. Scottish urban communities tended to be characterised by high mobility accentuated by the six-monthly house lets. The predominance of single-ends and two-room houses in tenements may have meant families were simply unable to take in needy children. And the extremes of poverty suffered amongst the working classes may have militated against accepting an extra mouth to feed on a long term basis unless the child was of working age. Nor did the proximity of an extended family guarantee that orphaned children would be kept out of a home as Meg Henderson demonstrates in an autobiographical account of her childhood in Glasgow's notorious Blackhill and Drumchapel council housing estates in the 1950s and 60s. Following her aunt Peggy's death in childbirth her husband placed the three children in care despite the presence of relatives residing close by who were helpless to prevent it.[65] The inability of the extended family to provide for a child was highlighted by William Quarrier who carried out extensive checks on alternative forms of family care before a child was admitted to his institution. The five King children were admitted to Quarrier's Homes in 1906 following the death of both parents within two weeks of one another. There was no-one else to take the children; the maternal aunt and uncle 'have families of their own and cannot help...the grandparents bring the children and sign...Paternal relations take no interest.'[66] More frequently, children — especially the younger ones — were placed in charitable institutions for a temporary period while the family got over a crisis. Those who experienced child care institutions first hand confirm this pattern of care. Arthur, born in Aberdeen in 1911, was one of five children. When his mother died of TB leaving her husband to manage the house and the children on the wages of a casual dock labourer:

> He couldn't cope and he went to the bottle, he went to the bottle, he was a dock labourer, he got paid by the day, daily payment...and I remember my aunty came and she got the cruelty man.[67]

Arthur, who was just eight years old, was taken along with his brother by the SNSPCC inspector to the local poorhouse but shortly afterwards all five children were found places at Aberlour Orphanage on Speyside. When Arthur was 12 his father married a local woman who already had two children of her own. Arthur was removed from the orphanage and returned home for a while to live with his father and stepmother but when she died of dropsy all three children were returned to the orphanage. This 'in-and-out' pattern of care was not unusual and although possibly traumatic for children certainly helped some families to weather temporary crises. An alternative was to send older children out to work. Evelyn Cowan recalled how, when her mother was widowed in the 1930s and left to survive in the Gorbals with eleven children aged between 19 years and six weeks old, the children of working age were forced to hunt for work thus saving any of the younger ones from the orphanage.[68] In fact it was very common for older children, especially girls, to be let off school at the age of twelve or so to work or to look after younger children at home in lone parent families.[69] But when all possibilities had been exhausted there was no alternative but to find accommodation for a child elsewhere as Mary Harrigan from Glasgow found when she asked for her youngest child aged four to be taken into the Whinwell Home in Stirling in 1914. According to her sponsor, Mary was

> a very decent woman…She has left her husband as he was cruel to her children and self. Two of her children are being brought up by her first husband's people…the eldest child has just gone into service, [her] mother will take the girl of eleven so there is just the little girl aged four, the child of the second husband to find a home for and then [she] can go properly into service herself…[70]

Of course the image of the caring, close-knit community where children were treated as everyone's responsibility can be taken too literally. Not all homeless children could be absorbed back into the community. The baby-farming scandal in the 1870s had already drawn attention to the fate of babies unknowingly given up by mothers to unscrupulous nurses, indicating that there were limits to the amount of disinterested care available to children in the community. Some private adoptions before the Adoption of Children Act in 1926 worked to the benefit of all parties, but there were inevitably casualties of such informal arrangements and the authorities or the charities were left to pick up the pieces. Deserted and abandoned children were left to be cared for by a variety of individuals and agencies. In 1910 a Glasgow man was charged with deserting two of his children but another four were discovered by investigators, none of whom were supported by their father.

> This is a disgraceful case. This man's 6 children are scattered all over. One Jessie (15) in St.Mary's, Hugh (14) on Training Ship, Catherine (10) with grandmother in Coatbridge, Mary (6) and Margaret (5) in Stobhill and Martha 3 months with mother, so that he is getting them

all brought up at the expense of other people while he has been away in Wales working by himself…He is a proper schemer and tries to deceive us whenever he is caught by pretending that he is bad with 'Asthma and Rheumatics' which is only a hoax.[71]

Paradoxically perhaps, in some instances the addition of a child to a family might aid its survival. Rural families often welcomed the opportunity offered by the policy of boarding out of pauper children to acquire a child who would contribute to the household economy by working the croft or engaging in other economic activities. At least until the First World War but probably for much longer in marginal agricultural areas, children were still regarded as an economic resource as well as a focus of affection and emotional satisfaction. A child who was an economic burden to a lone mother in the city was an additional pair of hands to an elderly couple working a marginal croft. In Scotland, the break up of one unviable family could mean another gained a new lease of life.

The Parish, Philanthropy and the State

Community care of children, ranging from temporary baby-sitting to long term unofficial adoption, was widespread and often effective in Scotland, but the depth and severity of problems encountered by some families ensured that from the early nineteenth century philanthropic and charitable bodies saw an opportunity to step into a vacuum created by the failure of statutory poor relief to come to the aid of those in poverty and distress and provide more permanent care of the child victims. At the same time the state, in the form of the poor law authorities, also began to adopt what might be termed a child-oriented philanthropy, influenced by a general shift in attitudes towards children and childhood which had been taking place since the early 1800s. During the course of the nineteenth century a 'modern' notion of the child was gradually formulated so that by the 1870s the concept of the child, as distinct from the adult, by nature of his or her ignorance, innocence and dependence, was firmly in place. This process of definition was shaped by a series of debates centring on child labour, child delinquency and education, formulated by the middle classes and then gradually imposed upon working-class children and their parents. The nineteenth century saw increasing regulation of working-class children's lives as an idea of childhood which centred on domesticity and the safety of the home was disseminated. The Factory Acts, which between 1802 and 1901 progressively forbade children from long hours of work, signified that children were now seen as requiring the protection of the state and childhood was increasingly seen as incompatible with wage-earning.[72] Previously, when thousands of children had been engaged in some kind of wage labour, the middle classes could claim that poor children had no childhood. The decisive form of middle-class intervention, though, was the introduction of compulsory and eventually free schooling. The 1872 Education (Scotland) Act obliged all authorities to provide compulsory education at primary level although it was not declared free of charge by the Scottish Education Department until 1889.

This emerging concept of childhood had less to do with age — although the 1908 Children Act defined a child as aged 14 or under — and more to do with responsibilities (or lack of them). Legislative reform in the 1850s and 1860s affecting so-called juvenile delinquents reinforced this view. For the first time young offenders were acknowledged as a separate category and more importantly as individuals who might not be responsible for their own actions. The proper place for a child was deemed to be within a 'family', protected and dependent, whether this be the child's natural family or a substitute. Henceforth, children found unattended outwith the domestic sphere, on the streets and in the wynds and closes, were deemed to be at risk and requiring rescue, notwithstanding the fact that in working-class neighbourhoods the tenements and courts were believed to be safe places for children, watched over by a community of 'mothers'. By the mid to late nineteenth century then, a fairly well-defined ideology of childhood had emerged amongst the middle classes. 'At the heart of this ideology', writes Hugh Cunningham, 'lay a firm commitment that children should be reared in families, a conviction that the way childhood was spent was crucial in determining the kind of adult that the child would become, and an increasing awareness that childhood had rights and privileges of its own.'[73]

It was against this background that a distinctive child welfare policy and practice began to be developed in Scotland. Institutions for the education of 'fatherless bairns' such as George Heriot's school in Edinburgh and Cowane's Hospital in Stirling had been established in the seventeenth century but these had really only provided for orphans of the middle and upper ranks. However, the mid to late nineteenth century witnessed the burgeoning of both philanthropic initiatives and state-sponsored child welfare provision directed towards the care, education and protection of the homeless working-class child. Parish provision was dominated by foster care or boarding out of pauper children with relatives or strangers. The Scottish Parochial Board — the central authority responsible for poor relief in Scotland — was averse to placing children in the poorhouse and only resorted to residential care for those who could not be found homes such as those assessed as 'imbeciles', older or 'unruly' children who were more likely to be admitted to industrial schools, reformatories or training ships. Roman Catholic children were also more likely to be placed in an institution owing to the shortage of foster parents of the same faith. Boarding out was most enthusiastically practised by the urban parishes in Glasgow, Edinburgh and Aberdeen and by 1910 90 per cent of pauper children in Scotland numbering more than 7,000 every year were cared for in this way.[74] The policy of placing children in receipt of parish relief in families rather than institutions was continued, especially by Glasgow Corporation, well into the 1960s.

Charitable provision for orphaned, destitute and neglected children, on the other hand, was shared amongst religious organisations and private individuals with a philanthropic — and usually evangelistic — mission. The most well known institutions of this type in Scotland were the Orphan Homes of Scotland (better known as Quarrier's Homes) at Bridge of Weir near Glasgow, established by William Quarrier in 1873 and housing over 900 children by 1897, and Aberlour Orphanage on Speyside, an episcopalian institution founded in 1875 by an Englishman, the Reverend Jupp, which saw over 2,000 children pass through its doors by 1914. In addition to these large voluntary children's homes, much smaller institutions were opened all over Scotland catering for all categories of homeless children. Smyllum Orphanage in Lanark was one of the few institutions catering for Roman Catholic children in the nineteenth century. The Stirling Creche and Home for Neglected and Destitute Children founded in 1883 and later known as the Whinwell Children's Home was typical of a small institution housing no more than around 50 children at its peak and entirely dependent upon charitable donations and contributions from parents and relatives of the children admitted. The cities of Glasgow and Edinburgh possessed numerous and varied homes, each with a specific remit in respect of the sex, age and social status of the children admitted. Some of these explicitly operated as reformatories and industrial schools, others provided for the mentally handicapped, whilst others still, like the so-called Magdalene Institutes, claimed to rescue wayward girls. From the 1870s private residential homes have played an essential although now dwindling role in the pattern of social provision for homeless and needy children. Although charitable homes were entirely independent of local authorities and were not subject to any form of official inspection and regulation until 1933, they were an intrinsic element of the wider child care web in Scotland, often arranging adoption, cooperating with the SNSPCC and parish poor law inspectors and, until the 1920s, participating in the child emigration schemes to Canada and Australia.

From the late nineteenth century then, an extensive pattern of voluntary provision complemented statutory poor relief. Indeed, the two systems operated hand in hand and between them established a web of care services encompassing children's homes, foster care and adoption, emigration and rescue and protection work. It was not unusual for children to be passed from the public to the private sector, facilitated by the fact that the two systems shared an ideology of the child which influenced welfare practice.

There is no doubt that in Scotland those involved in the alleviation of child poverty and in child rescue, that is both those in charge of administering poor relief and private philanthropists, largely adhered to the view that children were not responsible for their position or their actions and therefore should not suffer for the inadequacies of their parents. Children could be saved because they were innocent; they could be taught to become useful citizens; and they could be 'given back' their childhood which had been stolen from them by worthless, indigent parents. But the rescue agenda — rescuing children from appalling conditions of poverty and neglect, from exploitation and from vice — was less forgiving of the families and communities from whom the children had been saved. Not only Poor Law officials but evangelical philanthropists believed it was their duty to remove children — forcibly if necessary — from parents who were unable to discharge their responsibilities to their children (and to the state) and to protect children from such degrading influences for the remainder of their childhood. As Harry Hendrick points out for England, the Poor Law and the philanthropic child care organisations concurred in the policy that 'needy children were best brought up outside the influence of parents.'[75]

Child welfare workers have always negotiated a fine line between prevention and protection; that is, between intervention on behalf of the family as a whole, to prevent it from breaking up, and protection of the child at all costs usually involving the removal of that child from the family. By the 1880s prevention had become an important adjunct to the earlier protection activities. Poor Law children, writes Hendrick, 'occupied a transitional position between the State, as arbiter of rescue, reclamation and protection, and as the provider of services for children as publicly recognised citizens of the future.'[76] This shift in emphasis, from separation of the child from its parents to intervention on behalf of the family as a whole, demanded greater state involvement in the lives of children and their families. If a child's natural family was unable to guarantee protection and safety then the child could legitimately be removed and placed within an alternative family situation. Influenced by voluntary associations such as the SNSPCC which brought the issue of neglect and cruelty to public and government attention and actively campaigned for the criminalisation of child neglect, the state increasingly extended its powers in respect of all children at risk. These powers were enacted in positive and negative ways. On the one hand, from around the turn of the century, families were supported in their efforts to care for their children with the introduction of infant welfare measures, improved medical provision for mothers and infants, the promotion of breast feeding and the introduction of the school meals service (1906) and the school medical inspection service (1907). On the other hand, while implicitly blaming working-class mothers for high infant mortality rates and condemning working-class child care practices, the state increasingly impinged on the family's autonomy via a series of legislative measures designed to protect the child from harm.[77] Poor Law officials with the support of voluntary agencies became increasingly responsible for the policing of families, initiating prosecutions of parents who had deserted, neglected or abused their children. In the decade or so before the First World War then, the balance between the state and parents for the responsibility of children's welfare had shifted quite substantially towards the former. 'Deserving' parents were given limited support; the undeserving were not.

Despite the growing power of the state to intervene in the welfare of children, the dual system of state and private welfare of homeless children has been maintained until the present day. The groundwork laid down by the poor law and philanthropic endeavours in the late nineteenth century formed a solid foundation for the development of a sophisticated and comprehensive child welfare system which slowly adapted its methods and ideology to suit Scotland's distinctive mix of economic hardship and cultural diversity. In many respects, though, the policy and practice of child welfare in Scotland between 1845 and the present has mirrored trends in the rest of Britain. Certainly all the major child protection legislation was applied in Scotland and child welfare workers were influenced by ideas from England, Europe and North America. However, the Scottish experience does present something of a distinctive picture. To some extent the differences to be found in Scotland stem from Scotland's uniquely traumatic experience of industrialisation and urbanisation. The welfare system that emerged out of the crisis of the mid-nineteenth century was built on the foundations of urban and rural poverty and family breakdown and was designed to respond to local problems. Moreover, Scotland's pattern of religious affiliation and distinctive education and legal systems also had, and still have, a bearing on how needy childen were protected. Perhaps the most interesting feature of Scotland's difference in this field, however, is her geographical and cultural divide — between the urban centres and the rural Highlands. All of these distinctive features helped to structure a system of care characterised by the boarding out of urban children in the countryside, and by institutional care provided by religious charities with limited state intervention. It is a pattern that continued well into the twentieth century. At least until 1945 a Scottish child left homeless was far more likely than a similar child in England to be boarded out in a rural environment far away from his or her cultural roots or placed in a remote institution which sought to separate the child permanently from family ties.

Despite the longevity of nineteenth century structures which to some extent outlived shifts in ideology, there have been changes. Since 1945 the proportion of Scottish children cared for under the auspices of the child welfare system has declined dramatically. More effective welfare provision, less interventionist strategies of child protection that place greater emphasis on helping families to stay together combined with the closure of the large and impersonal children's homes and the decline in the birth rate has meant that although in 1998 more than 12,000 children in Scotland are recorded as being in the care or under the supervision of local authorities the vast majority — around 70 per cent — are still living at home. Yet the question of how Scotland's most vulnerable children are being and were cared for in the past has probably received more attention in recent years than ever before. A series of crises within the modern child welfare system, particularly concerning the quality of residential care but also focusing on the role of social services in investigating allegations of physical and sexual abuse, have raised searching questions about how our society protects its children.

The rest of this book will narrate the history of how Scotland cared for its most vulnerable children over the course of 150 years. Inevitably, some groups of children are not included in this study. Those who were offically adopted were swiftly removed from the child welfare system and deemed no longer to be 'homeless'. Children admitted to reformatories and industrial schools (later Approved and then 'List D' schools) are only mentioned in passing as their story has been told elsewhere.[78] 'Juvenile delinquents', child criminals, the mentally and physically handicapped were given special treatment outside the core care system. The story of those who do appear in these pages — the orphaned, deserted, homeless, neglected and abused — will be informed by the voices of those who experienced the system. Of course it is much easier to write about the policies affecting children and even ideas about childhood than about children themselves, their experiences and their emotions, their fears and anxieties and their moments of pleasure. This book places the child at the centre of the discussion by using the recollections of those who spent their childhood in an institution or boarded-out with a foster family. In addition, the personal files of hundreds who passed through the welfare network and the papers of the key organisations and charities involved in child welfare policy and practice have been tapped. Children are absent from most historical studies, especially in Scotland, yet by studying a group of Scottish children who did leave some record of their lives we may gain insight into society's attitude towards children in the past in an effort to understand how children are treated in Scotland today.

NOTES

1. SAS, PD 41: Whinwell Children's Home case files, M 74 (1902). Identification codes are my own.
2. The figure for England is estimated to be between 70,000 and 80,000 before 1914.
3. *B.P.P., 36th Annual Report of the Board of Supervision for the Relief of the Poor and of Public Health in Scotland, 1880–81*, 1881, Cmd.2971, p.xv; *40th Annual Report*, 1884–5, Vol.XXXIV, p.268.
4. T.M. Devine, 'Scottish Urbanisation' in T.M.Devine, *Exploring the Scottish Past* (East Linton, 1995), p.116.
5. R.L.Stevenson, *Picturesque Old Edinburgh* (Edinburgh, 1983), p.33.
6. T.M.Devine, 'Urbanisation', in T.M.Devine & R.Mitchison (eds.), *People and Society in Scotland, Volume I, 1760–1830* (Edinburgh, 1988), p.43.
7. M.Flinn (ed), *Report on the Sanitary Condition of the Labouring Population of Great Britain* by Edwin Chadwick, 1842 (Edinburgh, 1969).
8. J.Butt, 'Working-Class Housing in the Scottish Cities 1900–1950' in G.Gordon & B.Dicks (eds.), *Scottish Urban History* (Aberdeen, 1983), p.234.
9. R.Rodger, 'Crisis and Confrontation in Scottish Housing, 1880–1914', in R. Rodger (ed), *Scottish Housing in the Twentieth Century* (Leicester, 1989), p.29.
10. R. Rodger, *Housing in Urban Britain 1780–1914* (Cambridge, 1989), p.37.
11. See F.Worsdall, *The Glasgow Tenement: A Way of Life* (Glasgow, 1989) and J.Faley, *Up Oor Close: Memories of Domestic Life in Glasgow Tenements, 1910–1945* (Glasgow, 1990), pp. 476–80.
12. See J.Cunnison and J.B.S.Gilfillan, *The Third Statistical Account of Scotland: the City of Glasgow* (Glasgow, 1958).
13. J.B.Russell cited in M.A.Crowther, 'Poverty, Health and Welfare' in W.H.Fraser & R.J.Morris (eds.), *People and Society in Scotland Vol II, 1830–1914* (Edinburgh, 1990), p.283.
14. The mortality rate per 100 cases notified in Aberdeen was 6.8 for one-roomed dwellings and 3.0 for two-roomed in 1893–1902. W.L.Mackenzie, *Scottish Mothers and Children,* (Dunfermline, 1917), p.283.

15. For example, compared with an average number of overcrowded houses as a percentage of the total houses of 30.3% in 1935 and an average infant mortality rate of 98 infant deaths per 1,000 births, the figures for Hutchesontown were 48.1% overcrowding and 106 infant deaths, Gorbals 37.7 and 131, Parkhead 43.7 and 92. These contrast with Cathcart whose figures were 6.1 and 61. *The Third Statistical Account: Glasgow*, Tables 75 and 91.

16. See C.G.Brown, 'Urbanisation and Living Conditions' in R.Pope (ed), *Atlas of British Social and Economic History since c.1700* (London, 1989), p.176.

17. Mackenzie, *Scottish Mothers and Children*, p.430.

18. For example, R.Glasser, *Growing Up in the Gorbals* (London, 1986); G.Rountree, *A Govan Childhood: the Nineteen Thirties* (Edinburgh, 1993); E.Cowan, *Spring Remembered: A Scottish Jewish Childhood* (London, 1974); J.T.Caldwell, *Severely Dealt With: Growing Up in Belfast and Glasgow* (Bradford, 1993).

19. Cited in Crowther, 'Poverty, Health and Welfare', p.266.

20. GCA, D-HEW 27/3: Parish of Govan Combination, Children Act 1908 Part II, 18.3.1915.

21. SRO, GD 409/57/1: Annual Report of the Glasgow Society for the Prevention of Cruelty to Children, 1885.

22. GCU, RSSPCC Archive: SNSPCC Glasgow Branch Annual Report, 1910.

23. R.J.Morris, 'Urbanisation and Scotland' in Fraser & Morris (eds.), *People and Society*, p.83.

24. SAS, PD 41: Whinwell Case Files, G76 (1913).

25. *Third Statistical Account: Glasgow*, p.794; R.Mitchison and L.Leneman, *Sexuality and Social Control: Scotland 1660–1780* (Oxford, 1989), p.156.

26. A.Blaikie, *Illegitimacy, Sex and Society. Northeast Scotland 1750–1900* (Oxford, 1993), pp.141–5.

27. In 1858 the illegitimacy ratio for Scotland as a whole was 8.9 per 1,000 births but this figure hides wide variations. Particularly high rates were consistently recorded in the north east (especially Banffshire, 16.0) and the south west whilst the northwestern area recorded a rate of 4.6. See Blaikie, *Illegitimacy, Sex and Society*, p.11.

28. GCA, D-CH 1/1: City of Glasgow Children's Committee Minute Book no.1, 24 March 1857.

29. GCA: Half Yearly Report of the Inspector of the Parish Council, May 1909.

30. GCA, D-HEW 33/1: Criminal Officers' Reports Vol.VIII, Desertion 1910, case G10 1803.

31. GCA, D-HEW 33/17: Criminal Officer's Reports, Desertion, case 3/12/16418.

32. I.Levitt & C.Smout, *The State of the Scottish Working Class in 1843* (Edinburgh, 1979) pp.190–1.

33. Cited in I.Levitt, *Government and Social Conditions in Scotland 1845–1919* (Edinburgh, 1988), p.51.

34. See I.Levitt, *Poverty and Welfare in Scotland 1890–1948* (Edinburgh, 1988), p.32.

35. See E. Gordon, *Women and the Labour Movement in Scotland* (Oxford, 1991), p.25.

36. See E. Roberts, *A Woman's Place: An Oral History of Working-Class Women 1890–1940* (Oxford, 1984), pp.144–5.
37. Aberlour Child Care Trust: Schedule 201.
38. SAS, PD 41: Whinwell case files, G62 (1915).
39. Interview with Frances.
40. For example, in parts of Germany. See M. Lindemann, 'Love for Hire: the Regulation of the Wet-Nursing Business in 18th Century Hamburg', *Journal of Family History*, 6 (1981), pp.379–95.
41. See M.L.Arnot, 'Infant Death, Child Care and the State: the Baby-Farming Scandal and the First Infant Life Protection Legislation of 1872', *Continuity and Change*, 9 (1994), pp.271–311.
42. See H.M.Dunbar, 'Philanthropy in Twentieth Century Glasgow with Special Reference to Children', Mphil, University of Strathclyde 1987, pp.81–3.
43. 'The Traffic in Infants', *Glasgow Herald*, 5 January 1910.
44. Mackenzie, *Scottish Mothers and Children*, pp.120–5. On the operation of the Scottish magdalene homes see B.Littlewood and L.Mahood, 'Prostitutes, Magdalenes and Wayward Girls: Dangerous Sexualities of Working Class Women in Victorian Scotland', *Gender and History*, 3 (1991), pp.160–75.
45. SRO: GD 409/5/1, Annual Report of the SNSPCC, 1886.
46. See J.Treble, 'The Characteristics of the Female Unskilled Labour Market and the Formation of the Female Casual Labour Market in Glasgow, 1891–1914', *Scottish Economic and Social History*, 6 (1986), p.39.
47. Aberlour Child Care Trust, Schedule 1502.
48. GCA, D-HEW 33/1: Criminal Officers' Reports, Vol.VIII, Desertion 1910, case A 29245.
49. B.R.Mitchell and P.Deane, *Abstract of British Historical Statistics* (Cambridge, 1962), p.37. This figure was lower than in England and Wales where it stood at 156 in the same year.
50. Figures cited in O.Checkland, 'Maternal and Child Welfare' in O.Checkland & M.Lamb (eds.), *Health Care as Social History: The Glasgow Case* (Aberdeen, 1982), pp.126–7, 213.
51. See *Third Statistical Account: Glasgow*, p.884. In Glasgow, for instance, the infant mortality rate was 146 in 1903 and declined steadily so that it was only 96 in 1933 but after the war the rate declined dramatically to 36 in 1953.
52. *Ibid.*, p.119.
53. *Ibid.* pp.117–33; H.Tait, 'Maternity and Child Welfare' in G.McLachlan (ed), *Improving the Common Weal: Aspects of Scottish Health Services 1900–1984* (Edinburgh, 1987), pp.411–440.
54. T.M.Devine, 'Women on the Land, 1850–1914' in Devine, *Exploring the Scottish Past*, p.213.
55. R.Anthony, *Herds and Hinds. Farm Labour in Lowland Scotland 1900–1939* (Edinburgh, 1997), p.63 and p.163.
56. *Ibid.,* p.65.
57. Cited in Devine, 'Women on the Land', p.216.
58. See B.W.Robertson, 'In Bondage: the Female Farm Worker in South East

Scotland' in E.Gordon & E.Breitenbach (eds.), *The World is Ill Divided* (Edinburgh, 1990), pp.117–35.

59. L.Jamieson & C. Toynbee, *Country Bairns* (Edinburgh, 1992), p.26.
60. SAS, PD 41: Whinwell case files, H 39 (1899).
61. See E.Ross, *Love and Toil. Motherhood in Outcast London, 1870–1918* (Oxford, 1993).
62. A.Davin, *Growing Up Poor. Home, School and Street in London 1870–1914* (London, 1996), p.61.
63. *Ibid.*, p.43. See also Ross, *Love and Toil.*
64. Jessie Kesson, *The White Bird Passes* (Edinburgh, 1958).
65. M.Henderson, *Finding Peggy: A Glasgow Childhood* (London, 1994).
66. OHS: History Book 1905–6.
67. Interview with Arthur.
68. Cowan, *Spring Remembered*, pp.20–3.
69. See Davin, *Growing Up Poor*, p.99.
70. SAS, PD 41: Whinwell case files, H32 (1914).
71. GCA, D-HEW 33/1: Case G57346.
72. H.Hendrick, *Child Welfare: England 1872–1989* (London, 1994), p.25.
73. H.Cunningham, *Children and Childhood in Western Society since 1500* (London, 1995), p.41.
74. Figure cited in Levitt, *Poverty and Welfare*, p.209.
75. Hendrick, *Child Welfare*, p.80.
76. *Ibid.*, p.74.
77. See Ross, *Love and Toil.*
78. See L.Mahood, *Policing Gender, Class and Family. Britain, 1850–1940* (London, 1995), a study of juvenile reformatories in Scotland; A.Ralston, 'The Development of Reformatory and Industrial Schools in Scotland, 1832–1872', *Scottish Economic and Social History*, 8 (1988), pp. 40–55; M.Collin, 'The Treatment of Delinquent and Potentially Delinquent Children and Young Persons in Scotland from 1866 to 1937', PhD thesis, University of Strathclyde 1992.

CHAPTER 2

THE BOARDED-OUT CHILD

I remember Glasgow when I was two or three. I can still remember finding my grandmother dead. After that I remember these men arriving with big black coats on and bowler hats, and leaving in a black car with them...I can remember that, and the home in Castlemilk. But the next thing I can remember is being on the ferry coming to Uist...I remember arriving in Lochboisdale, that's very clear. Yes, and this woman saying 'this woman is your new mother.'

— Tom, boarded out on South Uist in 1950s, *Air Fasdadh*.

The Scottish Solution

It is difficult for us to imagine why a child victim of destitution, poverty or neglect should be placed in a foster home often many miles distant from his or her place of birth with guardians hardly better equipped to provide for the child's needs than the birth family. 'How could you expect', remarked one critic in 1945,

> children from the slums of our big cities where they have been accustomed to noise and bustle, crowds and the ever-changing excitement of the city, to be suddenly transplanted to the island of Mull, where one sees nothing but mountains and water, rain and snow, cattle and sheep?[1]

It is even more difficult for us to imagine the emotions of a child suddenly transported to some remote location and left with a strange family with little understanding of the reasons. This was the policy known as 'boarding out' which took children from centres of urban poverty and found them new 'homes' in rural districts. It found great favour in Scotland as a solution to the problem of large numbers of pauper children from the beginning of the nineteenth century until the 1960s. Despite consistent evidence from the early days of the system that some children found new homes in this way were likely to endure ill-treatment and cruelty, sometimes far worse than they might have suffered had they remained with family members or been placed in an institution, Scotland's child welfare professionals consistently rejected institutional care and advocated boarding out as the most appropriate method of caring for needy children. In 1946, the Clyde Committee's report on the care of homeless children in Scotland concluded 'that a good foster parent system should be encouraged as the best solution of the problem, as it is most suited to give the child the necessary individual attention, and scope for the development of its independence and initiative.'[2]

Many Scottish people today have memories of the boarded-out children housed in their communities. Known variously as the 'homies', the 'Glasgow orphans' or 'Glasgow kealies', these children were found foster homes in small towns, farming or crofting communities all over Scotland by the parish and later by the local authorities such as Glasgow Corporation. Indeed 'boarded outs' are regarded as so much a part of Scottish culture that they have been immortalised in Scottish popular literature and in non-fictional accounts of rural life. It is popularly believed that by rejecting the poorhouse and the impersonal orphanage, Scotland — unlike England — showed an enlightened and humanitarian attitude towards children in distress.[3] In the United States the boarding out of New York orphans with families in the mid-West aroused considerable public debate and controversy.[4] The death of a boarded-out child in England in 1945 sparked a campaign there to review the entire child welfare system. In Scotland, however, there appears to have been little public concern at the use of the same system even when a Fife couple — John and Margaret Walton — were convicted of wilful mistreatment of the boarded-out boys in their care in 1945. The reaction to this case in the Scottish press was to focus on the 'difficult' nature of the boys and the many other children requiring local authority care in the abnormal circumstances of the war and its aftermath, the implication being that the Scottish system itself was not at fault.[5]

The very existence of the 'Walton case' alerts us to the fact that the history of boarding out is much more complex and ambiguous than the story told by official reports and reinforced by popular literature. Recollections of foster care by those who experienced the policy first-hand reveal conflicting accounts. For some children boarding out was a successful and happy form of care; it provided an environment in which they thrived and many came to regard their guardians as their only family. 'I don't think it bothered me where my own family were or what they were doing' said Tom boarded on South Uist; 'I couldn't ask for better people to raise me so why should I be jealous of others?'[6] For others, as we shall see, the experience was more traumatic, characterised by ill-treatment, exploitation and emotional neglect.

Urban destitute children had been sent to country areas to live with a foster family at least since the 1770s, some at the behest of parish committees responsible for the care of needy children, others sent by their parents as a form of indentured labour. Early textile mills such as those at Deanston in Perthshire and Robert Owen's New Lanark mill, depended heavily on child labour and thus were happy to accept destitute children, accommodating them in a boarding house and employing them until the age of 15 or 16.[7] Moreover, fostering had always been a feature of Highland life, a form of a community response to the need for care of homeless children. In 1843 the Poor Law Inquiry Commissioners noted that 'orphans, foundlings, and deserted children were usually boarded either with relations or friends...or with strangers who were willing to take charge of them'.[8] However, it was not until the 1860s that parishes across Scotland but especially those in urban centres, adopted the boarding-out system as the primary means of finding homes for the orphaned, deserted and separated children dependent on poor relief, a policy affirmed by the 1876 Poor Law (Scotland) Act which laid down that 'no orphan or deserted child, and no child separated from its parents, shall be detained in any poor house for a longer period than three months.'[9] This followed the precedent of the boarding out of lunatics which was encouraged in Scotland by the 1857 Lunacy Act as a way of reducing the numbers in asylums.[10] By 1880, out of a total of just over 8,000 children dependent on poor relief more than 5,000 were boarded out, the majority with strangers in rural areas, the rest with relatives closer to home. On the eve of the First World War, as figure 2.1 shows, 86 per cent of Scotland's 8,873 pauper children were found homes with foster families.

It is not surprising to find that the overwhelming majority of the boarded-out children were those 'rescued' from the slums of Glasgow, Edinburgh and Aberdeen, but smaller and more rural parishes enthusiastically adopted the system too. In 1881 for instance, the county of Elgin boarded out 83 children, 50 of them with strangers and in Stirlingshire in that year 57 pauper children

Figure 2.1. Total Number of Children in Care and Number of Those Boarded Out, Scotland 1880–1993

Note: There are no accurate available statistics for the period 1940–1949.

The term 'in care' includes children under poor law care until 1945 and under the care of local authorities thereafter. Included in the total figures for 1971–1993 are children under local authority supervision, a large proportion of whom remain at home. The sharp rise beginning in 1976 may be explained by the inclusion of children who were previously excluded (such as those in List D schools). The fashion for assessing all children in care in special assessment centres may also have artificially inflated the figures.

Source: Annual Reports of the Board of Supervision and the Department of Health for Scotland; Scottish Abstract of Statistics.

were found homes with strangers.[11] The greatest supporter of boarding-out, however, was the county of Lanark which included the city of Glasgow. In 1881, for example, almost 1,500 children from that county were relocated from their homes, some of them as far as away as the Highlands and Islands. Certainly between

1845 and 1914 up to 90 per cent of Scottish children dependent on poor relief were boarded out and there was little change in the inter-war period.[12] Indeed, as Figure 2.1 shows, 1933 was a peak year for the number of children under poor law care as a result of the depression, when 8,150 children out of a total of 9,200 were found foster homes.[13] Moreover, as a consequence of the Second World War foster care maintained its popularity as a cure-all for the nation's problem children with the *Edinburgh Evening Dispatch* calling for foster mothers to come forward to take care of Scotland's 80,000 illegitimate children, many of whom, it was alleged, were the product of wartime romances.[14]

It was this policy of boarding out healthy children, many of whom, as we saw in Chapter One, had at least one surviving parent, that distinguishes Scottish child welfare under the Poor Law from the policy implemented in England and Wales. South of the border pauper children were more likely to be provided for in the workhouse where, it was believed, greater control could be exerted over the child's development. Some English Poor Law Unions did try to provide a quasi-family environment by creating so-called 'cottage homes' which grouped children together under the care of a house-mother or father. Boarding out children with individual families was never a popular or widespread solution however, and even when it was adopted on a limited basis towards the end of the nineteenth century it was always regarded as a relatively expensive and time-consuming solution because of the insistence upon an extensive inspection system which was not paralleled in Scotland.[15]

In Scotland there were no such qualms about the relative freedom permitted to children boarded out in the community. The rejection of residential care was wholehearted. In 1864 the Glasgow City Children's Committee turned down a proposal for the establishment of orphanages in the city and vigorously stated its support for boarding-out:

> For upwards of one hundred years Glasgow has adopted the plan of boarding children in carefully selected families...The family circle is the most natural one for the bringing up and training of children...These children look upon the heads of the family as their parents, and the younger branches as brothers and sisters — the best feelings of the heart are engaged, the affections are cherished and drawn out, not smothered in the child's breast as if among

strangers…they are satisfied that they are following the arrangements of the Sovereign of the Universe by placing these children in families where the moral, intellectual and physical training is calculated to fit them for that sphere of life which they are likely to occupy.[16]

William Peterkin's report to the government on the condition of children boarded on the Isle of Arran just two years previously had influenced Scottish opinion. He contrasted the poorhouse child with its 'pale face and inert expression' with the 'robust looking frame' and 'intelligent expression' of the boarded out child.[17] 'I think that pauper brought-up children are like stall-fed cattle, not natural' commented an observer of boarding out as practised by Glasgow's Barony parish, reflecting the predilection for comparing children with animals.[18] The Paisley Board had, in 1866, agreed to continue boarding-out on the grounds that:

> We believe that children brought up in public institutions, when at length turned out in the world, are, as a general rule, feeble in body and mind, and less able to fight their way through life than those who come from the common walks of society. At present our children are living amidst, and already form part of the labouring community in which their after life is to be spent…they are free from the enervating and depressing presence of pauperism. At home, in school, and in the playground, their ordinary routine of life is the same as that of other children…[19]

They were right to reject the poorhouse as an inappropriate form of care for young children. By the mid-nineteenth century poorhouses were becoming inhabited by a diverse group of inmates consisting largely of those who could not be maintained by outdoor relief: the elderly, the sick, the insane, and the inebriate. Such institutions could be frightening and even dangerous for young children and many did pass through them while awaiting a placement elsewhere.[20] Arthur remembered Aberdeen's Oldmill Poorhouse populated mainly by men and the elderly as a place where 'I was terrified because they stood in the corridor and to me like they were fearsome to look at.'[21] By 1893 when William Peterkin produced his second, more comprehensive report on the entire boarding out system in Scotland he was able to say that 'A marked preference has always been shown in Scotland for the system of dealing with pauper children in private dwellings instead of public institutions, and this has grown.'[22] The only pauper children to be placed in a poorhouse or some other institution were the sick, the disabled, the 'insane' and, before 1880, those who could not be separated from their pauper parents, a category dominated by illegitimate children. However parishes, pioneered by Barony in Glasgow, regularly separated poor law children from parents they regarded as immoral or dissolute and a judgement of 1885 gave parishes more leeway in such cases stating: 'In the case of children whose parents or other near relatives are of the depraved or criminal classes, and where the contact of the relatives with the children would be manifestly injurious to the latter, the Parochial Board would probably be justified in keeping the children apart.'[23] In 1891 the judgement was formalised denying automatic access to a pauper child by a parent and henceforth the separation policy was adopted by parishes across the country.[24] And in 1894 boarding out was extended to 'children of lunatic parents, children of parents in prison, children of parents who are dissolute and enter the [poor]house'. It was said that some parishes 'even assume the right to board the children out until the parents leave the house, to separate the children altogether.'[25] By 1898 more than 2,000 of Scotland's pauper children had been 'separated from parents'.

By 1914 boarding out was firmly established and there was no change in policy through the inter-war years. In 1945 almost 90 per cent of the 7,000 or so in local authority care were being cared for in this way. Clearly Ian Levitt is correct in asserting that 'it was the boarding out of otherwise healthy children that distinguished Scottish child care from English';[26] whether the seemingly progressive Scottish system was more effective or successful than the policy south of the border may only be judged by a close analysis of children's experience of boarding out.

Urban Slum to Rural Idyll?

To find the younger children...or others, after school hours, enjoying themselves on the sea beach, playing about the family hearth, running messages for the family to the nearest shop...or looking after the cows, or sheep or poultry, helping to plant potatoes, or engaged in any of the many rural avocations of crofters' children — amidst beautiful scenery, and in a healthy climate, with good lodging, wholesome food, and decent and sufficient clothing — is so great a contrast to the life of the children in the lanes and bye-streets of the great towns, or even in the well-regulated Poorhouses, *where restraint must be enforced and strict discipline maintained* — that, personally, I should regret if it should be found necessary...to interfere with the present arrangements.[27]

If there is one constant theme in the official discourse on boarding out from this paeon to its advantages by William Peterkin in 1863 through to the 1960s, it is the benefits of removing children from the urban slums to the rural districts where they might flourish away from the harmful influences of the city. Crofting society in particular was portrayed as a natural, healthy environment. The climate, and especially the fresh air and sea breeze in coastal areas, were regarded as invigorating for children, and crofting families could provide good, wholesome food: plenty of oatmeal, milk and potatoes. In view of the fact that pauper children were not infrequently malnourished, suffering from rickets and other acquired conditions as a result of urban conditions, such concerns were in the child's interests, but equally the emphasis on the environment was indicative of a romanticised view of the Highlands which contrasted with the image of the wicked and disease-ridden city. This anti-urban rhetoric owed much to nineteenth century evangelical preaching on the immorality of the industrial city. Thomas Chalmers, the inspiration behind the Free Church, was the leading proponent of this view in Britain. For Chalmers the city, with its culture of dependence (on poor relief), its profligacy and heathenism, stood in stark contrast to the pre-industrial rural community based on the ecclesiastical and moral unity of the parish.[28] The countryside of course, and especially the Highlands, was almost free of temptation. Public houses were few and far between and the strict presbyterianism of the Free Church which dominated in many Highland communities ensured that children would be reared to be hard-working, God-fearing citizens, lessening the possibility that they would become paupers in later life. 'The God-fearing farming and fisher folk did much character building' noted Glasgow's Children's Officer looking back on a century of boarding out, transforming children into 'good upright citizens.'[29] Thus, boarding out in crofting and fishing districts easily attracted support — who would not wish children to be brought up in such an environment? — but it thinly disguised a number of ulterior motives which may have compromised the quality of care received by at least some children removed under the policy.

Young boy with calf, Barra, c. 1920s. This picture suggests the happy side of rural life for the boarded out child. Comunn Eachdraidh Bharraidh.

The city parishes in Aberdeen, Edinburgh and especially Glasgow were the most enthusiastic advocates of rural foster care. In 1895 Glasgow's Barony parish had children boarded out as far apart as Dumfries and Castle Douglas in the south to the Black Isle, Tomintoul and Buckie in the north. Twenty-four children had been found homes on the Island of Islay, another 35 on Iona.[30] Very few, just 37, were with families in the city of Glasgow itself, and their situation was generally deplored by the parish visitors. 'Altogether we cannot report so favourably as to the general appearance of the children here as compared with those boarded with strangers in the country' wrote an inspector after visiting children residing north of the Clyde in 1883:

a few of the children are boarded with grandparents who are aged and infirm, and consequently unfit to take proper care of those under their charge. They are also exposed to the many evil influences and examples seen in a large city like this, and more especially in the crowded localities. The same healthy, robust, and cheery looks of the children boarded in the country is here absent, and a few of the children wore that peevish, languid look which plainly told the rearing up in a polluted and confined atmosphere, and the evil of too much tea drinking...[31]

Inspectors never missed an opportunity to reinforce their preference for rural placements and their heartfelt belief that children benefited from being removed from the city. Upon visiting three children boarded out in a cottar's cottage in a 'most picturesque situation' in Tombrae on Speyside, the inspector from Glasgow learned of an older sister who remained in the city hawking for a living.

We could not resist being struck by the difference of sphere, and the much better chance the three here have of growing up useful members of society than the older one, who has not had the good fortune to be thrown on the parish while of tender age when she would have had our care and attention.[32]

Glasgow continued to find rural homes for its city children as late as the 1950s and 60s. In 1953 there were 550 Glasgow children boarded out in the county of Inverness, another 114 in Ross and Cromarty and 130 in Argyll; in fact 27 of the 31 Scottish counties contained Glasgow's boarded-out children.[33] Indeed it was in the post-war period that islands such as Barra and South Uist were first opened up to receive children, primarily to help find homes for Roman Catholics who were difficult to place. Great care was taken to board children with a family of the same religious denomination; in fact it was forbidden to send a Catholic child to a Protestant home which meant that many Catholic children were far more likely to end up in a children's home, usually Smyllum Roman Catholic orphanage in Lanark, if they could not be found a family in one of the few pockets of Catholicism in rural Scotland, such as Arisaig or Castle Douglas. No distinction was made between the different presbyterian denominations and many children born into the Church of Scotland or the Scottish Episcopalian Church (or no church at all) found themselves in strict Free Church families or even with members of the Brethren where the Sabbath was rigidly observed and frequent church-going was enforced. 'Needless to say' recalled one man brought up in a Free Church family, 'myself and my two brothers could recite the Bible backwards.'[34] Registered 'Protestant' on his birth certificate, Frank was boarded in 1939 with a Salvation Army family in Peterhead and attended church three times on Sundays and on weekday evenings.[35] There appears to have been no attempt though to match children of other faiths with an appropriate family. A child born to a Jewish mother from the Gorbals in Glasgow was designated 'Protestant' and placed with a Free Church family in Aberdeenshire in the 1930s despite the existence of a Jewish orphanage in Glasgow since 1913 and the presence of Jewish foster parents in Glasgow.[36]

Undoubtedly one of the main reasons for boarding out children in rural districts some distance from their place of birth was, in the plain and honest words of Malcolm McNeill, Secretary of the Local Government Board for Scotland, so that 'dissolute relatives do not discover the child and visit it'.[37] Blood was thicker than water in the eyes of the authorities, and it was their intention to try to permanently sever the ties between an 'unworthy' parent and a child. Attempts by parents to make contact with their children were, understandably, not uncommon. While some parents were motivated by mercenary objectives — a child of 13 or 14 could be put to work — others who had been forcibly separated from their bairns must have yearned to know how they were getting on. In 1868 Glasgow Barony parish remarked on just such a case concerning Jane Summers boarded with a female guardian in Luss:

> They have both been much terrified and annoyed of late by the mother of the girl coming down from Glasgow in a state of intoxicated fury threatening them with vengeance and attempting to force the girl away with her...It will be a deplorable pity if this unprincipled mother should succeed in getting her daughter away from the wholesome influences under which she is living and introduced into circumstances where she will most probably be exposed to the withering seductions of vice and intemperance.[38]

The 'wholesome influences' referred not simply to the rural environment but the inhabitants of country areas. Children were believed to be in safe hands with these uncomplicated, hard-working, righteous, law-abiding, God-fearing folk who would take the children into their hearts and their homes, folk who could not be compared with the likes of Mrs Summers. A considerable number of boarded-out children were said to be suffering not only from poverty but also 'the vice of their parents.'[39] A new home with such people would restore these children to health but also good habits. Crofting communities were especially sought after. By the early nineteenth century the crofter had been rehabilitated in the eyes of the Lowland Scots. The image of the rough, papist Highlander had been replaced by the sympathetic victim of the Clearances and famine, and a strict Presbyterian to boot. In hailing the advantages of boarding with crofting families, the oatmeal-eating inhabitants of the Highlands were favourably contrasted with their Lowland and especially English cousins. 'The frugal and provident habits of the northern parts is a household word' opined J.J.Henley in 1870. 'Education has also made the northerner, if not a better man, at least a more intelligent being.'[40] It was said that such a class of people was virtually unknown in England. On Arran, for example,'the natural dispositions of the people are kindly and hospitable', a guarantee apparently, that the children would not be ill-treated.[41] Romanticised images of children boarded in crofting communities were regularly presented which reinforced particularly Glasgow's preference for homes in the crofting counties. These images were repeated well into the twentieth century. In 1947, Glasgow Corporation's Director of Welfare received a letter signed by a number of boys boarded at Roy Bridge in south-west Invernessshire. It was clearly written by a guardian or schoolteacher and was undoubtedly music to the ears of those implementing boarding out at a time when the system was open to some legitimate criticism:

> We are writing to thank you for the shinty pants and jerseys which you so kindly sent us. We will make good use of them. Already we have beaten two teams which gives us four marks. We are enjoying the fresh air in Roy Bridge. We are getting on splendidly at the bag-pipe practices. In Roy Bridge we have many open spaces to play in and our chief game is shinty. What a relief it is to get out of the town and into the country, where, instead of seeing nothing but buildings and grey smoke, you see green fields and trees and the silence is only broken by the soft twittering of the birds and the scurrying of the rabbits.[42]

The affection between the guardians in rural communities and the children was often commented upon. 'It sometimes happens that they prefer to keep them for nothing rather than part with them.'[43] 'It is no uncommon occurrence', remarked the Barony Inspector, 'to see children crying bitterly when taken from strangers with whom they are boarded to be handed to their own parents, preferring the parentage of the Barony board.'[44] By contrast colliery towns were consistently rejected, at least by Glasgow parishes, as unsuitable for boarded-out children. Upon a visit to Blantyre in Lanarkshire inspectors deprecated the housing conditions there, 'with large open public lavies and ashpits in front of their doors' and where 'the dungstead appears as the principal object in what might be called the street.'[45] Fife colliers in particular were classified as 'a class apart, [who] stand very low in the scale of civilisation.'[46] Moreover, colliers' houses and 'others who work in the night shifts' were regarded as a potential risk owing to the 'fact of the men remaining at home and in bed during the day.'[47] The mining town of Girvan on the Ayrshire coast provided a typical example of an undesirable location which contrasted with a crofting community. Upon a visit to that town in 1882 the inspector formed such a poor opinion of the inhabitants that he recommended the immediate removal of the children on the grounds that 'The tenants are of a low class and the females, young and old, appear slatterns who idly lounge about the close mouth and sit unseemly upon the outside stair heads…' Homes that were 'in disrepair, dirty and permeated by disagreeable smells, occasioned…by a neighbour who dealt in fish' and guardians who uttered 'profane, disgusting imprecations' were said to be commonplace in such places.[48]

Apart from the desire to remove children from the immoral influences of the city and their parents, the Poor Law authorities were well aware that by boarding children in country districts they were entering into a mutually beneficial economic relationship with the guardians and the local community. In an extensive report on the condition of children boarded on Arran in 1862 William Peterkin admitted that in addition to benefiting the children, 'the crofters and small farmers in Arran are not only benefited by the cash payments on their account, and enabled to pay their rents more easily than they could do without them, but also a present and prospective supply of servants and labourers, whose wages are at the lowest.'[49] Guardians at that time received between three and six shillings per child per week, depending on the child's needs, which was intended to cover board, food and other necessary items of expenditure. This was a definite saving for the parish since the cost of keeping a child in the poorhouse was estimated to be around four shillings and sixpence a week. In the short term then, in the case of a parish like Glasgow Barony with around 500 children boarded out in the 1880s and 1890s, the cost benefits were significant.

Although the authorities consistently denied that material gain was the prime motive for many foster parents it is undoubtedly the case that boarded-out children were expected to engage in some form of labour and were seen as a source of income. Barony parish's instructions to guardians stated, 'The children should be taught to cultivate industrious habits. They must not, however, be taxed with labour…'[50] Poor Law officials were attempting a careful balancing act. They recognised that guardians did not take the children 'out of pure philanthropy'. 'You see, the possession of a family is a valuable thing for a working man; they become wage earners very early; and so long as they remain under his roof it all adds to the family income.'[51] In fact in 1910 Glasgow, Govan and Edinburgh parishes boarded a fair proportion of their children, around 25 per cent, with families described as 'low income' where it was tacitly acknowledged that the payment received for the child was a necessary component of the guardian's income.[52] Of course most contemporaries were of the opinion that there was little wrong with children working within the household, that they should 'share the common life of the class in which they will have to make their way in after life.'[53] By this it was meant 'peats to carry, peats to dry, corn to stack'.[54] On the other hand, in the era of the Factory Acts which had succeeded in outlawing the most flagrant abuse of child labour by large-scale industry (although agricultural labour was largely unaffected) and the introduction of compulsory schooling in 1873, Parochial Boards were honour bound to try to ensure children were not exploited.

Favoured areas used by Glasgow parishes included Speyside, Banffshire and Aberdeenshire where foster families might be found amongst the relatively wealthy Lowland farmers, the fishing villages of the Moray, Banff and Aberdeenshire coast, and the crofting counties which included Argyll and the Highlands, especially parts of Inverness-shire, Arran, Islay, Iona and later the Outer Hebrides. The Western Isles and Skye, on the other hand, did not find favour with the boarding-out authorities, maybe because of their poor and rebellious reputation. A few children were placed in Caithness and Orkney but Shetland was probably too inaccessible. In most of these Highland districts agriculture was marginal with crofting — a combination of animal husbandry, cultivation of small plots of land supplemented by fishing or poaching or seasonal wage-earning — the main source of income. In coastal areas dominated by a thriving fishing industry — a third of the Scottish steam herring fleet was registered in Buckie in 1913 — vigorous single industry towns characterised by thrift and sobriety were the preferred destinations for boarded-out bairns.[55]

All children, not just the boarded outs, were expected to take part in general farm duties; in the Highlands and Islands there was always plenty of work to do. 'We had three cows and three calves. We'd be making stacks, lifting potatoes and everything', remembered Bernard boarded out on Tiree in the 1960s, adding, 'But we didn't like it. We'd rather be fishing.'[56] Similarly Seumas who spent his childhood on South Uist at the same time recalled kelping:

> We had to go to the shore. We had to keep an eye on the tide. We started when the tide was just going out. We started on the kelp — it was always wet. The muck was wet, the kelp was wet, we often got soaked at the kelp. Getting wet and lifting things — heavy armfuls of kelp. That made your bones ache without a doubt. We were cold and wet. We had to be out in all weathers to make a living from it.[57]

The economic reality in many crofting communities determined that children's contribution was crucial to the standard of living. Children were expected to help out when needed. 'Oh we all worked yes' remarked Betty, boarded on Tiree between 1943 and 1956. '…I look at it this way, it was part and parcel of life, and you were helping, you were needed…'[58] Lynn Jamieson and Claire Toynbee in their oral history of rural childhood in Scotland found that children carried out a wide range of jobs from stacking peats to beating for the grouse shoot, picking blaeberries, hoeing and even ploughing when they were older.[59] But they note that any payment was not usually for the child's personal use. However there was a fine line between reciprocal relationships between

Boy ready to bring home the peat, Barra, 1920s or 1930s. Creeling the peat was a common occupation for children and teenagers. Comunn Eachdraidh Bharraidh.

parents and children and exploitation. Personal recollections are instructive on this point. Although individuals understood the expectation that children would contribute to the household economy they judge the nature of their contribution in relation to the duties expected of other children — especially any natural children of the foster family. Boarded-out children were probably more likely to be treated differently. Peter spent most of his childhood between 1938 and 1949 boarded out in a village on the Moray Firth coast. He remembered trapping and skinning rabbits, looking after hens as well as being sent to the nearest farm during the school holidays to lift potatoes and turnips. Although his foster mother would have received regular payment from Glasgow Corporation for the children she took in, according to Peter they were inadequately fed and deprived of any home comforts. When asked why he thought she had taken in children — up to seven at a time — Peter replied:

> Purely money…Material gain because not just what they would be getting from Glasgow Corporation they were obviously gaining

something from sending us out to the farm to work, I mean we got nothing for it. We had to slave and do what we had to do so I mean she's bound to have got some reward from that…I mean there was no love no, it was just no contact other than at mealtimes or getting told you go and scrub the floor or you polish the stair or clean the henhouse out, that was all.[60]

This guardian also ensured any money Peter received from running errands for neighbours was handed over. 'Did they give you anything? Yes they gave me threepence. Right well hand it over.'[61] There is no shortage of evidence that boarded-out children were often worked harder than guardians' natural children. Peter's foster mother did not send her own son to work and Eileen boarded out in the Outer Hebrides commented:

Some of the work we had to do was really heavy. I'd say it was more for a man than for a child. But the summer was really harder. As soon as it was sun up you were up because you had to bring in the hay, the corn, whatever. It was us that done it. Their own daughters stayed at home.[62]

It would be easy to dismiss such stories as isolated examples but evidence suggests that especially in the more economically marginal areas it was not uncommon to treat boarded-out children as cheap labour. A member of the Tiree community remembered:

When I was young in the 40s and 50s there was poverty here. There wasn't much money. The Glasgow Corporation gave a small sum to those who brought up the 'boarded-outs'. They grabbed at it, and there was no assessment of the people taking the children. If you wanted 'boarded-outs' you got them. Whatever kind of person you were. And the crofters who were here when I was young worked their own children hard, working on the croft, but they were harder on the 'boarded-outs'. They were just what you would call slave labour for many of the crofters who were here.[63]

This point of view is supported by other first hand accounts. It was said that people took in boarded-out children 'to look after their children, do the housework, or farm duties.' 'You will get a weekly allowance for each and make them work. It is so easy to bluff the inspectors.'[64] Naomi Mitchison, in her capacity as a member of the Clyde Committee on Homeless Children in 1945, confirmed this impression. Having already visited Islay where she found the crofts to be relatively prosperous with little need for

Girls creeling the peats at Scaliscro, Lewis, 1920s or 1930s. Scottish Life Archive, National Museums of Scotland.

child labour, she found homes around Inverness by contrast to be very poor. 'Indeed, in many of them, the only money coming into the house would be that which the children bring...'[65] She continued, 'All the children on these crofts were working. We checked up on this by conversation with the children...these remote crofts depend almost entirely on primitive labour and the children will not learn anything which will be useful to them as modern agricultural workers.'[66]

It would be misleading to portray all guardians of boarded-out children as motivated by money. For some, especially women, although the extra money was welcome the chance to take in a child offered company, interest, and sometimes a replacement for children grown-up or dead. Frank's foster mother in Peterhead had lost her husband and three of her five sons at sea; '[she] took me as a child and I was effectively her "relief" from the terrible tragedy she had suffered.'[67] Betty was taken in by a middle-aged, childless couple on Tiree who treated her as their own child. 'I mean she was very very kind...I mean she was just over the moon about getting me, that must have been just what she wanted, she got this wee girl...'[68] Eleanor's foster parents had been unable to have children and treated her as their adopted child; 'I *was* to all intents and purposes their daughter.'[69] But even when the financial motive was uppermost, economic exploitation did not necessarily follow as Frances' story illustrates:

> I think I was boarded out because he [her foster father] didn't approve of women working so it was a bit of, you know, extra cash…that didn't make any difference, none at all, none at all to my upbringing because when we were married I said I don't want a white wedding, 'oh yes, the other two girls did so you're having one too'.[70]

Whether boarding out in the Highlands and Islands, particularly since the 1920s, was a deliberate attempt to repopulate these areas against a background of fears of rural depopulation and the disintegration of Highland society, is difficult to judge. Social organisation, especially in the Hebrides and more remote parts of the Highland mainland, was seen to be breaking down, assisted by the 'tyranny of religion' — in the main the strict Presbyterianism of the Free Church — and the decline of Gaelic culture and accompanying anglicisation, notably in the schools. The boarding out of large numbers of young children to these areas may have been seen as one solution to the problem and certainly the sheer numbers involved contributed to the survival of some communities and their culture through the maintenance of the local school.[71] Significantly, the recent departure for the mainland of one of Eriskay's first boarded-out children with his wife and young family has been said to symbolise the current problem of depopulation and ageing on some of the more economically marginal and inaccessible islands.[72]

Health and Happiness

> The child's first need is a stable background, true affection and understanding; cleanliness, food and clothing of course. The best homes are not necessarily the best furnished or those of the 'house-proud' type of woman. A kindly, warm-hearted guardian is the most important and can go a long way to make up for what the child has missed…Life in a home, in a household where a child is taken in as one of the family, has an advantage over any institution. It shares the ups and downs of family life and learns to give and take, and takes part in the pleasures and disappointments of the family. This is a far better preparation for life than to live in even a small institution…[73]

By the 1940s when this observation on the boarding-out system was penned, the middle-class image of the family as an affective, emotional unit which essentially provided children with a secure and protective environment, had gained ascendancy. Gone was the widespread expectation that children would contribute economically to the household and learn the habits of independence and industry; compulsory education and the removal of children from the labour force buttressed the conception of the family as a place within which the child would be nurtured and protected. Such a view of the family was a far cry from that envisaged by nineteenth-century child welfare professionals who, as we have seen, set great store by the external environment in which a child should be brought up at the expense of domestic circumstances. Until the 1930s and probably much later in some areas, the welfare of a boarded-out child was judged largely upon evidence of the physical well-being of that child. If a child was found to be healthy and robust by the parish inspector he or she was judged able to make his or her way in life and to shake off the traces of hereditary pauperism. Hence children were quite frequently removed from unsuitable guardians for reasons connected with their physical welfare. In 1889 for instance, the visiting inspector recommended the immediate removal of two Glasgow Barony children boarded in Tomintoul on the grounds that:

> The children's heads here are ill-kept and dirty. Mrs Forbes looks like a woman *not all there*. She is thowless and soft, and in our opinion unfit to be continued as one of our guardians. She has been found fault with before, but the heads are as filthy as ever.[74]

A visit in the same year to the children boarded out on Iona discovered Malcolm and William Carrick who were judged to be 'dirty and untidy, traces of vermin being observed on their skin.' Their clothes were found to be full of 'ova' upon close inspection.[75] Inspectors were similarly disturbed by what they regarded as 'undue and cruel' punishment. A case of a boy with an inflamed eye, apparently the result of a thrashing by his teacher with the tawse, prompted the inspector to remonstrate with the teacher. 'We pointed out to her that the Board would not, upon any consideration, allow her to abuse any of the children under her charge.'[76] While not an isolated case, in general inspectors and those higher up in the child welfare hierarchy were reluctant to accept the existence of adult cruelty towards children, especially in the case of foster parents.[77] Ill-use of a child was seen to be a vice of the urban classes. When asked in 1896 whether any cases of cruelty towards boarded-out children had come to light, Malcom McNeill replied: 'None' and continued, 'I may say that these associations for the protection of children exist only in the large towns…but it is only the low class of population in towns that are found to ill-use their children', thus perpetuating a long-standing myth that a child was safe in a rural community and that in the favoured areas community policing could be relied upon to protect a child from mistreatment.[78]

The obsession with appearance was not always at the expense of emotional well-being however. There is no doubt that the parish authorities wished boarded-out children to be treated no different from native children and to this end they went to great lengths to remove any distinguishing marks of pauperism, particularly in the form of distinctive clothing. It was always a matter of some considerable pride for Poor Law inspectors to contrast the appearance of 'their' children with those placed in institutions who could frequently be distinguished by a uniform or some form of 'pauper stamp'. Citing the example of the Edinburgh parish of St. Cuthbert's which boarded children in mid-Calder, Malcolm McNeill reported:

> When the children came first, the boys wore uniform of white moleskin, the girls of blue drugget — every article stamped St Cuthbert's Poorhouse. They were ashamed of it and of themselves, and the other children kept aloof from them; they were looked upon as pariahs — the stamp of pauper was on them and pauper they would have remained.[79]

Apparently once the badge of pauperism was removed from these children 'The hang-dog look of pauperism gradually disappeared from their faces — they saw themselves treated as other children and soon became as others.'[80] Similarly, inspectors in the Highlands remarked upon the fact that native boys were all dressed in kilts while those boarded out were clothed in fustian jacket and trousers.[81] Just a year later the situation had been remedied, the visitation report noting that 'the introduction of the kilt in the Highland as well as in some of the Lowland districts is a vast improvement both as to cleanliness and freedom of action…it entirely removes the pauper badge from them.'[82] The policy of providing clothing for boarded-out children continued until the 1960s but the problem of the children being marked out as different was never really overcome as the clothing never fitted properly. To a young child such things could be crucial to his or her sense of self respect. 'I remember well you'd get long trousers that reached well down past your knees', said Ian boarded on Tiree. 'They looked awful those trousers. The others boys in school had neat, short trousers and that was a pointer, you know, that these lads weren't the same as people's own sons.'[83]

The concern with children's physical well-being and outward appearance on the part of the parish authorities was genuine and well meant but it concealed fundamental flaws in boarding-out policy and practice. Many of the defects were highlighted in evidence received by the 1945 Clyde Committee on Homeless Children when boarding out was placed under special scrutiny following the death of Denis O'Neill in England that year. Clear evidence which pointed to the failures of the policy was quickly and easily accumulated. When Lady Margaret Kerr set off on a fact-finding tour to Aberdeenshire she discovered:

> Mrs Moira Campbell, Aucharney, Hatton. Accommodation: a but and ben, tiny sandwich room with window. Two members in the household: the youngest an infant of a few months (illegitimate child of the eldest girl) and three boarded out children, boys age 7, 4 and 2. Payment of 12/6d per week and 10/-. Eldest boy at school. House filthy. Bedding filthy and very inadequate. Guardian ill in bed. Girl of approximately 15 running the house. Boarding out authority Aberdeen. No record book of visits from inspectors. Home utterly unsuitable and should be black listed.[84]

Cases like this one were not uncommon. For a local authority like Glasgow with large numbers of children in need of new homes, boarding out was a convenient policy which gave the illusion that these children were receiving the best and most appropriate form of care. Few, then or now, would disagree with the basic premise that a child is better off being cared for by a family than in an institution, a principle accepted by the Curtis Committee in England who stated in 1946 that 'there is probably a greater risk of acute unhappiness in a foster home, but…a happy foster home is happier than life as generally lived in a large community.'[85] As we have already seen, foster care was cheaper than institutional care and children were being reared in a healthy environment and amongst a particular class of people such that the child would learn 'to battle with the world' and make his or her own way in life.[86] However, the process of selecting guardians and inspecting homes was slapdash and lax, exposing some children to mistreatment.

There was little attempt to vet potential foster parents; despite the protestations of Malcolm McNeill that local parish officers carefully selected and visited the homes of boarded-out children, evidence points to a far more relaxed state of affairs.[87] Glasgow parishes frequently loaded a large motor-car with children and set off northwards. Once beyond Perth they would stop at small towns, villages and crofts to ask for homes for the children. Sometimes local ministers or doctors would be asked to recommend potential foster families but all too often the car would simply draw up outside a house and the occupants would come outside to view the children on offer and choose those they liked the look of.[88] This would continue until the car was empty. One can only imagine the feelings of the last child to be found a home, an experience recalled by Betty taken to Tiree in 1943. Following a dreadful boat journey from Oban, the ten children were loaded into the ubiquitous black taxi and motored around the island with this respondent remembering how people 'just came out and shook their heads and went away again' before she was finally taken by the owners of the island post-office who took pity on her.[89] Robert, boarded out in Buckie in the 1930s and 40s remembered how:

> ...the Corporation they came up every three months religiously to check on the kids and times they had a kid with them, you see, to foster...so they came into Granny Gibson, Granny Gibson couldnae take him you see, oh but try Joan, my daughter, Joan down the brae you see...anyway down she goes and Joan says well she says I can't take him, I can't she says, but she says you can leave him here and do your travelling and come back for him and they ken that were all right...[90]

Of course the Corporation never came back for this child. Peter had a similar story to tell of his own experience. Initially boarded with a widow in a small village in Inverness-shire, he, his elder brother and several other fostered children were simply transferred to the care of the widow's house-servant when she died. There was no attempt to ascertain the suitability of this woman and the cruelty experienced by Peter and others in her care is testament to the lax procedures of Glasgow's boarding-out officers.[91]

The inspection of children, their guardians and homes was carried out by officials from the children's parish of settlement, usually the Inspector of Poor and a representative of the Children's Committee. There was no obligation on officials in the parish where the children were boarded to look after their welfare. The Board of Supervision, later the Local Government Board and subsequently local authorities, prided themselves on the efficacy — and no doubt cost efficiency — of this system. Inspections were supposed to take place two or three times a year without prior warning. They examined the children's appearance and state of health and inspected the dwelling, especially the sleeping arrangements. Comments were noted in a black book kept by the guardian. Successive inquiries questioning the ability of distant parishes to effectively protect the children in their care were complacently brushed aside despite an admission that inspectors for large parishes such as Glasgow and Edinburgh could not possibly visit all the children personally and therefore relied upon information gathered by local inspectors.[92] Glasgow employed just four inspectors between 1931 and 1948 when the number of children boarded out all over the country was around 2,500.[93] With the best will in the world inspectors could not uncover all cases of ill-treatment. Peter and his older brother who suffered a broken arm and a burst eardrum respectively at the hands of their guardian noted that these incidents were never uncovered by the inspector who was effectively bamboozled by a manipulative guardian and the fear of her charges.

> I mean Glasgow Corporation they sent an inspector once a year or something. They always must have told them when they were coming. They didn't arrive out of the blue. So we were all lined up the day beforehand and warned 'when the inspector asks you whether you like it here you'll tell him yes or you'll get another hammering'. So of course when the inspector [said] 'how do you like it here, do you like it here?' 'Oh yes', you know, you daren't say anything else...[94]

Whilst it would have been difficult for any inspector to thoroughly assess the conditions of a boarded-out child, the potential for not recognising cases of mistreatment was heightened by authorities' naive expectation that community self-policing would prevent cases of child abuse occurring thereby permitting them to keep costs down. '...It is very improbable', remarked William Peterkin in 1862, 'that any harsh treatment of any child should occur without being well known to the entire district.'[95] As we know today, child abuse is usually well hidden.

In their eagerness to separate children from dangerous influences, to remove them from the cities, and to prevent hereditary pauperism, the architects of the boarding-out policy appear to have underestimated the complicated machinery required to ensure that children who were being 'rescued' from poverty, homelessness and immorality were not placed in equally dangerous circumstances in the countryside. Although boarding out was a genuine attempt to substitute personal for institutional care, the policy was nevertheless driven by a political and economic agenda which paid little heed to the real emotional needs of the children. Considering that many of these children came from disturbed backgrounds, had experienced the death of one or both parents, had been neglected or had been forcibly separated from their family by the Poor Law officials and may have spent some time in a poorhouse or children's home, it would be surprising if their integration into a family and a community was smooth and untroubled. From the outset of the boarding-out scheme, the relationship between the children and their guardians was an ambiguous one. Foster parents were instructed that 'a kindly feeling should be cultivated between the guardians and the children, who ought to be treated, as far as possible, as members of the family in which they are boarded...', and yet guardians were reminded that the children who were 'orphans or have been deserted by worthless parents...should also be taught to cultivate industrious habits'.[96] Little or no information was provided to guardians on the background of the children, and whilst entreating parents to care for the child as one of the family there appeared to have been no policy on whether to inform the child of his or her status. As a result children could find themselves in a cultural and emotional no-man's land — neither recognised as one of the inner family circle nor as an outside — a position sometimes reinforced by wider community attitudes to the 'boarded-outs'. In fact, as we shall see, children's relationships with their foster parents and with the wider community were at best characterised by cultural misunderstanding and at worst by rejection and misuse.

A Home from Home?

When asked what he called his foster mother Peter recalled, after a long pause: 'I didn't call her anything...no I can't remember ever calling her anything, no, because you didn't speak until you were spoken to...'[97] This man's experience may not have been typical but his words spoke volumes about his relationship with his foster mother. It is only relatively recently that the importance of the mother-child relationship has been recognised and has influenced child welfare policy. Since the 1950s the writings of John Bowlby and others on the effects of maternal deprivation on a child's psychopathology have informed policy towards children in care. In the early days of boarding out however, as we have already seen, greater attention was paid to a child's physical well-being and material requirements at the expense of emotional needs. A loving relationship between foster parents and boarded-out child was almost a bonus; it was invariably commented upon by inspectors as did the Glasgow Barony children's inspector in 1864: 'I remember seeing an old man when parting with a boy saying, while the tears were running down his cheeks, "awed, awed Jock, it's na dout for yer guid yer gan to work, but its [hard] to part wa ye."'[98] But a close relationship between a child and the foster parents, and especially the mother, was central to the child's sense of identity and belonging. As two sisters boarded on Barra explained:

> I remember the night we got word of my mother's death in Glasgow. We felt very strange because our mother...was in front of us. She was with us so we didn't feel we had suffered any great loss...
>
> My mother came down saying how sorry she was that they'd heard that night that our mother had died. And we were all saying 'But Mum, you're here.'...it didn't put us up or down. Our mother was with us.[99]

Yet, in spite of the evident closeness in these cases it was rare for a boarded-out child to take the surname of his or her foster family. The child was legally in the care of the parish or local authority and only an adopted child might have a name changed by deed poll. The anomaly inevitably caused problems. When Frances was boarded as a baby with an Aberdeenshire family called Garrioch she kept her natural mother's maiden name, 'but then you see the Garrioch was always in brackets after everything, in anything official.' Frances had no idea she was a fostered child until the age of seven when, following the taunts of schoolfriends, she discovered the documentation under her parent's bed. The reason for her double surname was thus revealed, but Frances' sense of identity remained less confused.[100]

Within the foster home, relations with guardians' natural children and the pattern of everyday activities helped to determine a child's sense of belonging. There were the inevitable jealousies and rivalries when a new foster child arrived in the family. Frances recalls the relationship with one of her sisters as permanently difficult; 'all at once she realised she wasn't the baby you see, her life had been ruined by me she thought...right up to middle age she said her nose was out of joint with me.'[101] But tensions were not always so long-lasting. Robert referred to his guardian's children as well as her other fostered children as his 'brothers and sisters...it was the only family I ever knew you see.'[102] 'I was very much their daughter although they never adopted me or anything like that' remembered Betty.[103] However, in some families the boarded-out children were made to feel different and even treated as second-class citizens, prevented from eating with the rest of the family, given inferior and inadequate food and barred from certain activities despite a Department of Health instruction of 1931 stating 'distinctions should not be drawn between the children.'[104] Peter remembered never being allowed in the parlour where his foster parents and their natural son lived, ate and listened to the radio. There were other privations in this household too:

> [you] got your breakfast which was always porridge and if you didn't eat it at breakfast time it was waiting for you at lunchtime when you came in from school and if you didn't eat it then it was waiting for you at night. So of course you were starving when you got to bed so they had what you call the hen pail where they threw their old crusts and their stale bread and we used to creep down in the middle of the night and steal a crust and away back up to bed...[105]

The detested porridge was so thick you could 'stuff it in your pocket when you're going to school [and throw it] over the hedge.'[106] Similarly Eileen recounted how the boarded outs in her household were made to eat in the scullery. 'They had chicken soup, chicken, potatoes, the lot. Ours consisted of the bones of the chicken and the skin of the chicken. That was our dinner. You could've maybe got a slice of bread as well. You got used to it...'[107]

The confidence in the ability of the boarding-out system to provide a stable and affectionate family environment expressed by many in child welfare practice was not entirely misplaced despite these failures. For every child brought up in a loveless family there were those who were accepted into the homes and the hearts of their parents and siblings. Robert, boarded on Tiree in the 1960s when he was three and half years old, commented that 'I was happy and felt at home there. They were a nice family, and I never regretted being with them.'[108] The affections of many children lay with their foster family and the feelings were reciprocated. Paul from Tiree explained the potential for hurt when children were forced to leave the only family they had known at the age of 15 or 16, either to find work or because their natural parents had 'reclaimed' them, a far from uncommon occurrence, especially once the child had reached working age:

> Many think that a mother is the one who gives birth to you. But she's not. The one who raises you, that's your mother. I don't know why my parents wanted us back...But the pain we felt, the pain of my mother here, of my father, my grandmother after they had given us their love. They had no peace going to bed at night afraid they were going to lose us. That was breaking those people's hearts.[109]

The relationship between the family and the boarded out child was central to a child's sense of identity and self respect but this was also either reinforced or undermined by the attitudes of the local community to the children in their midst. Since the early days of the policy the Poor Law authorities had been made aware of local opposition to what the critics regarded as the 'dumping' of city children on small, rural communities; hardly surprising perhaps when small islands like Iona, Islay and Arran and later Tiree and Barra suddenly received an influx of city children. In the 1860s children had to be removed from Iona and Arran following objections by the landowners on the grounds that these children were 'not of a good class of society and had a bad effect on the native children.'[110] In the Arran case the factor acting on behalf of the Duke of Hamilton threatened guardians of the children with the result that some took temporary refuge on the mainland until it was considered safe to return. In a letter written in 1896 by Miss Margaret Campbell of Dunmore in Argyllshire to Glasgow Barony Parochial Board, the social and cultural gulf which existed between the rural elites and those engaged in finding homes for needy children was made crystal clear:

> For some time past you have sent a number of Poorhouse children to board in this neighbourhood, the cause of my letter to you now is to request you to remove these children and I will tell you why. There is a nice little school on this property that was built in order that the respectable rural population might have an opportunity of getting their children morally trained and educated, but since these children have come, the respectable parents complain bitterly that their children are learning many bad things from them, which is quite likely when we know that they come from the lowest of a town population, besides they are so dirty (to an extent that I can hardly mention) and have brought the *itch* into the school, a thing never known of before, so that many of the people about say they cannot continue to send their children to the school while these pauper children remain, it is the *meanest* of the people who could be tempted to make a profit out of poor children and indeed to make profit of what is paid for their board can only be done by starving the children and keeping them like pigs...Surely some country habitation could be got in your own parish and some one found who would look after these children properly, for it is a miserable business sending them here...the wrong is sending them in numbers to be farmed out.[111]

The members of Barony board must have been amused by the suggestion that they find a 'country habitation' in inner city Glasgow, and a visit to the district affirmed the policy of Barony board which merely agreed to limit the number of children boarded out there in future. Although there was some attempt to avoid turning villages into 'pauper colonies' the population of some small towns was boosted markedly by the influx of boarded outs.[112] In 1939, for example, there were no fewer than 82 Glasgow children boarded with families in Peterhead and more than 70 in Keith.[113] Such concerted opposition appears to have subsided in subsequent decades but late twentieth-century antagonism to the siting of youth projects, drop-in centres and children's homes in small towns and villages bears many similarities to earlier rejection of children on the grounds that street-wise city children would corrupt the rural young.[114]

Overt opposition to the boarding out of children was rare, however, and according to the editors of the *Poor Law Magazine* 'very much out of accord with the feelings of a country which has in a special sense taken the poor under its protection.'[115] For the most part the criticism did not reach the ears of the children themselves. However, children were the targets of taunts and accusations from fellow schoolchildren and their parents. Many respondents spoke of name-calling — 'Glasgow orphans', 'Glasgow kealies' and 'homies' — in the playground and in the community at large. 'Kids will be kids', recalled Robert, boarded in the fishing town of Buckie in the 1930s and 40s:

> and you used to get the brickbats at school, Glasgow orphan this that and you were called names and again — it wasnae so bad, it was acceptable to you as a kid, it was one kid to another idea but again you see if there was any devilment...the adult parents 'mine can do no wrong, it's those Glasgow orphans' and that you know that's what you're up against...there was a differential kind of system there you see.[116]

'I wouldn't say ostracised' remarked Peter, 'but you were looked on as being different.'[117] 'Even at school' remembered Betty, 'they would turn around and say "you're just boarded out."'[118]

Integration into the community was difficult when the boarded-out child stood out from other children in ill-fitting and sometimes old-fashioned clothing supplied by the parish and was visited by an inspector from the city two or three times a year. In some cases children had to learn a new language, Gaelic, a cultural shock graphically described by Bernard who was sent to Tiree:

> When my brother and I came here on the Oban-Tiree ferry we heard people speaking but we didn't understand what they said. We thought they were Germans but they were Tiree people coming back from the sales in Oban. We were a bit worried by this but in fact they were speaking Gaelic.[119]

'I remember my first day at school', recounted Caidlin boarded on the Catholic island of Barra; 'I couldn't speak Gaelic and I felt different from the others…I made sure I learned and worked out the meaning of every word so that I could speak Gaelic and be like the others at school.'[120] On Tiree, however, although Gaelic was the native language, English was widespread. 'When I went to school' remembered Betty, 'there was one lot spoke Gaelic and the other lot spoke English because there was a bigger percentage of boarded-out children on the island than there was of native speakers so there was English spoken in the school.'[121]

For some children the sense of being an outsider had long term repercussions. As Robert found, the absence of blood ties in the 'clannish' town of Buckie affected his search for employment at the age of 15:

> The thing was there was the slips, the boat building, there was the fishing, and it's a fishing community you understand, and they were clannish…and they looked after their own you see; now just take me I wanted to get in to serve my time as a joiner I did you know, but Willie was taken before Bobby because Willie's Dad was maybe in the shipyards, I didnae have that push, I didnae have that kick your backside into a job, but this is what you're up against and you accept it right enough…[122]

Robert's experience seems to support the view of the Church of Scotland's director of social service who remarked in 1945 that 'in country places where everybody knows everybody else, the boarded-out child tends to be regarded as an "in-comer", and often without justification, as an unwelcome intrusion into a rather class-conscious community.'[123] Anecdotal evidence also points to longer term consequences of the boarding-out policy, especially in small communities. While there are no statistics on the number of marriages between former boarded outs — and it would be surprising if there were none given the concentration of boarded out children in some communities — as one respondent put it, 'people would turn round and say well they married their own kind, they were maybe drawn together because of that…'[124] 'We're the same. We're in step as it were' commented Ian from Tiree on his marriage to a woman fostered nearby.[125] Moreover, some evidence suggests that the boarded outs will always occupy an ambiguous place in the history of the communities that took them in. 'To this day' remarked a resident of Tiree, 'some people here look down on the "boarded-outs". Recently one idiot said that no "boarded-outs" should be included in the roll of honour of this island…"Boarded-outs" died in the war as well as other men from Tiree. And some people don't want their names on the roll of honour.'[126] And yet the fact that large numbers of boarded-out children stayed in their adopted communities or returned in later life is a fairer testament to their place within Scottish rural life. 'They are at the heart of these islands', commented one observer. 'They have enriched our communities.'[127]

Reassessing Boarding Out

In Scotland the commitment never wavered to boarding out as by far the most humane solution for the majority of children in need. However, the policy was subjected to quite far-reaching re-assessment in the 1940s by which time considerable doubt was being cast upon the idea of the croft as the ideal home. In 1946 the Clyde Committee, although continuing to advocate that children should be boarded out with families whenever possible, was sharply critical of the placing of city children in remote areas.

> We strongly deprecate the boarding out of city children on crofts in very remote areas where they have no real contact with other children, where they have no facilities for learning a trade…or where the living conditions are bad. Investigation of conditions in Highland crofts has shown that the lack of sanitation and the absence of facilities for training the children in cleanliness and personal habits make it inadvisable to board out children in remote crofts in the Highlands, where economic conditions are such that the practice of taking in children is regarded as an industry, and the labour obtained therefrom often enables the guardians to maintain their crofts.[128]

The death of Dennis O'Neill in Shropshire and the prosecution of the Waltons in Fife jolted those responsible for child welfare, in England at least, out of their complacency, and two government committees were set up to investigate the entire system of welfare and protection of homeless children. In Scotland by far the majority of those institutions, local authority departments, voluntary organisations and private individuals who presented evidence to the Clyde Committee registered their continued commitment to boarding out; but by then the ideology of children as threats to society had disappeared and thus the incentive to place children in remote locations was less persuasive. The RSSPCC explicitly recommended that children should be found homes in their county of birth or residence.[129] Moreover, the perceived advantages of rural homes — the fresh air, the healthy environment and so on — were, by the post-war era, deemed less important for the child's development than access to a decent education and a range of work opportunities. Children were regarded as the country's investment in its future. There was concern that some children had been boarded in such remote locations that the possibility of them attending secondary school was almost impossible. The Scottish Association of Social Welfare Officers were persuaded that:

> the desirable thing is to have children boarded out in accessible places, if possible — accessible both in the matter of scholastic facilities and contacts with other children…that it is essential, if these children are to get the best out of life and to grow up like other children, they should have the opportunity of mixing in a community of children, going to school with other children, and playing with other children…[130]

Some felt that an upbringing on a croft or farm restricted children's choice of career. In the past boys had been expected to undertake farm work or go to sea while girls were found jobs in service. Of those Glasgow girls and boys who came off the parish roll between 1882 and 1902, 59 per cent of the girls found work in domestic service and 52 per cent of boys were employed as farm servants or in a variety of trades.[131] By 1945 these options were no longer so widely available at the same time as the horizons of many children themselves had broadened. With limited or non-existent after-care, even if a child did wish to pursue a particular line of work his or her opportunities to do so were limited by economic forces. Peter, who enjoyed school and passed his qualifying exam to attend Inverness Academy, had ambitions to work in journalism but the need to earn a living when he left care at the age of 15 meant he became a butcher's apprentice instead. 'We were all denied whatever chance we might have had to follow what we wanted to do. We just had to take pot luck.'[132] A study of 200 Glasgow children who left care in the 1960s shows that little had changed since the nineteenth century. None of the boys were engaged in skilled employment, the majority finding jobs in the armed forces, apprenticeships, farm work and labouring while 58 per cent of the girls were engaged in domestic service, factory or shop work.[133] Children boarded out on the smaller islands in the post-war period were probably the least well placed to find employment. If they had no interest in farm work, fishing or joining the merchant navy they were forced to move away, often back to the mainland. Betty, who wanted to go to Glasgow having spent most of her childhood on Tiree, was dissuaded from doing so by her foster parents and instead the local factor found her domestic work in the Duke of Argyll's residence. 'I didn't want to do that but I ended up doing it.'[134] For Betty and others like her choice was denied but some were given financial support to pursue their career choices. Glasgow Corporation paid for Frances to attend pre-nursing college in Aberdeen; her foster parents could not have afforded the cost of books and travel to Aberdeen every day. 'This is one advantage that…I had that the rest of the family didn't have.'[135]

By 1945 the climate in Scotland had changed. Foster parents were harder to come by. Some potential guardians had been deterred by the bad press given to the evacuation experience and by the highly publicised cruelty cases. In Fife in particular, the home of the Waltons, people were reported as saying, 'We are not going to take any more trouble now, because we know what can arise.'[136] Accepting a boarded-out child also made less economic sense.[137] The National Vigilance Association noticed that after the war 'women hesitated to appear to their neighbours in such a state of poverty that the little derived from the care of a baby was a necessity' and advocated giving 'the whole idea of fostering a new importance and dignity' so as to attract 'respectable upper working class women'.[138] In addition adoption became a more popular option suggesting that people were increasingly taking in children for emotional rather than economic reasons. Whereas only 812 children had been officially adopted in Scotland in 1938 by 1945 the number had increased to 1,875.[139] The views of those working in the child welfare field had also changed considerably by 1945; in particular their horizons for the children's futures had expanded. Boarded-out children were no longer merely expected to 'live by their physical labour' but were to be given the same opportunities as other children.[140] When Edinburgh Corporation stubbornly supported boarding out on crofts in 1945 the Clyde Committee expressed its frustration with the response: 'from the mental development and intellectual point of view isn't it a rather limited background?' they asked. There was also more concern for the psychological condition of children following information gathered from the experiences of evacuees during the war. Finally child care professionals had recognised the strength of bonds between children and their natural parents and the middle classes had been made aware that working-class children has psychological as well as physical needs. What had changed by 1945 was that the middle classes were beginning to apply standards they would expect of their own children to those less fortunate. Children were not to be denied a childhood and opportunity to excel merely because of their objective status as homeless, orphaned or neglected.

The Clyde Committee's recommendations for the improvement of boarding-out practice might have been predicted since they merely recognised the inadequacies of the system which had long been evident to anyone caring to look under the surface. Key recommendations included an improvement in the selection and inspection of foster parents; a standard rate of payment; responsibility for the welfare of the child to rest with the boarding-out authority, thus doing away with the confusion of responsibilities; children to be medically and psychologically assessed before placement and in the case of boarding out in another parish a suitable person in the vicinity to report on the progress of the child.[141] However, whilst the Clyde Report sought to tighten up the practice of boarding out, and it certainly pulled few punches in criticising the failures of the existing system, there was no attempt to look at the system from the child's point of view. No child witnesses were called and thus the question of the child's perception of his or her status within a family and community was not addressed. The Clyde Report essentially gave Scottish authorities the go-ahead to continue with boarding out in a modified form and slowly the practice of placing children in areas remote from their place of birth and remaining family ceased. By 1970 Glasgow had over 900 children with foster families within the city signalling a radical policy reversal.[142]

The Curtis Committee in England concluded in 1946 that boarding out was still preferable to institutional care even when there was 'probably greater risk of acute unhappiness in a foster home', thus clearly accepting there would always be some victims of the policy but that this was a price worth paying for the greater good of the majority of children who experienced a happy and supportive environment with a foster family. This research suggests, however, that although undoubtedly large numbers of children were placed with affectionate and caring guardians, throughout the period 1845 to the 1960s the number of children who suffered physically, emotionally and educationally from their boarding-out experiences has always been seriously underestimated. While concern was regularly and correctly expressed about the regimes in the larger children's homes, the 'boarded-outs' were hidden from sight, their voices were silenced. It is only in the last ten years as boarding out has belatedly received publicity in Scotland that those who experienced their childhood with a foster family have been able to reclaim their past. For some this has meant gaining a greater understanding of the circumstances which led to them being placed in care having spent most of their lives in the dark and a not infrequent recognition that had they not been placed in foster care their material and sometimes emotional circumstances might have been harder. 'Well I think compared to what my brother had I had a far happier childhood', explained Betty.

> Well he stayed with my mother…and my mother went out, she had to work, she worked for Barr's Irn Bru, she scrubbed the floors and she went out to the big houses and cleaned and Alex had to sit on the steps until she was finished you know, because she couldn't leave him, she had to take him with her, so look at the freedom that I had [on Tiree]…compared to him, you know when you look at it that way, alright he lived with his mother which I didn't which you'd suppose was better for him but on the other hand I had a happier childhood.[143]

Others have reassessed the care they received in the light of their later experiences. 'I went about with a chip on my shoulder for a long time' revealed one man who was treated cruelly and felt that he had 'lost his childhood':

> …why should that have happened to me, you know, why should I have been beaten from morning to night you know, I'm just an ordinary human being but…when you came out and seen how other people lived and started mixing with families and friends and you saw how they lived and were brought up you know it made you feel bitter…[144]

Similarly, memories of boarding out can be thrown into sharp relief by an individual's personal experiences of 'normal' family life:

> They never cuddled us, they never gave us a kiss. I didn't know how much I'd missed until I had kids of my own. Then I noticed the affection you should get back from children. Wee cuddles, wee kisses, things you're supposed to do with them. Ordinary living that other people take as everyday, we didn't get.[145]

The Scottish policy of boarding out may be seen as an early enlightened, humanitarian approach to child care which anticipated late twentieth-century policy which similarly tries to place children in foster families whenever possible. Yet this apparent continuity in child care practice disguises two inherently different ideologies towards children and the appropriate quality of material and emotional support. Although local authority child care provision, at least until 1948, suggests a template for the more modern systems of child care, early practice was essentially experimental and confused in its aims and objectives. Though the reluctance to place children in poorhouses and orphanages was well-meant and in some respects fully justified, the poor law authorities had other motives for so stubbornly pursuing a policy which although liberal in conception was potentially dangerous. In the first place boarding out was seen as a cost-effective means of providing for the thousands of children in need of care; secondly, it was widely perceived to be a remedy for the scourge of hereditary pauperism;[146] and thirdly it was thought to provide a more healthy environment for children tainted with the degradation and poverty of Scotland's urban centres. And while always denied by officials there is no doubt that like the indentured service scheme which preceded it, boarding out contributed in no small measure to the viability of the rural economy and individual households within it. Indeed, it might legitimately be regarded as an attempt at social engineering, especially after the First World War when fears were raised about depopulation in the Highlands and Islands. At the same time, however, one should not ignore the considerable sensitivity to the children involved on the part of individuals involved in the implementation of the policy and a genuine desire to find children homes where they might settle and experience 'normal' family life.

Any assessment of boarding out is bound to consider both the successes and the failures but attempting to balance the two would be disrespectful to both groups of children. In any case, the experiences of individual children are often remembered as ambivalent and contradictory. Gratitude for affectionate care received could be accompanied by a feeling of being different. Robert put it this way:

> We was better looked after than the bloody kids with their mother and father I can tell you that, we really were. I'd used to stand on a rostrum and tell them that you know and yet you was underdog you know in the playground and that you see, you were a Glasgow orphan (...) In fact you couldn't be bloody jealous right enough because you were better off than they were.[147]

At the end of the twentieth century, although foster care is still preferred to residential placement, the shift towards the recognition of children's rights and the emphasis on working together with the birth family has meant that foster care is now more likely to be regarded as a temporary respite for children who hopefully will be eventually re-united with their parents. Similar policy shifts have resulted in a massive decline in the number of children cared for in children's homes and the next chapter will explore the parallel institutional dimension of child care.

NOTES

1. SRO, ED 11/266: Evidence of Governor of Dumbarton Townend Hospital to Clyde Committee, 1945.
2. *B.P.P., Report of the Committee on Homeless Children (Scotland)*, 1946, Cmd.6911, p.32.
3. See, for example, Robin Jenkins, *A Love of Innocence* (Edinburgh, 1963), a fictional tale of two orphaned brothers sent to a Hebridean Island and Katherine Stewart, *A Croft in the Hills* (Edinburgh, 1960), the story of a crofting community in Inverness-shire.
4. See J.F.Cook, 'A History of Placing-Out: the Orphan Trains' in E.P.Smith & L.A.Merkel-Holguin (eds.), *A History of Child Welfare* (New Brunswick, NJ., 1996), pp.175-92.
5. For reaction to the Walton case see *Glasgow Herald*, 23 July–4 August 1945.
6. Tom Sloss (South Uist), *Air Fasdadh*.
7. T.Ferguson, *Children in Care and After* (London, 1966), pp.2–5.
8. *B.P.P.*, W.A.Peterkin, *Report to the Board of Supervision on the System in Scotland of Boarding Pauper Children in Private Dwellings*, 1893, Cmd.7140, p.2.

9. GCA, AGN 150: R.Brough, 'One Hundred Years of Boarding Out' (1959).

10. See H.Sturdy, 'Boarding-Out the Insane, 1857–1913. A Study of the Scottish System', PhD, University of Glasgow, 1996. It was noted in 1910 that 'defective children' were usually boarded out 'unless they are actual idiots' on the grounds that 'slightly defective children are "uplifted" by being placed among those of normal intelligence.' *B.P.P.*, C.T.Parsons, *Report on the Condition of the Children who are in Receipt of the Various Forms of Poor Law Relief in certain Parishes in Scotland*, 1910, Cmd.5075, p.54.

11. *B.P.P.*, *Report of the Board of Supervision (Scotland)*, 1888, Cmd.5500, p.217.

12. See SRO, ED 11/190: Department of Health for Scotland, Public Assistance Circular No.18, 1931; 'It is generally agreed that children should not be brought up in the environment of a poorhouse or similar institution...'

13. Figures from Levitt, *Poverty and Welfare in Scotland 1890–1948* (Edinburgh, 1988), p.209.

14. SRO, ED 11/162: *Edinburgh Evening Dispatch*, 25 May 1945.

15. In England children were to be inspected in their foster homes every 6 weeks compared with the Scottish practice of twice or three times a year. Foster homes were also to be within 5 miles of a committee member's home. Lady visitors were employed and children were assessed in reception homes before placement. See J.Stroud, *An Introduction to the Child Care Service* (London, 1965), pp.78–81.

16. GCA, D-CH 1/1: Glasgow City Parish Children's Committee Minute Book No.1, 1852–1865, 25 August 1864.

17. *B.P.P.*, *Report by W.A.Peterkin, Visiting Officer, on Pauper Children Boarded in the Island of Arran dated 21.4.1862*, 1863, Vol.XXXII, App.(A), no.4, pp. 3–8.

18. *Poor Law Magazine*, Vol.II (1868–9), p.614.

19. *B.P.P.*, *Report of J.J.Henley Esq, Poor Law Inspector, to the Poor Law Board on the Boarding Out of Pauper Children in Scotland*, 1870, Vol.LVIII, p. 9.

20. See the case of lewd practices towards young girls in Inveresk poorhouse in 1868 cited in Levitt, *Government and Social Conditions*, pp.85–6.

21. Interview with Arthur.

22. *B.P.P.*, W.A.Peterkin, *Report to the Board of Supervision on the System in Scotland of Boarding Pauper Children in Private Dwellings*, 1893, Cmd.7140, p.5.

23. *B.P.P.*, *40th Annual Report of the Board of Supervision*, 1884–5, Cmd.4559, p.260.

24. See Levitt, *Poverty and Welfare*, p.33.

25. *B.P.P.*, *Minutes of Evidence taken before a Departmental Committee appointed by the Local Government Board*, 1896, Cmd.8032, p.507.

26. Levitt, *Poverty and Welfare*, p.29.

27. *B.P.P.*, Peterkin, 1863, Vol.XXII App (A), No.4, p.650.
28. See C.G.Brown, '"To be Aglow with Civic Ardours": the "Godly Commonwealth" in Glasgow 1843–1914', *Records of the Scottish Church History Society*, XXVI (1996), pp.171–5.
29. GCA, AGN 105: Brough, 'One Hundred Years'.
30. GCA, D-HEW 24/6: Barony Parish, Allocation of Boarding Places, 1895.
31. GCA, D-HEW 24/1: Barony Parish Visitation Reports for 1883.
32. GCA, D-HEW 24/7: Barony Parish, Reports by Visiting Members for 1889.
33. E.Mackenzie, 'The Boarding-out of Children in Glasgow, 1770–1970', unpublished paper; GCA, AGN 105: Brough, 'One Hundred Years'.
34. Interview with Peter.
35. Correspondence with Frank.
36. On provision for Jewish children see K.E.Collins, *Second City Jewry: the Jews of Glasgow in the Age of Expansion, 1790–1919* (Glasgow, 1990), p.162. Glasgow did find Jewish guardians for some children, see D-HEW 24/41: Children boarded out 1930.
37. *B.P.P.*, 1896, Cmd.8032, p.713.
38. GCA, D-CH 2/2: Barony Parish Children's Committee Minutes, 20 July 1868.
39. GCA, D-CH 2/1: Report to the Education and Children's Committee, 30 May 1860.
40. J.J.Henley cited in *The Poor Law Magazine*, New series Vol.IV (1870–1), p.364.
41. *B.P.P.*, 1863, Vol. XXII App (A), No.4, p. 78.
42. SRO, ED 11/294: Homeless Children — Inspection of Boarded-Out Children (Glasgow Boarding-out System).
43. GCA, D-CH 2/1: Report by Glasgow City Inspector of Children, 27 June 1864.
44. *Ibid.*
45. GCA, D-CH 1/3: Glasgow City Children's Committee Minute Book 1890–1897, visit to children in district 2, 20 December 1893.
46. GCA, D-HEW, 24/7: Reports by visiting members for 1889. However, Edinburgh city parish found a number of homes amongst the miners of Midlothian. *B.P.P.*, 1896, Cmd. 8032, p.518.
47. *B.P.P., Report of J.J.Henley Esq. to the Poor Law Board on the Boarding Out of Pauper Children in Scotland*, 1870, Vol.LVIII, p.17.
48. GCA, D-HEW 24/1: Barony Parish, Visitation Reports for 1882.
49. *B.P.P.*, 1863, Vol XXII (App A) No.4, p.651.
50. *B.P.P.*, 1896, Cmd.8032, p.590.
51. *B.P.P.*, 1896, Cmd.8032, p.518.
52. *B.P.P., 1910,* Cmd.5075, p.72.
53. *B.P.P.*, 1896, Cmd.8032, p.512.
54. *Ibid.*
55. See P.Thompson with T.Wailey and T.Lummis, *Living the Fishing* (London, 1983), chapter 13.

56. Bernard Mac a'Ghobhainn (Tiree), *Air Fasdadh*.
57. Seumas MacUalraig (South Uist), *Air Fasdadh*.
58. Interview with Betty.
59. L.Jamieson & C.Toynbee, *Country Bairns: Growing Up 1900–1930* (Edinburgh, 1992).
60. Interview with Peter.
61. *Ibid*.
62. Eileen Leppard, *Air Fasdadh*.
63. Eachann MacPhail (Tiree), *Air Fasdadh*.
64. SRO, ED 11/154: letter from Mary Wallace to Clyde Committee, 1945.
65. SRO, ED 11/168: Report on visit to boarded out children around Inverness, 19 May 1946.
66. *Ibid*.
67. Correspondence with Frank.
68. Interview with Betty.
69. Correspondence with Eleanor.
70. Interview with Frances.
71. See K. Stewart, *A School in the Hills* (Edinburgh, 1996). She notes that falling school roles in primary schools in Inverness-shire in the 1950s was a result of fewer foster children in the area, p.18.
72. 'Hebridean Island Faces Loss of its Young Blood', *The Scotsman*, 11 August 1997.
73. SRO, ED 11/159: The National Council of Women, Scottish Standing Committee, Evidence to Committee on Homeless Children, September 1945.
74. GCA, D-HEW 24/7: Barony Parish Visitation Report, Tomintoul 1889.
75. GCA, D-HEW 24/7: Barony Parish Visitation Report, Iona and Creich, 1889.
76. GCA, D-HEW, 24/1: Visitation Reports by Managers for 1882.
77. See Hendrick, *Child Welfare*, p. 249–52.
78. *B.P.P.*, 1896, Cmd.8032, McNeill, p.513. Q: 'And you believe that the public opinion of the district is enough to protect children from any kind of ill-usage, starvation, or anything of that sort? A: 'I have not the slightest doubt of it, we should hear at once if there was anything of that sort.'
79. *B.P.P.*, 1896, Cmd.8032, p.514.
80. *Ibid*.
81. GCA, D-CH 1/1: Glasgow City Parish Children's Committee Minute Book, 15 September 1864.
82. GCA, D-CH 1/2: Children's Committee Minute Book, 21 Sept 1865.
83. Ian Mac an Fhleisdeir (Tiree), *Air Fasdadh*.
84. SRO, ED 11/165: Committee on Homeless Children; Report on homes for boarded out children in the Aberdeen area visited by Lady Margaret Kerr on 29 March 1946.
85. *B.P.P., Report of the Care of Children Committee* (Curtis Report), 1945–6, Cmd.6922, paras 134–5, 418–22.

86. GCA, D-CH 2/1: Barony Parish Education Minutes, Report by Inspector of Children, 27 June 1864.
87. *B.P.P.*, 1896, C.8032, McNeill, pp.508–9.
88. For example, on a visit to children boarded out in the Fort William area, a medical inspector reported that 'it came out casually in the course of conversation that the foster parent had not intended to take so many children but that a car had arrived on a cold October evening with a poor child for whom no home could be found...' SRO, ED 11/294: Report by I. Seymour, 11–13 November 1947.
89. Interview with Betty.
90. Interview with Robert.
91. Interview with Peter.
92. *B.P.P.*, 1896, Cmd.8032, Peterkin, p.593.
93. Mackenzie, 'The Boarding Out of Children from Glasgow', p.2.
94. Interview with Peter.
95. *B.P.P.*, 1863, Vol XXII (App A.) No.4, p.650.
96. *B.P.P.*, 1896, Cmd.8032, Peterkin, p.590.
97. Interview with Peter.
98. GCA, D-CH 2/1: Report by Glasgow City Inspector of Children, 27 June 1864.
99. Veronica NicNeill and Caidlin Bhoid (Barra), *Air Fasdadh*.
100. Interview with Frances.
101. Interview with Frances.
102. Interview with Robert.
103. Interview with Betty.
104. SRO, ED 11/190: Department of Health for Scotland, Public Assistance Circular No.18, 29 June 1931.
105. Interview with Peter.
106. Interview with Peter.
107. Eileen Leppard, *Air Fasdadh*.
108. Raibeart Mac'Ille Ghlais (Tiree), *Air Fasdadh*.
109. Pol MacCaluim (South Uist), *Air Fasdadh*.
110. GCA, D-CH 2/1: Barony Parish Education Committee Minutes, 20 February 1865; 21 August 1865.
111. GCA, D-CH 2/2: Glasgow City Children's Committee, 11 October 1869.
112. *The Poor Law Magazine*, 3 (1875), p.470.
113. GCA, D-HEW 24/50: Boarded Out Children, 1939.
114. See *The Observer*, 17 August 1997.
115. *The Poor Law Magazine* 6 (1878), p.396.
116. Interview with Robert.
117. Interview with Peter.
118. Interview with Betty.
119. Bernard Mac a'Ghobhainn (Tiree), *Air Fasdadh*.
120. Caidlin Bhoid (Barra), *Air Fasdadh*.
121. Interview with Betty.

122. Interview with Robert. See Thompson, *Living the Fishing*, pp.250–4.
123. SRO, ED 11/159: Rev L.L.L.Cameron, Memorandum on the Care of Children Deprived of a Normal Home Life, September 1945.
124. Interview with Betty.
125. Ian Mac an Fhleisdeir (Tiree), *Air Fasdadh*.
126. Eachann MacPhail (Tiree), *Air Fasdadh*.
127. An Canon, Aonghas MacCulmhein, *Air Fasdadh*.
128. *B.P.P., Report of the Committee on Homeless Children (Scotland)*, 1946, Cmd.6911, p.21.
129. SRO, ED 11/159: RSSPCC Memorandum to Clyde Committee, 1945.
130. SRO, ED 11/266: Minute of the Meeting of the Committee on Homeless Children, 4 December 1945, Appendix III.
131. Figures from H.Macdonald, 'Boarding-Out and the Scottish Poor Law, 1845–1914', *The Scottish Historical Review*, LXXV (1996), p.211.
132. Interview with Peter.
133. T.Ferguson, *Children in Care and After*, p.95 and p.99.
134. Interview with Betty.
135. Interview with Frances.
136. SRO, ED 11/266: Scottish Standing Committee National Council of Women evidence to Clyde Committee, 1945.
137. SRO, ED 11/267: Ayr Social Welfare Committee, 5 July 1945, who not only commented on the evacuation experience but noted, 'unfortunately such children are frequently physically or mentally under standard or ill behaved.'
138. SRO, ED 11/158: National Vigilance Association of Scotland and International Guild of Service for Women memorandum to Clyde Committee, 1945.
139. *Glasgow Herald*, 30 July 1946.
140. GCA, D-CH 2/1: Report by Glasgow City Inspector of Children, 27 June 1864.
141. *B.P.P.*, 1946, C.6911 (Clyde Report), p.32.
142. Mackenzie, 'The boarding out of children from Glasgow', p.3.
143. Interview with Betty.
144. Interview with Peter.
145. Eileen Leppard, *Air Fasdadh*.
146. See H. Macdonald, 'Boarding-out and the Scottish Poor Law', pp.197–220.
147. Interview with Robert.

CHAPTER 3

THE ORPHANAGE CHILD

When you stroll up to the orphanage the very first day,
You would think it was nice and that you would just like to stay.
After several years your heart fills with sorrow,
    your eyes fill with tears,
The matrons they thrash as people can see,
    especially the matron they call Miss Mc…

> — Former resident of Aberlour Orphanage,
> *Childhood Days at Aberlour.*

A Hidden Existence

Girls and boys sent to a children's home are Scotland's forgotten
children. The promotion of boarding out as the most appropriate
solution for the majority of homeless children throughout the
nineteenth and for much of the twentieth century effectively
consigned orphanage children to a hidden and silent existence.
The 'home' was a place to be feared; the visit of the 'cruelty man'
a grim portent of institutionalisation.[1] Since Scotland had rejected
the poorhouse for its needy children, it was widely assumed that
only 'problem' children were sent to an institution: the disabled,
the 'insane', the unruly and the 'dangerous'. Even today, children
suffer from the ignorant assumption that those cared for in
childen's homes must have done something wrong. 'Oh were you
a bad lassie?' was the question frequently asked of one girl who
recently left residential care.[2] Certainly in the past many children
categorised in this way by the courts did find themselves inmates
of reformatories, industrial schools, asylums, magdalene homes
and training ships — indeed a whole range of institutions designed
to discipline and reform the body and mind of the child. And by
the turn of the century Scotland was amply provided with so-called
'reforming' institutions, with Glasgow alone having in excess of
3,000 places for boys and girls.[3] Yet, the majority of children placed
in institutions had not been categorised as 'problem' children —
or at least not explicitly. Rather, their parents, relatives, a child
saving charity or the parish or local authority had placed them in

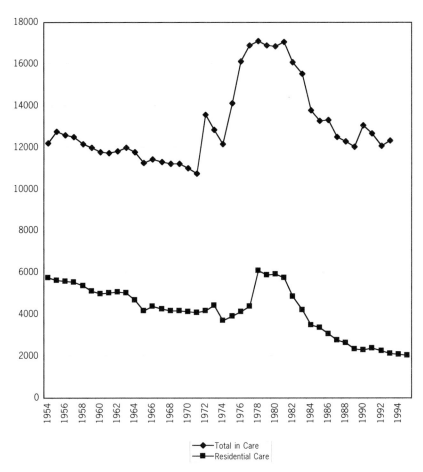

Figure 3.1. Total Number of Children in Care and Number of Those in Residential Care, Scotland 1954–1995.
Source: Scottish Abstract of Statistics; Digest of Scottish Statistics; Scottish Office Statistical Bulletin.

any one of a vast range of orphanages, some of them run by the local authority but more often operated by charitable, and usually religious organisations. Most of these institutions were small, capable of housing no more than 30 or 40 children, but Scotland also had two very large children's homes: namely Quarrier's Homes at Bridge of Weir and Aberlour Orphanage on Speyside. But in addition, by the inter-war period there were at least 275 institutions for homeless children and young persons across the country, more than 100 of them located in Glasgow and Edinburgh.[4]

Between the 1880s and 1960s thousands of Scottish children passed through institutions; some were to be temporary residents while others remained until their teenage years. It is impossible to estimate the true figure since no-one made any attempt to count the number of children in the unregulated voluntary homes until the 1940s. A minimum of 2,000 children were resident in voluntary homes at any one time between 1880 and 1940; this means that over 60,000 young Scots stayed in such homes between those years. As Figure 3.1 shows, since the 1950s there has been a steady decline in the proportion of homeless children placed in residential care with a particularly marked decrease occurring during the 1980s — a period following the closure of the large voluntary homes when child care professionals attempted to minimise the number of children placed in institutions.

Despite the sheer size and turnover of the population of residential institutions, especially before 1945, we know very little about the lives of those who spent their childhood in the company of strangers. In the wake of recent allegations of physical and sexual abuse in a number of homes this one disturbing facet of institutional care has come to light. But the day-to-day life of thousands of Scottish children still remains in the shadows. No-one has written their history. Few of the children themselves have spoken publicly of their experiences; a number still regard the fact of being brought up in a home as a stigma, something they rarely reveal to strangers. Yet, reminiscences of childhoods spent in children's homes reveal the multi-faceted role played by these institutions in Scottish society as well as a range of experiences and emotions as varied and as complex as the individuals themselves.

A Place of Refuge and Respite

Since the seventeenth century there had been a limited degree of private, charitable provision for homeless children in Scottish towns. Edinburgh, Aberdeen and Dundee all possessed orphan homes by 1830 funded by philanthropic initiatives. Aberdeen in particular was noted for the extent of its residential provision for orphaned children, whilst a number of small residential schools such as the Glasgow Institution for Orphan and Destitute Girls, founded in 1825, provided education and training for the destitute.[5] By the late nineteenth century most of these isolated institutions had been amalgamated with the school system or had become unfashionable as parish authorities sought to find foster homes for the majority of their child paupers. Poorhouses were still used, especially by the smaller local authorities for whom it was uneconomic to build a special institution for children alone, but more often as a temporary shelter before a child was found a more permanent home.[6] However, in a parallel development, philanthropic institutions filled the gap of mass residential provision for the orphan children of the respectable working and middle classes and the child victims of neglect and abuse. Glasgow's City Chamberlain described Scotland's orphanages in 1885 as 'the most marked philanthropic feature of Scotland in the present day...a powerful lever for lifting neglected children of the slums into something akin to real home life.'[7]

The Whinwell Children's Home in Stirling, Aberlour Orphanage and Quarrier's Homes — the three institutions chosen for detailed analysis here — all opened their doors in the 1870s and 1880s, meeting a genuine need for homes for orphaned, destitute and neglected children across Scotland. All three institutions closed almost exactly 100 years later as a response to the decline in the number of children requiring residential care as well as a common belief that large homes were no longer appropriate. The Whinwell Home was founded in 1883 by Annie Croall, a local evangelical philanthropist. With beds for around 40 boys and girls, it was typical of the small town orphanage, well known in the community and almost totally reliant on donations for support. Aberlour Orphanage, by contrast, was able to accommodate almost 500 children at the peak of its activities in the 1930s. Founded in 1875 by an English minister, the Reverend Charles Jupp, this episcopalian institution saw some 6,000 children pass through its doors between its founding and closure in the 1970s. Unlike Whinwell and most other Scottish children's homes, Aberlour with its vast collection of buildings housing a school, a church, a farm and residential accommodation, formed its own village entirely separate from the small town of Aberlour by which it lived cheek by jowl. On a similar scale and almost as isolated was The Orphan Homes of Scotland better known as Quarrier's Homes, built on farmland in the Renfrewshire countryside. The story of William Quarrier's life from apprentice shoemaker in Glasgow to wealthy businessman and philanthropist is well known in Scotland.[8] Having become a Christian at the age of 17 he sought a means to provide for Glasgow's street children which combined Christian charity with a form of business philanthropy. His so-called Brigades of shoe-black, parcel and newspaper boys provided hundreds of homeless and destitute Glasgow boys with a home, education and training and it was from this venture that William Quarrier planned his children's home following the example of Thomas Barnardo in London. The first home at Renfrew Lane in Glasgow took in 93 children in its first year; in 1878 he moved to a green-field site at Bridge of Weir to open a cottage-style home similar to Barnardo's home at Barkingside in Essex. By 1890 Quarrier had created a 'children's city' with 46 buildings including a church with a capacity of 1,000, a school, and 34 cottages, able to accommodate over 800 children at one time.[9]

The founders of all three orphanages shared a sense of evangelical mission combined with genuine compassion for the children in their care. 'We believe that it is not the Will of God that any one of the enslaved victims of sin and shame should perish' wrote Annie Croall in 1884, 'and far less is it His will that the innocent blameless lambs should be left to run in the same paths of vice and shame.'[10] Hence 'the great aim of our work, and the desire of our heart, is their CONVERSION, that they may be rescued from the paths of vice and wickedness…'[11] To Miss Croall the children she 'saved' were simultaneously innocent victims and potential threats who could only be rescued from their own 'passionate, self willed, stubborn and sinful' natures by good education and training.[12] The work of William Quarrier and Charles Jupp was also guided by a deep Christian faith. They each accepted boys and girls from all backgrounds and denominations,[13] and supported their efforts almost entirely by charitable donations in cash and in kind, maintenance contributions by parents and relatives and some payments by Poor Law boards and local authorities. Aberlour's Reverend Jupp pioneered what came to be known as 'Jupp's sales', huge jumble sales attracting buyers from far and wide for goods donated by well-wishers. Annie Croall, in addition to using lady collectors, sent her children to perform at fêtes and galas to raise much needed money for the Whinwell Home.

Orphanages had many different groups of client children. Most of the charitable orphanages such as Quarrier's Homes, Aberlour Orphanage and especially the Catholic Smyllum Orphanage at Lanark, did accept some 'parish' cases — children in receipt of poor relief. But the majority of their inmates consisted of orphans and other needy children who were the victims of family crisis and for whom admission had been requested by a lone parent not eligible for poor relief, or a relative, an employer or churchman. By the turn of the century child victims of cruelty and neglect were also found places within institutions at the behest of the SNSPCC. Right up until the 1960s children's homes played a crucial and central role in the child welfare web, despite the anti-institutional rhetoric of Poor Law officers and child welfare professionals. Most children who were eventually found a foster-home spent a short period in a children's home before being boarded out. Orphanages and other voluntary homes provided a place of refuge and respite for children of poor families at times of crisis such as the death of a parent or long-term illness. Institutions were used as places of safety for children removed from cruel or neglectful parents. They were also the preferred solution for the respectable poor — those who might wish to avoid reliance on poor relief and the stigma of pauperism in order to preserve their dignity. The charitable home was a favoured solution too for mothers of illegitimate children or deserted women who were unable to combine gainful employment with care of a child.

Consequently, charitable orphanages had many different groups of client children, but actually contained very few true orphans. The majority of residents were, as we shall see, so-called 'deserving' children: the children of widows and widowers, children of the respectable poor and physically and mentally sound children who were victims of family circumstance. A significant proportion of parents and relatives who placed their children in a home apparently did so with the intention of retrieving them at a later date. Indeed, few regarded the home as a permanent solution and some did manage to remove their children when family circumstances improved. The charitable children's home, then, was often an intermediate agency. Indeed, the orphanage could resemble a railway station waiting-room as children passed through on their way to be adopted, fostered or transferred to another institution such as an insane asylum or home for the physically handicapped, or were sent away to Glasgow or Liverpool en route for Canada and Australia.

An examination of the admission records of three quite different Scottish children's homes reveals a great deal about the children admitted, the circumstances which necessitated their being placed in residential care and the role of the orphanage itself.[14] All three institutions shared similar objectives yet each children's home met a rather different social need in the context of family crisis in Scottish society revealed by the different profiles of children in each institution, the reasons for their admission and the length of time children typically spent in the home. Stirling's Whinwell Home was the only residential care institution in Stirlingshire untainted by associations with pauperism and 'delinquency'. It was widely regarded as a respectable Christian children's home for the innocent victims of poverty, neglect and immorality. The over-whelming majority of children brought to its doors hailed from Scotland, mostly from towns and villages in the county of Stirling-shire, with only five in the sample hailing from south of the border. The home admitted very few infants — its policy was to accept children under the age of one year for immediate adoption only — but otherwise at admission boys were aged between two and seven years and girls between two and ten. Aberlour Orphanage, on the other hand, had a much wider constituency. Although it primarily attracted children from north-east Scotland, as an episcopalian institution it was advertised farther afield. The majority of children there came from locations across Scotland but its size enabled it to take in entire families and hence regularly received children from the cities of Glasgow, Edinburgh and Dundee. Aberlour also took in few very young children before the First World War, although infants were more readily welcomed when a nursery was added. The majority of Aberlour's admissions, amounting to 60 per cent of the sample, were of children aged 6 years and over. An even larger proportion of Quarriers's children, 90 per cent, were already of school age when admitted despite the fact that Quarrier's Homes offered a place to any genuine needy child between the ages of one and 14 from any part of the country. The fact that fairly strenuous investigations were carried out into the child's extended family in order to discover whether an aunt or grandparent might take responsibility before admission was agreed along with its active emigration policy may help explain the age profile at Quarrier's.

Who were the children admitted to these homes? An almost equal number of girls and boys were placed in the care of Whinwell Home whilst there seems to have been a preponderance of boys at Aberlour although the random nature of the sample may not provide an accurate reflection of the sex ratio. Quarrier's Homes consistently accepted more boys than girls. Whether boys were more likely to be placed in care is an open question. In some families girls were useful as child-minders and housekeepers, especially if the mother was dead or sick, but in other circumstances boys as potential wage-earners may have been kept at home. None of these institutions openly discriminated against illegitimate children, but the majority of those admitted to both Whinwell and Aberlour were legitimate (73 per cent and 89 per cent respectively of the samples) and from what is already known about the position of mothers of illegitimate children it is likely that their children were more likely to be boarded out by the parish. Much more revealing of the ways in which these children's homes were used by families and the role such institutions played in the Scottish child care system are the reasons given for childrens' admission, the length of stay and their eventual destination upon leaving the home. A glance at the socio-economic background of the parents of the children admitted confirms the impression that voluntary homes were used by members of the working classes, predominantly the respectable employed. Occupations of fathers of Aberlour residents between 1898 and 1914 reflected the range of male employment in the north east especially, ranging from a trawler captain, a post-office superintendent and spirit merchant to a variety of artisanal jobs such as butcher, blacksmith, wagon-wright, milkman and farm labourers and draymen. Occupations listed for fathers of Whinwell children are similarly representative of the male working class including 12 labourers, 6 carters, 4 miners, 3 joiners, 3 soldiers, as well as a cattle-dealer, coppersmith, engineer, foundry worker, ploughman and shipwright amongst others. The majority of mothers of Whinwell children for whom an occupation is listed were employed in a more restricted range of ocupations, the majority in some form of domestic service; only four women were engaged in millwork which is surprising given that in Scotland as a whole 21 per cent of the female employed were engaged in the textile industry and as late as 1921 11.6 per cent of the occupied female population in Stirling worked in that sector.[15] However, while mill-workers may have been able to find child-minders, domestic service and child care were incompatible. When an analysis of the reasons given for children's admission is carried out, a fuller picture emerges of the place of the children's home in the family life cycle.

Orphanages were not full of orphans. As the table shows, of the three orphanages Quarrier's Homes had the largest proportion, but this only amounted to 37 per cent. Just three children in both the Whinwell and the Aberlour samples had lost both parents. However, half the admissions in all the orphanages had lost one parent. In the Whinwell sample, 38 per cent of children had no mother and 12 per cent had lost their father, whilst in Aberlour the numbers were 51 per cent and 8 per cent. The key to explaining

Number of Orphans and Children with One Parent upon Admission to Residential Care

	Whinwell		Aberlour		Quarrier's	
N=	169		80		94	
	No.	%	No.	%	No.	%
Orphans	3	2	3	4	35	37
Father Dead	20	12	6	8	30	32
Mother Dead	64	38	41	51	11	12
Parents Separated*	—	—	—	—	16	17

*This category includes men and women who have deserted, been imprisoned or otherwise detained.

Sources: *Whinwell Children's Home case files; Aberlour Orphanage case files; Orphan Homes of Scotland History Books.*

a child's admission to a children's home, though, was not the death of a parent as such, although this was certainly a critical moment in the life of a family, but rather a combination of circumstances which conspired to make the single-parent working-class family a non-viable unit. At Aberlour the absence of one parent, or the inability of the remaining parent to cope with the children, were the overriding reasons given for placing the children in the institution. In 25 per cent of cases the absence of the mother or her failure to take care of the children due to drunkenness, insanity, illness or desertion were the prime reasons for admission while half were admitted by widower fathers. The picture at the

Whinwell home also supports the thesis that the single-parent family was vulnerable and most likely to resort to a children's home in the absence of alternatives such as family or community support. Men who had lost the mothers of their children or whose wives were deemed incapable, and women who had been deserted by their husbands or who were unable to provide for their children without the help of a male wage-earner, comprised a significant proportion of those who brought their children to the doors of the Whinwell Home. These were parents who were either ineligible for poor relief or who did not wish to rely on the parish — indeed many were gainfully employed — perhaps because they feared their children would be permanently removed and boarded out with strangers. The children's home was a last resort for those parents in desperate circumstances but they also believed that their children would be well looked after and many hoped they would take their children home once family circumstances improved.

A typical case is that of Christina and James Hamilton, two of a family of six living in Cambuslang, who were admitted to the Whinwell Home in 1898 at the request of the Glasgow branch of the SNSPCC shortly after the death of their mother. Their father was a labourer in the steelworks, suffering ill-health and unable to provide for his children. 'They are greatly neglected for want of attention' commented the SNSPCC officer, 'but the man has not the means to pay for a housekeeper.'

> He is a sober man as far as I ever saw, the children get plenty of food and I never knew him to be cruel to them in any way…They are entirely wild for want of attention…I consider it would be an act of charity to place these children where they would be looked after. I don't think the man will ever be able to maintain himself besides being afflicted with 'lumbago' he is blind of an eye.[16]

Men such as Mr Hamilton — and his case was far from uncommon — were at their wits end attempting to care for several children while holding down a job. Housekeepers were difficult to obtain and they had to be paid. In a similar case the five Strachan children were admitted to Aberlour in 1903 at the request of a local woman who took an interest in the family. 'There is a sad case of a working man's family in this parish', she wrote.

> They are very much neglected as no suitable housekeeper can be got when there is so little money she can be given as wages. The father is employed at a farm and gets £16 in half year but finds it impossible to keep things going and is in debt.[17]

A lone mother was no less vulnerable than a father left on his own to manage without a wife. Before the advent of the social support net provided by the welfare state after 1945, single mothers — widows, deserted wives and unmarried women — had to struggle to keep their children. Single women with illegitimate children were probably the most in danger of being separated from their bairns, either by the poor law authorities who, by the end of the nineteenth century, preferred to find foster homes for illegitimate children leaving the woman to find employment, or at the behest of employers who might promise to keep a woman on if she agreed to place her child in an orphanage. In an unusual twist to this common tale, the employer of Annie Mackinnon who died leaving her child Murdina in 1900, agreed to find a situation for the girl once she had been educated and trained by the Whinwell Home.[18] Employers' obligations to their female servants and their offspring rarely extended as far as this.

Although the case notes kept by the institutions rarely record the emotions of those involved, heartbreak must have been felt by many mothers and fathers driven to hand their children over to an institution. Some continued to pay small amounts of maintenance for their children indicating an ongoing concern for their welfare. We should not assume that despite parents' relief at finding a place for their children that they did so with a cold heart. Many parents made no effort to stay in touch with their children once they had been admitted to an institution, but others wrote and some visited as regularly as they were permitted. James Davidson, a widower from Aberdeen, was clearly distraught at having to place his two sons in Aberlour a month after his wife's death in 1914. Just over a week after leaving them he wrote to ask after their welfare:

> Just a few lines to ask you how my two boys John James and Alexander Davidson are getting on. I have been very anxious about them since I was up with them a week past Thursday especially Alex the youngest as he cried to get away with me when we parted. I don't think he is a strong boy, he is very nervous…John again is more

robust but I feel for them both as it grieves me to have to part with any of them...[19]

When war broke out James was sent with the infantry to France but he continued to write to his boys:

> I came out of the trenches the other day and we are going back again soon. I may tell you it is something terrible out here and the weather is very wet and cold. How is my little ones, let them know where I am and get them to write me a few lines. I hope they have had a merry Christmas...

James Davidson was reported missing in action in April 1918 and the children eventually left the orphanage to be cared for by their grandmother and an aunt. There is no way of knowing whether the children received news of their father as he would have wished. This was a desperately sad case. So was that of Rebecca Anderson whose children were admitted to Quarrier's Homes in 1930. Rebecca, who was twice widowed and then deserted by her third husband, was suffering from TB and being cared for in a sanatorium in Arbroath. She had already given up the two children from her first marriage to Aberlour Orphanage and her remaining five boys were temporarily boarded out. The woman was clearly devastated at having to lose her four eldest boys to Quarrier's Homes, presumably on account of her continuing ill-health. She wrote to them repeatedly:

> Just a note to ask if you would be as kind to let me know how the four children are getting on since they went away...I miss the boys so much but I hope they are happy and good as they were good at home. Well matron I hope Walter is keeping well as he had a lot of illness since he was a baby...
> God Bless Thomas xxxx
> God Bless Alex xxxx
> God Bless Walter xxxx
> God Bless George xxxx
> Love to them all from Ma xx.[20]

Although Quarrier's staff did relay reports of the boys to her, they found her repeated letters an irritation, stating that 'we have really grown rather tired of replying direct to this woman's repeated enquiries particularly as there is seldom anything different to report.' Her anxiety was to be short lived as Rebecca Anderson died in Arbroath Sanatorium shortly after.

Children's homes did not encourage contact between parents and children. Despite their willingness to accept financial help from parents and relatives most children's home directors believed that children were better 'brought up outside the influence of parents', thus sharing the predominant view of those administering poor relief. Upon admission to the Whinwell Home a child's parent or guardian was obliged to agree to give the principal 'the power to send the child to any situation either in this country or abroad, or dispose of the child in any way the principal and her representatives think best for the child's future good.'[21] William Quarrier asked guardians to sign a similar undertaking which, at least in the 1870s and 1880s, invariably meant parents and relatives consigning children to an almost certain voyage overseas with an emigration party. Requests for information about children were usually answered politely if not always truthfully. 'Miss Croall has much pleasure in stating that the boy is in a very comfortable home, enjoys good health and is very happy' was the reply, which may have had little basis in fact, to one mother's request for details of her son who had been sent to Canada just one year after he was admitted at the age of six in 1902.[22] As we shall see in the next chapter, news from the colonies was intermittent and generally censored. Homes were suspicious of the motives of those enquiring after, or as they saw it interfering in, the lives of children they had given over to the care of others. Maggie Higgins, admitted to Whinwell Children's Home in 1910 along with her younger sister, was almost immediately dispatched to Canada from where she tried to maintain some limited contact with her father. Miss Croall, however, strenuously discouraged this contact, writing to Maggie in 1913:

> I have repeatedly told you it would be better not to communicate with your relatives until you were older and able to stand on your own. It is now three years since we found you and Isabella in utter destitution and starvation…We took you in when no-one else would…We were at the cost of bringing you here, rigging you out for Canada etc costing us about £20. Then think of your long illness in Liverpool and the trouble and anxiety you gave there. And now you kick up your heels and undo all the good that has been done…I am sending an inspector to Airdrie to visit your father and to tell him how cruel he has been to write such letters to you, instead of encouraging you in your work and to do well…Your father is only

imposing on you, and only keeps in touch with you for what he can draw from you and is not truthful with it at all...[23]

Undoubtedly some parents placed children in a local institution with the intention of removing them when they were in a position to provide a home once more. The children's home was in one sense being used as a life-raft, providing temporary care for children when the family ship struck an iceberg. The high turnover of children at the Whinwell home and the small proportion remaining until they left to find work is indicative of this pattern: 61 per cent of the sample left the home within a year. Aberlour Orphanage, on the other hand, was a long stay institution; it was a temporary refuge for relatively few with well over half the children remaining there for more than 6 years. In contrast, the majority of children admitted to Quarrier's Homes were moved on relatively quickly; the great majority of those — 42 per cent — staying for less than one year were sent to Canada within a few months of their arrival. These differing patterns are partly explained by the locations of each institution and the categories of children admitted. Aberlour was geographically isolated which discouraged continued contact between children and their families. It accepted almost any child for whom admission was requested and therefore housed a high proportion of children who might have been rejected by smaller and more selective institutions. The Whinwell Children's Home, on the other hand, served a local community and due to its small size could be fairly selective. Children placed here may have been more likely to have been retrieved by parents or relatives. Out of 169 children in the Whinwell sample, 41 (24 per cent) were removed by members of their family, 33 within a year of admission. Twenty-five or 15 per cent were adopted — the majority of these would have been under 5 years old — and 43 or 25 per cent were emigrated. By contrast, almost 50 per cent of the Quarrier's sample joined an emigration party and just 26 per cent returned to family members or stayed in the home until an age when they were old enough to be found employment. Although the information for Aberlour orphanage is partial, it appears few left the home before school leaving age. The contrasting fates of these sets of children are striking. A child admitted to Aberlour was much more likely to remain there until he or she was old enough to be found employment, usually in farm or domestic service. The Whinwell

Home, on the other hand, adopted a much more active role, passing 'unsuitable' children on to other institutions such as industrial schools and homes for 'imbeciles', finding adoptive families for the youngest and emigrating any who were sufficiently fit to go. Relatively few children remained in this institution until leaving age.

The key factor explaining the differing fates of children was emigration. Whinwell, Quarrier's and Aberlour had different attitudes towards this most permanent form of separation. Few parents were aware that this could be a fate in store for their own children. Philanthropists in the child welfare business could not forget that most of their children were victims of poverty and were unable to rid themselves of the taint of urban destitution and idleness. The best way of severing a child's ties with the family was to send the child overseas. Of the children admitted to Whinwell between the ages of two and five, 53 per cent were sent overseas, and 38 per cent of those who had been admitted at 6 years or older embarked on a voyage. Whinwell was a small home; it only had beds for around 40 children. If it was to continue providing a refuge for the needy children who were brought to its doors without physically expanding, children had to be moved elsewhere and the emigration programmes operated by Barnardo's and the Waifs and Strays Society in England provided this opportunity. Altogether around 200 children were sent to Canada and Australia from the Whinwell Home via Liverpool and London during the peak years for child emigration between the 1880s and the 1920s. Quarrier's Homes also adopted an enthusiastic approach to child emigration. Indeed, whole classes of girls and boys in groups of up to 100 embarked upon the journey to distant parts of the Empire. Of the first 300 children admitted to the William Quarrier School between 1894 and 1906, 108 left to go overseas.[24] In fact almost 7,000 children, 35 per cent of all children admitted to Quarrier's between 1871 and 1933, were emigrated. But Figure 3.2 shows that emigration was becoming a less popular solution for Quarrier's children after the 1910s, as children were increasingly returned to stay with friends and relatives. Aberlour, on the other hand, never embraced the policy of child emigration; only around 50 children were sent during the entire history of the orphanage, the directors believing that the home itself could provide a sound upbringing. As a result Aberlour was forced to

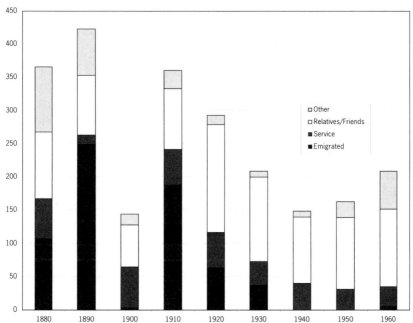

Figure 3.2. Destination of Children Leaving Quarrier's Homes at Decennial Intervals, 1880–1960.

Note: Quarrier's temporarily halted emigration between 1898 and 1905.

Source: The Orphan Homes of Scotland: *Narrative of Facts.*

expand almost continuously in order to take in the children asking for admission.[25]

The place of the children's home in Scottish society, at least until the Second World War, was to provide a place of respite and refuge for orphans but more especially for children of single-parent families and child victims of neglect and cruelty. The children's home acted as a safety-net at times of family crisis, allowing parents to find a temporary home for their children while attempting to reconstitute their lives and their families, although not infrequently it became a permanent solution. The orphanage provided a crutch for fragile families. When Helen's parents separated in the 1930s she was sent to Aberlour Orphanage along with her brother. Twin sisters had already been given up for adoption. Helen's mother subsequently married a man who already had six children in the orphanage but although one of his girls did run away back to her father and his new family, Helen remained at Aberlour until age 15.[26] These institutions also acted as intermediaries in the child welfare network. They posed as unofficial adoption agencies, they interacted with parish authorities, they co-operated with the child rescue organisations like the SNSPCC, and they liaised with the emigration societies. In addition to this multifarious role, children's homes existed to provide children with a substitute family within an institutional setting. Whether the residential regimes were able to provide an adequate substitute for the child's natural family may only be ascertained by listening to the experiences of those who spent much of their childhood within such an institution.

One Big Happy Family?

> There should be no longer a great house in which sixty of these motherless girls would be herded together, clad in some dull uniform generally divested of prettiness; but little cottages should arise, each of them presided over by its own 'mother' and in which all the members of the family could be clad as working people's children were under ordinary circumstances....There family life and family love might be reproduced, and gentle, modest ways would be made possible in the retirement of the cottage with its four or five rooms, and under the influence of godly women...[27]

William Quarrier's vision of a home run on family lines was borrowed from the Dr Barnardo's cottage experiment at Barkingside although the original idea for the cottage home had been pioneered in Hamburg, Germany, by Johann Wichern in the 1830s. Quarrier's belief that each cottage would function as a family unit supervised by an adult and accommodating up to 30 children of different ages was realised at Bridge of Weir in 1878. The 'children's city' he created certainly bore no resemblence to the form of residential care symbolised by the poorhouse. 'There is nothing here to remind us that we have come to an asylum for the destitute', commented Quarrier's biographer in 1902. 'There is not the slightest trace of the straight lines and the gaunt, icy, architecture of the workhouse.'[28] Instead, the village was said to resemble a rather elegant city suburb, an image it retains to this day.

Charles Jupp similarly portrayed the orphanage at Aberlour as one big happy family despite the more conventional regime adopted there based on dormitories for each sex and age group.

Children with staff in the grounds of Quarrier's Homes, c. *1930.*
Heatherbank Museum of Social Work.

> We have a large home with nearly 300 children in it, but it is really
> so many houses connected by a passage, there are separate
> entrances, separate mothers...The consequence is that we are able
> to get a maximum of family life at a minimum cost. We sometimes
> take whole families and they are brought up as brothers and
> sisters...it keeps up the family association, and family love.[29]

'Aberlour Orphanage aims at being a Home and not an Institution'
stated the Jubilee brochure in 1925, 50 years after its founding,
'and it succeeds in that ambition.'[30] 'Visitors frequently remark that
the children do not look in the least like Institution children. They
wear no uniform, are not hampered by unnecessary and unnatural
rules, and run about the place as freely as if they were in their
own homes.'[31] Yet, there is little evidence to suggest Quarrier's
Homes or Aberlour were entirely justified in their claims to provide
a substitute family life; one would be surprised if they were
bearing in mind the size of these two institutions. In 1896 there
was one 'mother' to around 60 children at Aberlour, a ratio which
prompted some probing questioning of the warden regarding his
claim to provide a substitute family life.[32] By the time voluntary
residential homes were subjected to rigorous government
inspection in the 1930s no pretence at reproducing family life

could be maintained in the light of inspectors' findings. Personal reminiscences of life in these homes also support the impression that the larger institutions were characterised by discipline, religion, physical violence and material and emotional deprivation. 'It was a strict, uniformed, episcopalian upbringing', remembered one former Aberlour child, 'where cleanliness, discipline and religion were adhered to.'[33]

Everyday life in the majority of children's homes until relatively recently was characterised by regimentation and routine. 'Things go on as if by machinery' was how the Whinwell routine was described in a rather jolly poem published in the home's Annual Report in 1891:

> At seven a.m. all are astir
> With bright and happy faces;
> And when the bell for worship rings
> The children take their places.
> Porridge and milk they have at eight,
> Then into school at nine,
> A break is made for 'piece and jam';
> At one o'clock they dine.
> Two hours allowed for games and fun,
> One hour to knit and sew;
> The tea and supper come in one,
> Then splash from top to toe.
> We keep good hours: at seven o'clock
> Each little prayer is said,
> The little ones are left with God
> To guard each little bed.[34]

Being a small home the Whinwell may have been able to tolerate a more relaxed atmosphere as this poem tries to convey but it conveniently omitted to mention the 'housemaid's catalogue of duties' performed by girls aged between six and thirteen who every morning before school hours made 20 beds, swept and dusted 8 rooms and ensured all the hallways, stairs and bathrooms were clean.[35] Most homes, large and small, ran on fairly strict lines, governed by a range of rules and punishments designed to maintain some control over the high-spirited, potentially noisy and unruly children. Thus almost every minute of the day was accounted for, children were kept busy, given little time to themselves, denied privacy and observed at work, at the table, at their prayers and at play. Annie, who spent several years in Bethany House in Aberdeen recalled the girls having little time to themselves:

> Well, [we] wouldnae really had much time to talk because eh at breakfast time after we'd the dishes to wash before we went to school, there was scrubbing to do, er, the dormitories to be cleaned out and er you never got time to talk about things and then you was in your bed at 6 o'clock at night.[36]

Children were kept busy to keep them out of mischief, to ensure they never had idle hands. There was little chance of that, especially for girls who, in most institutions, were expected to carry out most of the daily chores. 'We rarely "played" as normal children do', wrote one woman who was sent to 'a very famous Scottish orphanage'; 'we had no time to play because *all* domestic duties were done by us.'[37]

The pervasiveness of this regimentation and discipline is made clear in the memories of those who spent their childhood in residential care. They can still recall in detail the typical daily routine, the clothing, their personal identification number and the daily menu as well as the treats — at Aberlour this was plum duff and pocket money on a Wednesday and the occasional outing to Lossiemouth. The regularity with which oral respondents speak about the diet they received suggests food constituted an important element of their experience. Institutions supported solely by charitable donations often found it difficult to provide a healthy and sufficient diet for growing children. It goes without saying that porridge featured prominently on all children's home menus — it was cheap and filling and, served with milk, nutritionally valuable but monotonous if served everyday. At Aberlour not only did children crave variety in diet, there were undoubtedly times when children went hungry. Christine, who spent seven years at Aberlour between 1928 and 1935, described the daily diet in graphic terms:

> ...breakfast would be about 8 o'clock, porridge and this dry scone with no tea and er it was all tin, tin bowls and enamel in these days...and then home for our lunch which was soup and our pudding, uuuugh the soup uuuugh, there used to be a big basin in the kitchen that everybody put their old bread into it and that was broken up and put into our soup, we used to call it floaters oooooh,

> and then sometimes we used to pinch a bit of hard bread we were so hungry sometimes you know and er the puddings were dreadful, sago and tapioca and I think one day in the week we got a stewed pudding which wasn't so bad…but I can never remember much eating meat…[38]

This diet and the vulgarity of the eating arrangements was roundly criticised in 1934 by Scottish Education Department inspectors. Dirty kitchens, dirty tables and a lack of refinement in the serving of food was thought to be degrading. 'The tea was served in pails', and 'thick soup was served in enamel bowls' noted the visitors, 'and after they had finished the pudding was put into the same bowl without it being washed.'[39] The distaste felt by these middle-class ladies for the communal eating arrangements of the children is obvious but the children themselves found ways of varying their diet. Stories of unwanted porridge being tipped down the back of the wood panelling in the dining hall, jam roly-poly being stolen from the oven by a group of girls and replaced with pig-swill, girls secretly toasting cheese over small gas lights and later on the radiators, and all children grabbing the chance to eat wild berries and sweet leaves on walks in the country suggest they cared less about the enamel bowls and more about the quantity and variety of food on offer.[40] 'We were hungry, yes I'd say that' recalled Christine, 'they did their best for us but…'[41]

It did not go unnoticed that many larger homes operated a regime which stifled children's natural exuberance. One progressive psychopathologist called as an expert witness before the Clyde Committee in 1945 was outspoken in his criticism of the disciplined regimes which only benefited those charged with the children's day-to-day care:

> One of the great difficulties is that these big homes are unnatural. They are too clean, too orderly, and too quiet. Naturally the supervisors want orderliness and cleanliness and quietness, but sometimes it is absolutely pathetic. You see groups of boys playing football and never a sound. You see large rooms of toddlers 'playing' and never a sound. Everything is polished to the highest degree. Everything is clean and neat and tidy. No wonder the poor kiddies get complexes.[42]

He might have been describing any one of many Scottish children's homes. On a visit to the Catholic Smyllum Orphanage the inspectors noted 'enormous dormitories, far too big', and 'it is

The boys' dining hall. Aberlour Orphanage, 1925. This photograph gives an impression of the sheer scale of the institution and its impersonal nature. Heatherbank Museum of Social Work.

all very like an *institution*, very clean and polished and inhuman with just a few religious pictures etc.'[43] Another visitor to a number of homes around the country graphically described the sensation upon entering one of these older institutions: 'it is as if a technicolour film suddenly turned into black and white.'[44] Neither did the Duncarse Home in Dundee impress the Clyde Committee visitor: 'There seemed to be a lack of imagination in the treatment of the children, the rooms were very clean but the bedrooms were austere and the playrooms dull.'[45]

At Smyllum the emphasis upon religious worship went without saying, with religious teaching at the primary school, daily mass in the chapel, confession on alternate Fridays and weekly instruction from a visiting priest. Similarly, Bethany House in Aberdeen, an episcopalian institution run by a female religious order, operated a spartan and very strict regime which allowed the girls little freedom and plenty of religion.[46] At Aberlour, also episcopalian, religion pervaded the everyday routine and children came to regard going to church and saying prayers as a chore like any other. 'One real complaint of mine was the church and all the prayers' wrote one respondent; 'you had them at breakfast, dinner and tea, and supper and bedtime...on a Sunday you went to church at 7 a.m., 11 a.m. and 6 p.m. as well as the prayers every day.' This man's reaction to enforced religious worship was typical. 'Forcing religion down the throat does not do any good, it certainly put me off.'[47] 'It was sort of thumped into you really', recalled David; 'I think that's why you went against religion when I actually left the orphanage.'[48] Until the 1940s few spoke out against religious teaching in residential homes. After all religious institutions were key child welfare providers and most involved in child care would have applauded the attempts by these missionary philanthropists to inculcate children with Christian values. But some did recognise that excessive religious instruction could have a negative effect on the children; 'religious instruction [should not] be so spoon fed and violently compulsory as at many establishments' commented one submission to the Clyde Committee; 'the present system tends to turn the child's mind and like eating the same food at every meal causes sickness effect.'[49] A similar sentiment was also being expressed by official agencies. 'We are always a little anxious where excessive church going is demanded of the children', commented a Scottish Home Department official in 1945. 'It seems unwise to risk making what ought to be a real pleasure and privilege into another dreary duty.'[50]

Charity and religion went hand-in-hand. Although most residential homes received some income from local authorities for the maintenance of children under their care and some parents and relatives managed to pay small sums towards the children's upkeep the majority of their finance was raised by appeals for gifts and donations. Lady collectors worked the streets and lanes of Scotland on behalf of children's homes, responding to the appeals to 'every right woman's heart' to support God's work.[51] Aberlour's wardens travelled far and wide to speak about the orphanage and evangelise on its behalf. Every orphanage magazine and annual report contained thanks to donors and the names of those who had generously given their time and money. 'This afternoon the members of the Mothers' Meeting at St.Andrew's Cathedral, Inverness, listened with interest to a lantern lecture, with films, given by the Warden on the work of the Orphanage', reported the 1935 *Aberlour Orphanage Magazine*. 'The members of the Mothers' Meeting are most devoted in their labours and most generous in their gifts on behalf of our large family.'[52] By the 1960s Aberlour's running costs had reached around £60,000. In order to raise this substantial sum the orphanage relied upon subscriptions to the magazine, legacies, endowments and bequests, covenants and donations of money and in kind.[53] Although Quarrier's Homes did not beg for money it was well supported, especially by the adjacent community. Quarrier's was a household name and public collections such as one carried out at Greenock Cinema which raised money for much needed equipment, in this case two complete football strips.[54] The public success achieved by all of these charitable institutions inevitably influenced the children's perception of the care they were receiving. The atmosphere of charity was ever present in some, especially the religious homes, prompting one of the most astute observers of the Scottish child welfare system to note in 1945:

> These children are asked to be grateful for the things that are done for them, and it really should be the other way around...The number of homes...where the children are made to pray morning and night in gratitude for the lovely home they have got and so on is absolutely disgraceful.[55]

The orphanage regime was designed to prepare children for life after care which, until the Second World War, was assumed to be domestic service for the girls and farm service or manual labour for the boys. However, the domestic chores commonly undertaken by orphanage children lay heaviest on the girls' shoulders. Boys were not exempt — 'you had to do your duties, you had to do your chores, like cleaning the big dormitories...'[56] — but older girls were commonly used as domestic servants to carry out some of the more onerous tasks. In Aberlour the 'working girls' were those who stayed on at the home for a year after their schooling finished at the age of 14. During this year they were paid a small amount and given extra 'privileges' — smaller dormitories, smart uniforms, one free afternoon a week and permission to do what they wished with the money earned — in return for jobs dressed up as 'work-experience': looking after the younger children, working in the laundry and the kitchen.[57] Quarrier's Homes operated a similar system whereby boys and girls were removed from school at age 14 and given employment for a nominal wage;

Girls in the washing room, Quarrier's Homes, c. 1900. Laundry work was one of the chores assigned to girls in the year before they left the home. Heatherbank Museum of Social Work.

this was a situation deplored by Scottish Office civil servants.[58] Although those who recalled their experiences as 'working girls' appear not to have resented being put to work in this way there were some who did see it as exploitation. 'I expect you know all work is done in this orphanage by the children', wrote a former employee of the home in a letter to the Scottish Education Department in 1946.

> Now there are 28 to 30 girls known as 'working girls', 13–17 years. They also do excessive work. They get paid at 13 years the handsome sum of 1/- per week rising to 2/6d., 5/-…they pay for all breakages, are fined 1/- every time they speak back or are defiant. In the world these girls would get £2.10/-. If this is not child labour at its worst then I don't know what is…Nor should they be able to hold these 17 year old girls in there as slave labourers, put to bed at 8.30 with lights out and not given their freedom.[59]

The regimentation, the household chores and the routine of residential life all combined to create a disciplinary environment for children who had committed no crime. Everyday life in some children's homes differed little from the daily routine to be found in industrial schools and reformatories; they shared a regime which emphasised a strict routine, numerous rules and 'appropriate' forms of punishment. Linda Mahood points out in respect of Industrial Schools that it was often difficult to negotiate the fine line between rational discipline and cruel punishment.[60] Although children who had been boarded out were notionally protected from excessive use of corporal punishment, those in children's homes were guaranteed virtually no protection from disciplining verging on the vicious and vindictive. In most residential homes children were subjected to a degree of violence, usually in the form of physical punishment, as a matter of course. Rules governing the use of corporal punishment were not formalised until 1918 — these legislated for a limited number of strokes to the hand or the 'posterior' and required residential schools to record all acts of corporal punishment — but there is no doubt that these rules were not universally adhered to.[61]

A flexible disciplinary system mainly consisting of physical punishment and withdrawal of privileges was operated in most children's homes. The rules were designed to allow the staff to maintain control — no speaking after lights out, no answering back to the house-mother or father, no going out without permission — rules that were easily broken, especially by children like Christine who readily spoke out when she recognised an injustice was being perpetrated, either to herself or somebody else. 'I spoke up...if I thought I was being cheated I said and if somebody was being caned I said what a shame and I would get the cane again...'[62] Christine also recalled the system of withdrawing privileges at Aberlour:

> ...you only got your penny a week [pocket money] and I mean if you were naughty you had a mark, matron had a book, you got a mark or another mark and if you had two marks you only got a halfpenny a week but if you had four marks you got nothing...quite a few weeks I got nothing and then you sort of had to get a bite [of chocolate] from somebody else...[63]

But what today would be regarded as random and unnecessary violence — usually strokes from the strap or the cane — was regularly inflicted for a wide variety of petty misdemeanours from failing to learn a psalm off by heart and stealing apples to behaviour which, far from being punished, should have been dealt with sympathetically, such as bed-wetting and running away.[64] Few seemed to have questioned the reality that many staff, in beating children, were merely replicating the kind of treatment some children had received from their own parents and from whom they had been 'rescued'. The Aberlour Orphanage Magazine claimed that 'obstreperous and mischievous boys' were treated sympathetically on account of their 'psychological conditions', and that corporal punishment was only resorted to in cases of extreme and wilful misconduct such as the breaking of windows and violence against the person when 'a sound spanking is more often than not the most efficient and effective punishment'. Yet former girls and especially boys recall corporal punishment being administered by housemasters in a far more cavalier fashion.[65]

> [W]e got punished for being generally unruly or whatever, just being bad, you'd get the strap…I remember when my brother ran away…I remember we got the strap, and he eventually got caught the people who knew got the strap as well…and I couldn't understand for the life of me why we got the strap, in fact my brother didn't get the strap, he got a severe reprimand. The only people who got the strap really was the people that knew about it, because we didn't reveal it to them.[66]

After 1945 there was some official relaxation of the disciplinary regime in residential homes. More liberal, enlightened views regarding the treatment of children were taken on board at the government level and at the large orphanages, in part due to the recognition that a high proportion of home children came from disturbed and troubled backgrounds. Even the Aberlour staff accepted that children labelled 'delinquent' were often psychologically disturbed; 'punishment for these cases is rarely successful and only creates a feeling of resentment'.[67] Corporal punishment for 'hooligan' girls was seen by 1947 as 'worse than useless as a means of training'.[68] Smaller homes had already adopted a softer approach to discipline; a Fife children's home for instance stated that it did not believe in corporal punishment and did not permit the housemaids to smack the children.[69] Alternative forms of treatment were pioneered, especially for 'high-spirited lads', consisting of energetic sports presumably to dissipate their energy and make them more manageable. Five girls caught on the Aberlour school roof in 1958 would in earlier years have been soundly punished but the magazine reported in its familiar jovial tone:

while we felt inclined to scold we could not but admire the spirit of daring and adventure which inspired these girls. Certainly if ever a female paratroop regiment is formed, we can offer potential candidates from amongst our hundred lassies.[70]

However, while the orphanage magazine professed an enlightened approach to discipline, children were still being subjected to cruel treatment and often suffered in silence. At least one house master was forced to resign in the 1940s when his violent and 'unorthodox' treatment of boys was exposed by one of his colleagues and yet another was prosecuted and convicted for the abuse of the boys in his care in the 1950s.[71] As we are now discovering, in spite of the Clyde Committee recommendations in 1946 that all children's home staff should receive professional training, the absence of meticulous checks on those employed to work with children allowed abuse to occur on a massive scale. This aspect of the residential child care system will be discussed more fully in Chapter Six.

An Isolated Life

In 1945, the Clyde Committee on Homeless Children heard evidence from Dr Seymour who had visited a number of children's institutions on behalf of the Department of Health in Scotland. His observations led him to a consideration of the essential conditions for normal development in a child, commonly present in family life 'which are so difficult to supply in institutions.'

> These three things are parental affection, which calls forth the response of the child and starts normal emotional development; the second thing is the intimate personal interest which parents can take in each child, which encourage it to develop its capacities and train its character, and enables it, in fact, to become an individual in the community instead of just a member of a herd, as happens too often in institution life; and the third thing is preparation for and gradual introduction to independent life.[72]

This assessment led to a series of recommendations including the provision of greater individual attention for each child, the introduction of family groups in the larger institutions, the provision of facilities for free play and imaginative games and the introduction of after-care. His observations and recommendations were astute and reflected a more general shift of opinion amongst child care professionals in the 1940s towards a more child-centred and family-oriented approach to care. In Scotland, institutionalised children had been somewhat ignored owing to the obsession with boarding out, and change of this kind was long overdue.

In the previous chapter we saw how Poor Law officers made great efforts to ensure boarded out children were not distinguishable from other children by means of their clothing, and castigated children's homes and poorhouses for dressing children in a uniform which suppressed a child's sense of individuality. Most children arrived at the gates of the orphanage with only the clothes they were wearing: 'It was blue costume, pleated skirts, I think I see it yet...a double breasted jacket with brass buttons, and a black velour hat, black stockings and shoes' recalled Annie of her arrival at Aberdeen's Bethany House with her sister when she was just eight years old in 1914. 'We went into the home in that and I never saw it again. It was taken from us and we just got a dress and a pinafore on.'[73] The girls used to hitch up their long skirts when they were away from the nuns and Annie would pick out the eyelets from the boys' boots she was forced to wear but there were few other ways for girls in this home to express their individuality. At Aberlour all boys were provided with a kilt for Sundays and special excursions which immediately identified them as orphanage children. David remembered how tourists used to take photographs of them: 'Yes you sort of stood out from the crowd, you had short hair and people did look at you, you did feel a bit different...I used to hate the kilt...the time of the Beatles and that sort of thing.'[74]

This sense of being different was continually reinforced by the segregation of orphanage children from the world around them. Quarrier's Homes and Aberlour Orphanage were situated in isolated, rural locations and children were discouraged from contact with members of the local community. Children in these institutions attended a separate primary school — there were too many of them to attend the village schools — they also had their own church and leisure organisations such as scout and guide troups. Aberlour was accused of fostering a monastic atmosphere, 'and every obstacle is placed in the way of children in the orphanage making friends and chumming up with the village children.'[75] Following an unannounced visit to Aberlour in 1948 the Education Department official noted that 'like all institution children they lead an isolated, sheltered life, mix only with children and do not hear conversations or views of adults.'[76] Letters in and out of the orphanages were censored and children were rarely informed that their parents and relatives had inquired after them. Quarrier's operated a ticket system; only parents in possession of a ticket were permitted access to their children, the rest were blacklisted. Former residents speak of being cut off from the outside world for most of the time. Annie who was denied books, newspapers and comics commented: 'You didn't know anything about the outside world you see, you just thought that that was your life...'[77] Special day trips and holidays provided limited experience of the world outside the orphanage but Aberlour children did not travel much further than Lossiemouth, Hopeman and Elgin. As the headmaster of the Orphan Homes of Scotland school made plain in 1946, 'the isolation problem is a very big problem.' Mr Gellatly was clearly quite disturbed by the restricted outlook fostered by the Homes. 'You don't realise how little background these children have, especially during the war years...They hardly know what a bus is except what they see passing by.' Moreover, he added, 'The boys are shut in and frustrated so often.' Although permitted to play football on an inter-cottage basis they were not part of a league. 'They won't allow the boys out to play return matches.'[78] By the 1950s orphanages did have radios and television and the influx of older children imported outside interests — such as support for the major football teams — but when David left Aberlour for Aberdeen in 1967 Elgin was the largest place he had seen; not surprisngly he experienced quite a culture shock:

> It was actually when I came out of the orphanage into this big world I suddenly realised I was alone because I was put in digs away on a council scheme...it was there suddenly well you're on your own David now...it was secure in the orphanage, it was a wee world of your own...it was your only world...You weren't really aware of things, because you were in your own wee world, that was another world you know...[79]

Even when children were encouraged to integrate into the local community they remained 'a class apart' according to the headmaster of a boys' residential school near Dumfries. 'They are invited to join in the sports of other boys...but very few have responded. In the playground they associate only with one another.'[80]

The confinement of children within the grounds of these large orphanages, however picturesque, certainly restricted their personal development and this was further constrained by perpetual communal living. It was difficult, if not impossible, to give children the personal attention they would have received in a natural family environment. 'We were more or less treated as a "herd" not as individuals' was how one woman described her experiences.[81] In the larger homes it was acknowledged that with the best will in the world staff were unable to give affection to all of their children in their care, there were just too many of them.[82] In the post-war era there was a recognition that children needed to be treated as individuals rather than regimented and disciplined as part of a crowd. The Educational Institute of Scotland was explicit on this issue, remarking that the child:

> ...has a need too for a certain amount of freedom and leisure time. He needs a place of his own to keep his personal treasures; this is more important than it seems. His affection and tenderness should be developed by the opportunity of keeping pets...The opportunities for further education should be many, as in ordinary family life — wireless, gramophone, films, books, gardening, dramatics and concerts. Encouragement should be given to the cultivation of individual hobbies.[83]

Few children's homes were able to provide this degree of individual attention and freedom but by the post-war era many did try to provide boys and girls with a range of activities — boxing, stamp and chess clubs, indoor games and dancing — and the 'birthday aunt' scheme, which paired a child with a kindly person who would send a birthday card or present and maybe something at Christmas, was an attempt to cultivate at least some degree of personal contact with someone outside the institution.

By the 1940s, following the institutionalisation of many children during the war years, there was sound evidence to demonstrate that long term residential care affected children's sense of self and their ability to form relationships with others. 'In the case of institution bred children', noted one child welfare worker, 'the lack of a sense of "belonging" and the lack of a sense of counting as an individual is at times very marked. I am struck when I visit these institutions...by the desire of children for personal notice and their desire to talk of their relations...'[84] Her observations mirrored those made by Dorothy Burlingham and Anna Freud in their influential study of children cared for in residential nurseries during the war. The absence of a mother's influence and the intimate family setting, they suggested, caused children — many of whom had already experienced the trauma of separation — to develop severe behavioural patterns such as a demanding attachment to each new mother figure who might give affection. They developed auto-erotic habits such as thumb-sucking, head-knocking and persistent rocking as a consequence of sudden separation from the mother. As they grew older children developed a tendency to exhibitionism, showing-off in order to gain attention.[85] Visitors to children's homes had already noticed children's 'curious sense of detachment' which inhibited their ability to make friends.[86] Individuals' memories of residential care confirm these research findings. 'I remember my young brother who was about 2 yrs' wrote one woman who spent some time in a home during the 1940s, 'sitting in a cot just rocking back and forth against the bars of a cot.'[87] Children entered the homes in a state of bewilderment only to be separated from their brothers and sisters. Boys in particular seem to have had difficulty forming close friendships. 'I thought I lived in Aberlour with crowds' said Arthur, '[but] there was only one or two people I would speak to and confide in…'[88]

Burlingham and Freud also discovered that older children were prone to abnormal relations with their peers characterised by extremes of aggression, indifference, jealousy and envy. One might argue that relationships amongst children are always characterised in this way but the sense of either belonging or of being an outsider were accentuated in an institution. 'There was quite a lot of fighting went on actually, especially in your wee group, who's the master', recalled David. Boys and girls who did not fit in could be relentlessly bullied but of course unlike most children the home child had few means of escape. Having brothers and sisters in the home was no guarantee of protection as the sexes and age groups were usually separated. Although David knew his younger brother and sister were being bullied he could do little about it; 'I didn't realise it, I was in my own little world anyway.'[89]

The exclusion of the child who was 'different' in some way was one of the consequences of the abnormal relationships formed amongst groups of girls and boys in the larger homes.

Aberlour, unlike most other children's homes, tried to accept any child for whom admission was requested and therefore probably had a higher proportion of children with a variety of physical and mental difficulties which it could do little to alleviate or support. Children with physical impairments such as speech impediments, buck teeth, club feet and so on, could be harried relentlessly by other children but also by staff. Dorothy Haynes, whose book *Haste Ye Back* famously recounted her years at Aberlour, was later able to reflect upon the cruelty children could mete out to others:

> There were the unfortunate ones who mentally or educationally were not quite up to the mark; the children who were always behind, dragging along with all sorts of handicaps which at that time had to be endured rather than alleviated. At first these children had shocked me. I was sorry for them, but I didn't want to associate with them. I kept myself aloof from the bed-wetters forever washing and drying their soiled sheets, and the girls whose heads were shaven because of ringworm. Suppose I were to catch it and have my head shaved?[90]

Although Dorothy Haynes subsequently acknowledged her own callousness, at the time nothing could compensate a child for bullying treatment by other children and particularly staff. Evelyn described acts of abuse perpetrated against her by other girls and staff which included being tied to the bed, locked in cupboards for long periods and having her hair pulled 'from one end of the road to the other.' As a result Evelyn spent a profoundly unhappy childhood in the home which had a lasting impact on her life.[91]

Not all children coped with the isolation and confinement in the same way and some evidence points to a gendered response to residential care. While boys adopted an individualistic, competitive and sometimes aggressive mode of behaviour, girls on the other hand tended to formulate a collective response to problems and experiences. Christine's memories of Aberlour in the 1930s celebrate the friendships amongst the girls and the support they gave one another:

> ...I suppose you're unhappy...but you just don't remember very much about it because there's so many of you together and you're all telling each other your sad stories you know...and if somebody was crying we'd say what's wrong, I'm thinking of my Mum so we'd give her all our toys and then the next day it'd be her turn to give them all back to somebody else...[92]

Although other contemporaneous accounts suggests this support was not extended to all girls, there are few indications that boys were similarly supportive. Girls remember shared experiences: a group of girls sneaking out of the orphanage to the village to buy sweeties, falling in love with the Italians who came to lay the new terrazzo flooring, giggling about boyfriends, country dancing and picnics. Girls also seem to have developed a rather morbid fascination with death and dying which, as Dorothy Haynes speculated, had its roots in their 'collective past'. As they sat darning stockings before bedtime she recalled the girls sang:

> I am a poor wee orphanage girl,
> My mother she is dead,
> My father he is far away
> And cannot buy me bread.
> Alone I stand at the window
> To hear the church bells ring,
> God bless my dear old mother,
> She's dead and in her grave.
> Ding, dong, my castle bell!
> Farewell, my mother!
> Bury me in the old churchyard
> Beside my eldest brother...[93]

Boys, on the other hand, appear to have made few firm or lasting friendships with other boys, were more likely to engage in competitive activities and appear to have dealt with institutionalisation on a more solitary level. Despite or maybe because of being constantly in the company of large numbers of children at the same time as being separated from siblings, some experienced profound loneliness. Arthur was separated from his elder brother, his sister and twins upon entering Aberlour. 'I felt very lonely being separated from the rest of the family', he wrote, 'and I felt myself wanting to be with them.' He was not to see the twins again until they all went on a day trip to Lossiemouth but by then he 'felt a stranger with them.'[94] Similarly, David who was admitted to Aberlour in 1955 with his four brothers and sisters remembered that he 'never really thought about my brothers and sisters, there was just me and that was it.'[95] Although there was no encouragement to any children to talk about the past or keep in touch with family members, boys appear to have been particularly reticent in speaking about the reasons they were in a home. Christine, on the other hand, talked of trying to help the girls who had been in the home since babies, 'these were the ones that we used to feel sorry for you know',[96] but boys seem to have shared little that was personal, preferring to adopt psychological defenses against the repressive regime. 'We never spoke about it, you were just there and that was it', remarked David; '...nobody says "my Dad did this" or "my Mum did this" or whatever, never discussed it...nobody asked you so you didn't really speak about it.'[97] Boys had to look out for themselves. Fights were common, some boys belonged to gangs and in order to survive a boy had to stand up for himself. As David said, 'You did fight a lot actually, there were quite a few fights and you had to look after yourself, any sign of weakness and you got a wee bit of abuse.'[98] His strategy was to resort to jokes and cheekiness to deal with the threats but as he readily admitted the home bred in him a defensiveness which he was unable to shake off when he left.

The reproduction of family life was impossible in these institutions and although the cottage system with its house-mothers and fathers at Quarrier's Homes potentially obviated some of the worst experiences of isolation and exclusion this was no substitute for the close relationships formed within the family. John Bowlby's pioneering research in the 1950s and 60s into the mother-child bond which itself drew upon the findings of those who had observed the impact of separation of children from their parents during World War Two's evacuation programme, drew belated attention to what he termed 'maternal deprivation'. In his influential study *Maternal Care and Mental Health* published in 1951, Bowlby argued there was a connection between a child's separation from the mother and that child's later mental health. However, the psycho-analytical approach to child care pioneered by Bowlby and others at London's Tavistock Clinic only began to have an impact following the 1948 Children Act. Before the war, as personal reminiscence graphically demonstrates, emotional deprivation was a key feature of the large residential institution.

A kindly house-mother with responsibility for 20 to 30 children could at least obviate some of the worst feelings of loneliness and isolation but not all of these figures possessed 'motherly' qualities. Trained staff were thin on the ground before the 1948 Children Act required staff in children's homes to undergo training. According to one former orphanage resident, 'apparently the only qualification necessary to become a mother in this institution was that she had to be a good Christian…'[99] And in spite of the best intentions of staff, they could not replace the children's natural parents. 'They were just motherly sort of people' was how the house-mothers at Aberlour were described by one group of women although as one pointed out, 'the only thing we missed was parental love.'[100] In one home it was said that at bathtime children were 'passed along as if on a conveyor belt, with none of the little friendly individual gestures so essential for their personal development…'[101] When a journalist with a Scottish popular newspaper travelled around the country visiting child care establishments in 1946 she was struck by the absence of the 'mother temperament' in some, where babies were 'miracles of clinical well-being. In their "time-table" is 30 minutes "mothering" daily. It is just too bad if Baby No.1 isn't drowsy at the end of his half hour. he is dumped back into his heat controlled cot to yell his head off if he likes, because it is time for Baby No.2 to be "mothered".'[102] Some house-mothers and fathers and staff in other institutions must have struggled to maintain control of their young charges, many of whom were deeply traumatised by events in their past. Few would have experienced any formal training in child psychology but the staff who are remembered with affection are not the best educated but those who showed children kindness and affection. One boy who used to have recurring nightmares described how 'Miss Harold used to come through and comfort me and put a bit of fresh air in the window…You just needed a bit of comfort and it sort of settled you down.'[103] When Dean Wolfe replaced Canon Jenks as Aberlour's warden, former residents remember the atmosphere around the orphanage changing. Wolfe was, by all accounts, a kindly man who related well to children (not an attribute possessed by all children's home directors). The Educational Institute of Scotland had recommended in 1945 that orphanage wardens should ideally 'have a personal knowledge and understanding of, and intimate contact with each individual child…' This was crucial in the Institute's opinion, 'Because the emotional life of a homeless child is less stable, more open to distortion, leading in adulthood to a warped attitude to society and life itself…'[104] When Scottish Education Department officials made an unannounced visit to Aberlour in 1947 they particularly commented on the fact that 'whenever the warden and the matron appear amongst the children they are surrounded by the children who run to them and laugh and joke with them.'[105] There is no doubt that Dean Wolfe was held in considerable affection by many of the children at Aberlour and must have represented for many of them an idealised father figure with his pipe, his dogs constantly at his side and his kindly demeanour. 'In fact he used to play games with us' recalled David, the children calling out 'what's the time Mr Wolfe?'[106]

Former residents speak of the loneliness they experienced amongst strangers, the suppression of individualism, the absence of close relationships with other children or with the staff and the void where a mother and father's love should have been. One vocal critic of Aberlour described it as 'one of those cold and forbidding abodes' which could 'never fill the place of a normal home with the intimate family life cycle, in the life of a child.'[107] He continued in the same vein:

> The Orphanage despite its proud boast of providing a 'homely' home for children in the first place is structurally unable to live up to its boast...When a boy is admitted to the orphanage he ceases to be an individual, his personality is submerged...In a short time he has become as mediocre, listless and apathetic as the other boys in the house...Through time he becomes used to the cold impersonality of the place and becoming so used to it, people mistake it for happiness.[108]

Children who spent a few years in a residential home did become institutionalised to some degree. They became used to the routine and discipline and in some homes infantilised by the lack of independence and contact with the outside world. Few speak of profound unhappiness however and some look back with fondness and nostalgia. Christine has genuinely happy memories of Aberlour in the 1930s: 'you know it was great, and we were really quite happy — you know I look back and I think gosh, how lucky', and her experience, or her adult recollections of those experiences, are not isolated. There is a tendency to project one's own present day expectations of care onto past regimes whereas for Christine and many like her, although they perhaps lacked individual attention and parental love, they were otherwise well looked after.[109] And it should be remembered that many children placed in residential care had only limited, if any, experience of a 'normal' home life, a fact that was to influence their retrospective judgement of the care they received . '...I wouldn't say I was unhappy' said Annie who spent several years in a strict religious home for girls, 'because we didn't know what it was to be happy you see...it was just an existence from morning to night.' After leaving the home to stay with an aunt she commented, 'I thought it was wonderful to be in a home with other people you know.'[110]

A Necessary Evil

The memories of childhood in residential homes provide an eloquent reminder of why so many of the larger institutions were harshly criticised and eventually closed in the 1960s and 1970s. Orphanages founded by religious and voluntary organisations at the end of the nineteenth century to provide a sanctuary for homeless and destitute children had largely achieved their aim of meeting children's material and physical needs. But the emotional care they could provide was usually inadequate, thus justifying the long-standing rejection of residential care by Scottish authorities since the early nineteenth century and articulated repeatedly since then. In 1917 Sir Leslie Mackenzie, in his monumental survey of the condition of mothers and children in Scotland, expressed a gut feeling that institutional care could never provide an adequate substitute for family life.

> They are at the best a necessary evil. They cure nothing...They make a certain relatively good life possible; they keep the children for the time in safety; but equally they take the children out of their place in normal society, and, by that fact, tend to unfit them for a return to it. This is true of all institutions, however good.[111]

Sir Leslie anticipated the shift in the inter-war period towards supporting the family in urging those responsible to seek 'some other method of preserving a mother and a father to the child and of preserving the child to its parents.[112] After World War Two there could be no more pretence that the institution could act as a substitute family. Public debate on the quality of residential care for children was catalysed by Lady Marjory Allan's letter to *The Times* in July 1944 in which she drew attention to the 'repressive conditions and the chilly stigma of "charity" ' characterising children's homes.[113] Child care professionals loudly called for reform of the system so that it recognised children's spiritual as well as material needs. Susan Isaacs, whose studies of evacuated children during World War Two had been so influential, summed up the new mood in a letter to *The Times* in 1944:

> It is an established fact, not a matter of sentiment or opinion, that 'mothering' and close human contacts are as necessary for full welfare in childhood as are a proper diet and medical care. Nor can character, personality and sound social attitudes develop without the experience of personal affection and understanding treatment in the early years. Institutional life as such is terribly impoverishing to the spirit unless skill and knowledge are there to overcome its great disadvantages.[114]

As with the analysis of boarding out, it is difficult to reconcile the range of experiences recorded by former residents of children's homes. There is no doubt that these institutions filled a necessary gap in the child welfare system from the late nineteenth century onwards, and that they provided a place of safety or refuge and respite for children who had been left homeless as a result of poverty, death or mistreatment. This need continued through the inter-war years as the effects of the First World War and the Depression exacted a heavy toll on the working-class family. Throughout this period charitable and voluntary homes were largely unregulated and the Scottish authorities paid little attention to the poor relation of boarding out. The Clyde Committee's 1946 investigation of residential care was the first time Scottish voluntary and local authority homes had come under serious scrutiny and on the whole they fared badly. In its report the Committee made its feelings clear on the large institution:

> The answer is certainly not to be found in the large Institution. That is an outworn solution, and some of them have left a bad impression upon the Members of the Committee who have visited them. The uniformity, the repression, the impersonality of these cold and forbidding abodes afford no real consolation to the children who grow up in them, and constitute a sorry preparation for entry into a world where the child must ultimately fend for itself.[115]

A series of changes were recommended, including the break up of the large institutions and the large cottage-style homes — a maximum capacity of 30 in each cottage was mentioned — the relocation of remote homes to inhabited areas, the training of staff in child care work, the provision of nursery accommodation and education and the provision of effective after care, which sounded the death knell for the older homes like Aberlour Orphanage and Quarrier's. It was envisaged that in future residential care would be modelled on a 'normal' family life, with greater emphasis being given to a child's individual needs.

Residential child care continues to be regarded as the poor relation of foster care and recent crises prompted by allegations of physical and sexual abuse in residential institutions have damaged the reputation of this necessary form of care even further. As a result, residential care has been in retreat since the 1970s. In 1970 Scotland had 179 children's homes with accommodation for up to 4,103 children. By 1995 there were just 164 establishments capable of accommodating a maximum of 2,175 children.[116] The majority of these are small establishments accommodating fewer than 20 children; large orphanages are no longer deemed acceptable. Yet, in the wake of decades which have witnessed the rapid decline in both the number of children's homes and the number of children placed in residential care, at the end of the twentieth century there is recognition that such care still has a place within the child care system as a whole. For some children, especially those who have had traumatic family experiences, a residential placement will always be the most appropriate form of care. In 1997 the Utting Report on young people in care in England and Wales recommended that despite the catalogue of abuse that has recently been uncovered, new and more specialised homes are needed in order to deal more effectively with the full range of children entering the care system.[117] In Scotland there appears to be less concern about the number and quality of residential care places available, but it has recently been stated that foster placements have reached a plateau prompting a reappraisal of the mantra that foster care is always preferable to residential care. 'A good experience of group care', writes Roger Kent, 'is better than going to the wrong foster home, and infinitely better than going to a succession of foster homes.'[118] Residential care should no longer be judged as second best but as a positive choice.[119]

NOTES

1. See Jessie Kesson, *The White Bird Passes* (Edinburgh, 1958) for a vivid portrayal of this fear.
2. *Scottish Women*, Scottish Television, 9 June 1997.
3. Mahood, *Policing Gender, Class and Family*, Appendix B.
4. SRO, ED 11/211: List of Certain Institutions for Children and Young Persons in Scotland (1934).
5. See Checkland, *Philanthropy in Victorian Scotland*, pp.16–18.
6. For example, Zetland County housed a very small number in the poorhouse, just 3 for 8 weeks in 1945 and similarly Inverness Poorhouse could accommodate 3 children. SRO, ED 11/267.
7. T.Ferguson, *Scottish Social Welfare 1864–1914* (Edinburgh, 1958), pp.572–3.
8. See Rev.J.Urquhart, *The Life-Story of William Quarrier* (London, 1902).
9. See A.Magnusson, *The Village: A History of Quarrier's* (Glasgow, 1984).
10. SAS, PD 41/1/1: Whinwell Children's Home Annual Report, 1884.
11. SAS, PD 41/1/1: Whinwell Children's Home Annual Report, 1898.
12. SAS, PD 41/4/5: *Fifty Years on a Scottish Battlefield, 1873–1923*, p.41.
13. William Quarrier strenuously denied charges of proselytism, claiming that all children in the homes were brought up 'in the fear of God'. Urquhart, *The Life-Story of William Quarrier*, p.277.
14. 169 individual case files were sampled from admissions to Whinwell Children's Home; 80 from Aberlour case files and 103 from Quarrier's Homes.
15. See A.J.McIvor, 'Women and Work in Twentieth Century Scotland' in A.Dickson & J.H.Treble (eds.), *People and Society in Scotland Volume III, 1914–1990* (Edinburgh, 1992), p.140; C.G.Brown and J.D. Stephenson, 'The View from the Workplace: Women's Memories of Work in Stirling c.1910–1950' in E.Gordon & E.Breitenbach (eds.), *The World is Ill Divided* (Edinburgh, 1990), p.10.
16. SAS, PD 41: Whinwell Case Files, H25 (1898).
17. Aberlour Child Care Trust: Schedules 421, 422, 423, 424, 425.
18. SAS, PD 41: Whinwell Case Files, M17[A] (1900).
19. Aberlour Child Care Trust: Schedules 1506, 1507.
20. OHS: Case 1,2,3,4/30.
21. SAS, PD 41/1/1: Whinwell Children's Home Annual Report, 1914.
22. SAS, PD 41: Whinwell Case Files, A11 (1902).
23. *Ibid.*, H 41 (1910).
24. GCA, SR 10/3/1446/1: William Quarrier School, Admission Register, 1894–1906.
25. Aberlour Child Care Trust: Orphanage Record Book, 1875–1988.
26. Correspondence with Helen.
27. Cited in Magnusson, *The Village*, p.27.
28. Urquhart, *The Life Story of William Quarrier*, p.328.

29. *B.P.P., Minutes of Evidence taken before a Department Committee appointed by the Local Government Board* (Mundella Report), 1896, Cmd.8032, p.532 (Rev.Jupp).
30. *Aberlour Orphanage Jubilee Year 1925*, p.10.
31. *Ibid*.
32. *B.P.P.*, 1896, Cmd.8032, p.534. A.J.Mundella to Rev.C.Jupp: 'Where does the family life come in when you have 60 children in a home and 20 sleeping in a single dormitory?'
33. Letter from David.
34. SAS, PD 41/1/1: Whinwell Children's Home Annual Report, 1891.
35. *Ibid.*, Annual Report 1897.
36. Interview with Annie.
37. SRO, ED 11/154: Anonymous letter to Clyde Committee on Homeless Children, 1945.
38. Interview with Christine.
39. SRO, ED 11/443: Aberlour Orphanage, Annual Returns, 2 July 1934. The chipped enamel was still in use in 1946!
40. See the reminiscences collected in *Childhood Days at Aberlour Orphanage*, video and booklet produced by Speyside High School, Aberlour. Also SRO, 11/443: Aberlour Orphanage Annual Return, 11 December 1948.
41. Interview with Christine.
42. SRO, ED 11/266: Evidence of Dr R.D.MacCalman, Aberdeen University.
43. SRO, ED 11/168: Visit by Dr Wattie and Mrs N.Mitchison to Smyllum Orphanage, November 1945.
44. SRO, ED 11/162: *Scottish Daily Express*, 13 November 1946.
45. SRO, ED 11/168: Visit to Duncarse Home, 28 February 1946.
46. Interview with Annie.
47. Correspondence held in Speyside High School Collection.
48. Interview with David.
49. SRO, ED 11/154: Letter from A.Williamson to Clyde Committee on Homeless Children (undated).
50. SRO, ED 11/155: Memorandum by Miss H.R.Harrison, Scottish Home Department.
51. SAS, PD 41/1/1: Whinwell Children's Home Annual Report, 1892.
52. *Aberlour Orphanage Magazine*, Vol.LIII, March 1935.
53. *Aberlour Orphanage Magazine*, Vol. LXXXI, March 1962.
54. OHS: *Narrative of Facts*, 1951.
55. SRO, ED 11/266: D.R.MacCalman, evidence to Homeless Children Committee, 1945.
56. Interview with David.
57. Correspondence with Helen.
58. SRO, ED 11/269: Memorandum from Mr Gellatly to Clyde Committee, 1946 and Minute of 1 February 1946.
59. SRO, ED 11/443: Letter to Scottish Office Education Department from Miss Somerville, 22 April 1946.

60. Mahood, *Policing Gender, Class and Family*, p.92.
61. *Ibid.*, p.94.
62. Interview with Christine.
63. *Ibid.*
64. See the allegations made against the staff of two Aberdeen children's homes recently publicised by the press, 'Nuns in Child Cruelty Probe' and 'Suffer the Little Children', *Evening Express*, 10, 11 June 1997.
65. *Aberlour Orphanage Magazine*, Vol. LXX, Jan–Feb 1951.
66. Interview with David. This type of group punishment was commonly carried out, presumably in an attempt to impose a kind of group discipline. Girls who committed the 'crime' of speaking in the bedroom were all caned if the perpetrators did not own up; *Childhood Days at Aberlour*, video transcript.
67. *Aberlour Orphanage Magazine*, Vol.LXX, Jan–Feb 1951.
68. SRO, ED 11/443: Scottish Home Department to Warden of Aberlour Orphanage, 7 November 1947.
69. SRO, ED 11/158: Fife Children's Home Questionnaire, 1945.
70. *Aberlour Orphanage Magazine*, Vol.LXXVII, July–Aug 1958.
71. SRO, ED 11/154: letter from R.Cardno, 25 January 1947; Interview with David.
72. SRO, ED 11/266: Evidence from Dr Seymour, Department of Health for Scotland, 1945.
73. Interview with Annie.
74. Interview with David.
75. SRO, ED 11/154: R.Cardno, A Survey of the Report of the Committee on Homeless Children, 1946.
76. SRO, ED 11/443: SED Report on visit to Aberlour Orphanage, 31 August 1948.
77. Interview with Annie.
78. SRO, ED 11/266: Evidence of headmaster of Orphan Homes of Scotland School, 1946.
79. Interview with David.
80. SRO, ED 11/154: Headmaster of Noblehill School to Clyde Committee, 19 June 1945.
81. SRO, ED 11/154: Anonymous letter to Clyde Committee on Homeless Children, 1945.
82. SRO, ED 11/266: Dr D.R.MacCalman to Clyde Committee, 1945.
83. SRO, ED 11/159: Memorandum submitted by the Educational Institute of Scotland, November 1945.
84. SRO, ED 11/161: Lilian Russell, Organising secretary moral welfare work, the Episcopal Church in Scotland, 16 November 1945.
85. D.Burlingham and A.Freud, *Infants without Families* (London, 1944).
86. SRO, ED 11/161: Lilian Russell.
87. Letter from Jean.
88. Interview with Arthur.
89. Interview with David.

90. D.Haynes, *Haste Ye Back* (London, 1973), p.76.
91. Interview with Evelyn.
92. Interview with Christine.
93. Haynes, *Haste Ye Back*.
94. Letter from Arthur.
95. Interview with David.
96. Interview with Christine.
97. Interview with David.
98. *Ibid*.
99. SRO, ED 11/154: Anonymous letter submitted to Clyde Committee on Homeless Children, undated.
100. *Childhood Days at Aberlour.*
101. SRO, ED 11/158: Memorandum from National Vigilance Association of Scotland and International Guild Service for Women, 1945.
102. SRO, ED 11/162: *Scottish Daily Express*, 23 December 1946.
103. Interview with David.
104. SRO, ED 11/159: Memorandum submitted by Educational Institute of Scotland to Clyde Committee, November 1945.
105. SRO, ED 11/443: Report on Visit to Aberlour, 23 April 1947.
106. Interview with David.
107. SRO, ED 11/154: R.Cardno evidence to Clyde Committee, 1946.
108. *Ibid*.
109. See *Childhood Days at Aberlour Orphanage*.
110. Interview with Annie.
111. Mackenzie, *Scottish Mothers and Children*, p.190.
112. *Ibid*.
113. *The Times*, 15 July 1944.
114. *The Times*, 18 July 1944.
115. *B.P.P., Report of the Committee on Homeless Children (Scotland)*, 1946, Cmd.6911, pp.14–15.
116. *The Scottish Office Statistical Bulletin: Social Work Series*, SWK/SC/1996/5, November 1996.
117. *The Guardian*, 31 October 1997.
118. R.Kent, *Children's Safeguards Review* (Edinburgh, 1998), p.23.
119. *Ibid.*, p.24.

CHAPTER 4

THE EMIGRANT CHILD

Don't forget the Orphan Homes of Scotland,
Don't forget the dear friends here;
Don't forget that Jesus Christ your Saviour
Goes with thee to Canada.

And remember we are still a-praying
That your life will be good and true,
And that you may find a blessing
In the land you're going to.

> — Farewell song sung by children at Quarrier's
> Homes to those departing for Canada

Journey into the Unknown

In the summer of 1872 the first expedition of Quarrier's children to Canada departed from the Broomielaw in Glasgow on the *St David* en route for Quebec. The lads were excited at the prospect of their 16 day journey. 'There was nothing earthly that could have fired the laddies' hearts...What boy is there that would not have been thrilled by the hope of a voyage, and of seeing foreign lands?'[1] Certainly children — and especially boys — were not disabused of a popular view of the empire as a land of adventure inhabited by cowboys and Indians and wild animals, the stuff of comics and *Boy's Own* annuals. The boys were each kitted out with a Bible, a copy of the *Pilgrim's Progress*, a purse and a pocket knife to add to their outfits and a Band of Hope total abstinence pledge card 'to give the little ones a start up the right way'.[2]

On the day prior to departure the 'lucky ones' from Quarrier's Homes, sometimes more than 100 girls and boys, would gather in the village and prayers would be said for the emigrants. They were then taken to one of Quarrier's Glasgow homes close by the docks where they spent the night. On the morning of departure the band of children, aged between three and fifteen years, set off on foot to Govan attracting crowds of relatives and well-wishers. 'They march in procession along the Govan Road, and sing a hymn as they go down to the quay...'

Whither pilgrims, are you going —
Going each with staff in hand?
We are going on a journey;
Going at our God's command.

The sound of the children's voices brought people onto the streets. It seemed as if the neighbourhood was on holiday for the occasion.[3] The departure of so many children was a spectacle which aroused mixed emotions amongst those who went along to wave goodbye. 'Stifled sobs are heard from some of the women; one, miserably clad, catches a little bare-footed boy she has brought with her to her arms...She hears nothing of the hymn or prayer; she only hears her boy's voice, and sees him parting from her forever':[4]

Star of peace to wanderers weary,
Bright the beams that smile on me —
Cheer the pilot's vision dreary,
Far, far at sea.

Emotions were running high as the children made their way to embarkation. 'Clash! Clash! the gates are closed...Then we hear long and loud ringing of a bell.' As the young boys and girls made their way onto the ship, there was a realisation amongst the well-wishers that they would soon be gone for good. 'There is a confused mass of weeping faces, intermingled with waving hats and handkerchiefs; some struggle to get forward for a last grasp...' People threw oranges, sweets and biscuits to the children waving from the deck.[5]

The steamer is underway! 'Mind and write Willie. God A'mighty bless you' a porter shouts...straggling groups of men, women and children line the banks as far as Govan...Down the river we steam — the children forgetting the sadness of parting in the novelty of the situation...the gun is fired, a farewell huzza, a group of young faces, another waving of hats, handkerchiefs, the cheer growing fainter as we recede, the steamer with her bow pointing to the bright horizon, her stern to the dark foulsome river in the distance — fit symbol of the past and future of the little ones on board...[6]

According to one who accompanied the first band of emigrants in 1872, the boys were 'boisterous and romping, and full of fun' on board ship.[7] 'The children were as happy as larks', reported another accompanying a later voyage, spending their time 'swinging, singing, rope-skipping, marching, knitting, playing and romping; watching for whales, and seeing the porpoises and ships and icebergs…'[8]

> New sights began to astonish the little travellers as soon as the inevitable sea-sickness was got over, and the sea-legs had been developed. The apparently unlimitable ocean, with its unvarying horizon as the good ship rushed on, was in itself an experience which brought them face to face with the vastness of nature…to our great delight we were shown two icebergs…Bye-and-bye the cry got up: 'Whales! Whales!'…I need not picture the delight of all the children![9]

However, the excitement at seeing whales and icebergs was undoubtedly tempered by the conditions aboard ship. Descriptions of the 'wonderfully comfortable stowage — fresh, clean, plenty of room, airy and wholesome'[10] which appeared in the newspapers and was repeated in the orphanage magazine, presumably helped to allay the concerns of relatives, the general public and potential donors. But first hand accounts of the voyage commonly speak of the squalid, cramped conditions on board. 'The trip was appalling, horror-laden, fraught with unconcern and disdain from those on board' remembered one child who sailed to Canada in 1911. 'We were all put in a large holding area in the ship and treated like cattle.'[11] Memories of rough seas, chronic sea-sickness, rats and the foul air of steerage-class accommodation pervade accounts of the voyage of two weeks or so. William Doyle, a local government inspector whose 1874 report was harshly critical of the emigration programme, described children lying 'like herrings in a barrel around the funnel on deck, in nooks under the small boats; some too bad to be hauled up the ladder…'[12]

Upon arrival in Canada, the initial excitement at seeing land once again must have been counter-balanced by trepidation as the children were transported to the distribution homes run by the emigration charities — either Knowlton in Quebec or Belleville, Niagara, Galt or Brockville in Ontario. In the case of later parties to Australia children were more likely to be sent to residential farm schools and orphanages. A sense of bewilderment pervades emigrants' accounts of their arrival on foreign shores, in stark contrast to the excitement of departure. 'It wasn't very pleasant. It was *frightening* really, a strange country.'[13] Another twelve year old described his emotions upon arrival in Canada:

Before we left the ship they had a big do for us, gave us ice-cream cones. And then we boarded the train to Belleville: it took five or six hours. We were put in the Home then and taken up to our rooms and put in bed. I was frightened. I was sorry I had left and I cried and cried as I wanted to go back. I wanted to go to Canada but when I got there I wanted to go back…[14]

The emotions of this boy sum up the experience of emigration for many of the tens of thousands of children who left British shores between the 1870s and the 1960s. Although it had been described as an adventure and an opportunity, for many young emigrants it was an adventure best experienced through the pages of a comic book.

It has been estimated that between 80,000 and 100,000 British children were sent to Canada between 1870 and 1930; in total around 150,000 children were forcibly emigrated to distant parts of the Empire including Australia and South Africa over the course of 350 years.[15] It is not known precisely how many of these were from Scotland although Quarrier's Homes alone was responsible for the emigration of almost 7,000 children. Many more, including around 50 from Aberlour Orphanage, 200 from the Whinwell Home and an unknown number from local authority institutions, were found new homes overseas, predominantly in Canada but also in smaller numbers in Australia and South Africa. There was nothing peculiarly Scottish about child emigration. In fact its most enthusiastic promoter was Dr Barnardo whose homes throughout Britain provided more than 30,000 of the young migrants. In William Quarrier, though, Scotland had a willing accomplice so that homeless children north of the border who found refuge with a voluntary charitable organisation were just as likely as their English cousins to be sent to the so-called promised land.

Today this policy is regarded as at best misguided and at worst inhumane and immoral. Children as young as three years old were transported away from their surviving parents, brothers, sisters and relatives, on a long and uncomfortable voyage across the ocean to a country where they were often treated as cheap labour. The discovery that the self-styled child-savers were responsible for the mass transportation of so many of the country's children as late as the 1960s — children who had done nothing wrong — is still greeted with shock and disbelief.[16] It was one thing to board out homeless children to rural areas some considerable distance from their place of birth and cultural roots; it was quite another to forcibly emigrate them to another country. A few outspoken contemporaries did oppose what they saw as an act of cruelty and inhumanity; one called child emigration 'a disgrace to the Christian world', comparing the mass transportation of young children with sending cattle to market.[17] Their trepidation about the programme was confirmed by a damning report describing conditions in Canada by a local government inspector in the 1870s. Yet the policy seems to have had few public detractors until the 1920s when the Canadian Council on Child Welfare coordinated an organised attack on child immigration, although it has to be said this was motivated primarily out of consideration for Canadian children who, they alleged, were being infected by the United Kingdom's rejects. As a result, in 1928 the Canadian government enacted a permanent moratorium on the admission of school-age children to Canada. The Canadian scheme thus came to an end although small numbers continued to be sent to Australia and South Africa. In Scotland, as elsewhere, the child emigration schemes were seen as a sensible, practical solution to the problem of the mass of homeless, 'dangerous', working-class children who were threatening to undermine the social fabric.

The history of child and juvenile emigration is one of the better researched areas of child welfare policy, both from the point of view of those who were responsible for sending homeless children overseas and from the perspective of the children themselves, many of whom have committed their memories to paper and tape.[18] Emigration is one of the most ideologically driven child welfare policies incorporating a series of contradictions which could never be resolved. A natural harmony was assumed to exist between the needs of the mother country and the opportunities offered by the Empire: Britain was over-populated and suffering from urban degeneration, the Dominions offered plenty of open spaces and jobs in rural occupations. Yet, the emigration of children could not be an easy or natural element of this vision. To begin with, as Joy Parr points out, the children were caught in a contradiction between punishment and salvation.[19] Initially emigration conveniently served both to rid Britain of her unwanted 'refuse' in the form of pauper children and to offer the migrants the opportunity to redeem themselves in a new, untainted environment. Later on, philanthropists like Barnardo and William Quarrier claimed to be sending 'the flower of the flock' who would benefit from what Canada had to offer and at the same time would contribute to the development of that country. But the children could not cast off their labels in the middle of the Atlantic and arrive on Canadian shores as innocent angels. To many Canadians the child emigrants would always be Britain's unwanted children. The second contradictory element of child emigration policy was contained in the twin objectives of child welfare and imperial settlement. Notwithstanding the efforts of the child savers to ensure their children were satisfactorily cared for, they were unable to guarantee the children's welfare when their hosts held an entirely different conception of the value of the child. As we shall see, denied the protection of British legislation aimed at safeguarding and extending childhood, children quickly became adults upon arrival in Canada, subjected to demands no longer tolerated in their home country. Moreover, empire settlement was driven partly by economic demands — the desire for cheap rural labour — to which the needs of the children were subordinated. Child welfare and labour market requirements were mutually contradictory.

Clearly then, emigration was an inappropriate means of ensuring children's welfare. Children were essentially pawns in a policy which had more lofty objectives. Prominent child savers like Dr Barnardo and Quarrier conceived of child welfare as redemption. By removing children from degrading environments and sending them to work at rural pursuits and domestic service they were saving them from probable debasement and offering them a chance to work to redeem themselves. However, this conception of child welfare based on a strong if naive religious faith, was subordinated to the economic needs of Canada and later Australia, and the home country's imperial ambitions.[20] This was not a recipe for success and it is not surprising that the contradictions inherent in child emigration are reflected in the experiences of many children.

Slaves, Paupers, Workers, Colonisers

Indentured labour schemes, whereby boys were sent to the colonies — for example the South African Cape, Virginia and Bermuda — had been in existence since the seventeenth century.

THE ORPHAN COUNTRY

The forcible removal of unaccompanied, homeless children to the colonies began on a significant scale in the 1830s, pioneered in England by the Children's Friend Society. Between 1830 and the 1850s hundreds of poor and labouring children left British shores for the colonies. In 1848, at the time of the potato famine, at least 1,000 Irish girls were sent to Australia.[21] In the main these early child emigrants were not street children, the notorious 'street arabs', but children of the state — children who, through no fault of their own, resided in a poorhouse or ragged school and had been separated from their parents. They were not delinquents, merely homeless children who had been made dependent on the state for their well-being although, as Elaine Hadley points out, observers frequently blurred the distinction between the pauper and juvenile delinquent. They believed all poor children to be capable of, if not predisposed towards, criminal behaviour thus helping to legitimise the emigration solution.[22] Upon their arrival in their new home they were indentured as apprentices and domestic servants on farms and put to work.

Evidence of exploitation and comparison with slaves of children sent to the Cape put an end to the emigration activities of the Children's Friend Society in the 1840s although a smaller number of boys continued to be found apprenticeships in New Brunswick.[23] But the rapid increase of pauperism in the 1860s and the failure of the Poor Law to provide adequately for the children of paupers encouraged supporters of emigration to again promote the colonies as a solution to the crisis of overcrowded poorhouses and insufficient reformatories, industrial schools and children's shelters. Such children, some believed, were

> like the seaweed on the shores of our island, sometimes attached to the rock, sometimes washed off; and frequently the want of any education of the affections (not to speak of the absence of religious and moral principles), leaves them Arabs of social life, selfish, disappointed, and depending for daily bread on apparent accidents — useless, if not detrimental, to society.[24]

Regarded as dangerous and open to temptation if left on the streets, their institutionalisation was designed to rescue them by means of education, training and discipline. Between 1854 and 1890 more than 600 children were emigrated to Canada by Scottish reformatories and industrial schools.[25] By sending such children overseas, voluntary agencies and charities could continue to subject these children to the discipline of employment while at the same time ostensibly providing them with the opportunity to escape their origins and make a new life for themselves in a rural environment. Such sentiments, a combination of fear and loathing for the 'dangerous' child and a philanthropic impulse to save the children from themselves, was often conveyed in a melodramatic tone such as in these verses published in 1887:

> Take them away! Take them away!
> Out of the gutter, the ooze, and slime,
> Where the little vermin paddle and crawl
> Till they grow and ripen into crime.
>
> Take them away! Take them away!
> The boys from the gallows, the girls from worse;
> They'll prove a blessing to other lands —
> Here, if they linger, they'll prove a curse.[26]

Emigration was said to confer moral and physical advantages akin to the boarding-out system already prevalent in Scotland. It provided 'the great advantage of a better practical education for future life, [it was] less expensive, and [led] to an earlier introduction to remunerative labour.'[27] Emigration made economic sense. It was cheaper to educate and maintain a child in the colonies and he or she would be in remunerative employment by the age of 13, if not sooner, a year or so before a child would expect to be put out in Britain. It also, allegedly, conferred certain physical and moral benefits upon the child by providing him or her with a new start in life in a predominantly rural environment. Placed far away from the centres of temptation and vice, permanently removed from 'depraved' and worthless relatives, the child would be trained to industrious habits so that he or she might make an independent start in life. There was clearly no distance at all separating the rhetoric which supported boarding out and that which permitted involuntary child migration. Indeed, overseas migration offered all that boarding out with a rural family could provide, and more. It removed children from an unhealthy environment *and* it was a financially prudent means of disposing of the homeless. It made sense for someone like William Quarrier or Annie Croall to transfer responsibility for their charges to others for a one-off payment, just the cost of the journey and kitting out.

'There is no piece of philanthropic work on behalf of destitute children that accomplishes so much good at so little cost as does the emigration' admitted William Quarrier in 1882.[28] It was estimated that it cost around £12 per year to maintain a child in an institution at the end of the nineteenth century whereas for a single payment of £15 a child could be removed to the colonies and cease to be a burden on the poor rates or charity.

By the early twentieth century, however, evangelical and economic justifications were overlaid with imperial ideology. Child migrants were 'bricks for empire building.'[29] The Empire was seen first and foremost as an opportunity. Those who proposed imperial solutions to domestic problems not only believed the overseas colonies and Dominions should come to the aid of Britain in dealing with its own internal tensions but that Empire also offered opportunities for those who could not be successfully absorbed into British society.[30] Empire was seen as a solution to urban problems and homeless and abandoned children figured prominently in this discourse.

Transporting healthy British stock to Canada, Australia, New Zealand and Rhodesia would help to populate the colonies with white children who could be moulded into good citizens. This combination of motives was spelled out by Thomas Barnardo in his memoirs:

> Well-planned and wisely conducted child-emigration, especially to Canada, contains within its bosom the truest solution of some of the mother country's most perplexing problems, and the supply of our Colonies' most urgent needs...First it relieves the overcrowded centres of city life and the congested labour markets at home, while, at the same time, it lessens in a remarkable manner the burdens of taxation. Second, it supplies what the Colonies are most in want of — an increase of the English speaking population...Third, it confers upon the children themselves unspeakable blessings...[31]

One of the most influential exponents of the bricks for empire idea was Kingsley Fairbridge whose Child Emigration Society, motivated by imperial rather than evangelical ambitions, was responsible for sending parties of children as 'farm trainees' to Canada, Australia and Rhodesia.[32] The first Fairbridge Farm School was established in Pinjarra, Western Australia in 1912. Although Kingsley Fairbridge died in 1924 his farm school project was revived in the 1930s, perhaps somewhat surprisingly at a time when the antichild-emigration movement was in full voice. However, the Fairbridge Farms project was established at a time when juvenile migration was seen as an option for families in economic distress. During the Depression years the chance to start a new life in Canada or Australia was held out as an opportunity to unemployed young men and women in Britain's cities and for some the offer was too good to miss. 'I left school at age 13 for purely financial reasons' recalled James Drummond. Having heard about emigration opportunities on the Monday morning from a work colleague he decided to enquire.

> Wednesday — interviewed, given a physical, given 35 shillings for clothing. Thursday — bought 'farm' clothes, suitcase. Friday at nine in the morning I was at Waverley station to Glasgow to Greenock...Monday morning to Friday at eight in the evening. It still surprises me...One week later we anchored off Saint John...We wandered around amazed at the snow, in piles seven feet deep...[33]

More than 300 British children, the majority economic migrants including 25 from Scotland, were sent to Fairbridge's farm school in British Columbia from the 1930s through to 1948 when it was closed down although Fairbridge farm schools in Australia remained open into the 1980s.[34]

Today, child emigration is regarded as an extreme, radical and inhumane solution to the problem of homelessness but few would have regarded it as such at the time. It should be remembered that by the late nineteenth century the Empire was seen as an integral element of British, and especially Scottish, identity.[35] Scots had invested heavily in the Empire; they were active imperialists with thousands of entrepreneurs, professionals, administrators, skilled artisans and presbyterian ministers leaving Scotland's shores. Between 1830 and 1880 almost 650,000 Scots had emigrated to all parts of the Empire and almost 30 per cent chose British North America.[36] Scottish society in the late nineteenth and early twentieth centuries was extremely mobile. Numerous families had relatives overseas; the Empire was not a foreign country.

Canada, in particular, was not unknown territory; it was regarded as an extension of Scotland and had been used by Scots to enhance Scottish institutions and selective Scottish ideals such as temperance and presbyterian morality.[37] British and Scottish civil society, founded on Protestant roots, had arisen on Canadian soil in a predominantly rural form which echoed evangelical calls for a return to countryside ways. Canadian society was idealised. It was predominantly presbyterian, sober and industrious. Rural Canada was honest farming country; the land was owned by the farmers themselves rather than by oppressive landlords. For evangelicals, who believed in the individual as a free moral agent, Canadian society provided the ideal environment for a fresh start and offered prospects for an honest future. Thus, it took no giant leap of imagination to believe that children could easily be transplanted to a country where so many Scots 'kith and kin' had already successfully made their fortune and their home.

To the Promised Land

In 1869 the first sizeable party of English pauper children, 76 girls, left Liverpool for Canada. They were shepherded by Maria Rye who, together with the Scots Quaker Annie Macpherson, was the pioneer of child emigration in the early years. A year later Annie Macpherson took another 100 children to Canada just as the Poor Law Board approved emigration as a strategy for the care of pauper children on the grounds that it permanently removed children from the intemperate and immoral temptations of the city and set them on the road of industrious habits. In this sense then, child emigration was simply an extension of the boarding out policy which was already the preferred method of caring for pauper children in Scotland. It did not require a great leap of faith to condone the sending of children overseas and by 1889 more than 50 agencies were involved in the transportation of British children to Canada for domestic and farm labour. William Quarrier embraced emigration as an integral element of his child-saving operations as early as 1872. In that year 64 children were sent from Glasgow to Canada, followed by more than 200 in the following three years.[38]

In 1875, following considerable disquiet about the fate of youngsters sent to Canada, an official report by the Local Government Board Inspector, Andrew Doyle, caused the temporary suspension of the emigration programme for pauper children. Doyle, who was an outspoken supporter of institutional care in workhouses, had spent three months in Ontario where he independently assessed the emigration system as it was being conducted by Maria Rye and Annie Macpherson. Although recognising that all those involved had the best of intentions, Doyle was scathing in his criticisms of the entire process: he described the gaining of consent to emigration from the legal guardians of the children as 'loose and informal', the treatment of the children on their arrival at the so-called 'distribution homes' was unsatisfactory, the assessment of potential applicants for the children appeared to offer the child no protection against exploitation or ill-treatment, and the absence of supervision once a child was settled in a home similarly put children at risk.[39] Doyle's misgivings were made quite plain and were to be prophetic. He was amazed at how the Misses Rye and Macpherson could 'express so much confidence in the immediate and ultimate results of a system of which they can personally know so little.'[40] All in all, he was dismayed by the cavalier approach to the distribution and subsequent supervision of children.

> The little emigrants have been set afloat, and too many of them let to 'paddle their own canoes', until...some of them have gone over the rapids, and others are already lost sight of in the great human tide of the Western cities.[41]

'Of these results', he commented, 'it is impossible to speak with any degree of confidence.'[42]

And yet confidence in the emigration project was hardly dented. Against a background of perceived urban crisis, particularly after 1880, emigration not just of homeless children but of entire families and willing individuals — and especially single women — was promoted by organisations such as the Church Emigration Society and the Salvation Army.[43] Although there was a suspension of the emigration of official pauper children as a result of Doyle's criticisms, voluntary organisations, especially those of an evangelical persuasion, continued to send hundreds of children across the Atlantic Ocean. William Quarrier for instance sent almost 3,000 boys and girls overseas between 1875 and 1890, initially using the services of Annie Macpherson although eventually he established his own distribution centre, Fairknowe Home at Brockville, Ontario.[44] In fact at least half of the children admitted to Quarrier's Homes in the early years were emigrated; most left Glasgow within a year of their admission to the Homes. And Barnardo's similarly embraced emigration in these

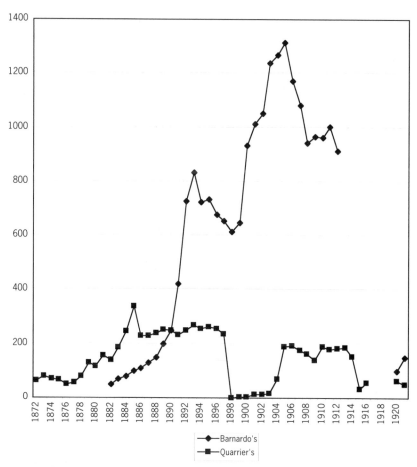

Figure 4.1. Child Emigration to Canada by Barnardo's and Quarrier's Homes, 1872–1921.

Note: Quarrier virtually ceased emigration between 1898 and 1905.

Barnardo's figures for 1882–1890 are estimates. Approximately 1,000 children were emigrated by Barnardo's during these years.

Source: G.Wagner, *Children of the Empire* (London, 1982); M.Harper, *Emigration from North-East Scotland, Vol.2* (Aberdeen, 1988).

years with great zeal, sending more children than any other charitable organisation, almost 20,000 between 1882 and 1905.[45] As Figure 4.1 shows, the peak year for child emigration to Canada was 1905 when Barnardo's and Quarrier's emigrated more than 1,500 children between them accounting for around half of all the emigrants that year. For children's homes such as Quarrier's and even smaller homes like the Whinwell Children's Home in Stirling, emigration was the solution to the inevitable consequences of an open door principle. No orphanage could continue to admit children — with the exception of Aberlour orphanage which expanded inexorably to meet demand — without finding homes for able-bodied children who could not be adopted, boarded out, or transferred to another institution. As William Quarrier admitted, 'By this means [emigration] we hope to be enabled yearly to rescue a fresh set of boys and girls, whilst, without this providential outlet, we should be stocked up with the same set of children for four or five years and unable to rescue more.'[46] In fact 35 per cent of the 20,219 children admitted to Quarrier's Homes between 1871 and 1933 were emigrated.[47] At the same time, however, emigration fulfilled a second purpose; it presented parents and guardians deemed unsuitable with a *fait accompli*.

After 1897 William Quarrier stopped sending children to Canada. The Act to Regulate the Immigration into Ontario of Certain Classes of Children, introduced in the wake of the death of a child who had been apprenticed in Owen Sound in the north of the province, sought to control the influx of children, to protect the children from ill-treatment and neglect and protect Canada from the importation of 'defective' and 'diseased' children. The Act put in place a more rigorous inspection system which placed the Home children under official control as soon as they set foot on Canadian soil. William Quarrier took exception to this implicit criticism of his own operation which he, maybe justifiably, believed was efficient and thorough, and refused to cooperate. However, following Quarrier's death, juvenile emigration resumed from the Orphan Homes of Scotland; more than 2,000 children were sent to Canada until the authorities there closed the doors to child migrants in 1928.

After the First World War the British state explicitly condoned, even supported juvenile emigration, although migration of children under school-leaving age was seen as more problematic. Government assistance for the emigration of those under school-age was withdrawn but at the same time the emigration agencies were supported by subsidies by means of the Empire Settlement Act of 1922 and new migration initiatives were encouraged, such as the Boy Scouts' Association Migration Department which sent around 5,000 scouts overseas between 1922 and 1932.[48] Juvenile migrants were seen as 'the most desirable settlers' since they were the most adaptable and thus schemes which provided apprenticeship and farm training in Canada and Australia were tacitly encouraged as providing 'great opportunities' for 'suitable boys'.[49] Many fewer girls were going overseas at this time, a regrettable trend in the eyes of the British Government which was appreciative of the fact that 'the need of women for women's work in the household, and as wives and mothers, is urgent throughout the Dominions', a shortage which was 'retarding the growth of the populations and preventing development.'[50] However, there were no positive measures to encourage the emigration of these prospective mothers of the new world.

At the start of the Second World War a scheme to evacuate children overseas with their parents' consent was run for a time. These children were not welfare cases however. The Children's Overseas Reception Board assisted the passage of between 15,000 and 20,000 British children until the programme was halted in 1940 on safety grounds. In September of that year a ship carrying hundreds of children to Canada was torpedoed killing most of the children and effectively bringing official overseas evacuation to an end until the cessation of the war. The renewal of the Empire Settlement Acts and the assisted passage agreement with Australia in 1946 once again facilitated emigration to that country as well as to Southern Africa. This renewed enthusiasm for child migration, sponsored by a number of emigration societies including Fairbridge Farms, the Catholic Emigration Society and the Church of Scotland, occurred in the face of the Children Act of 1948 which not only set out strict guidelines governing child emigration but made clear the preference for family care as opposed to institutionalisation. Australia was now the favoured destination for homeless and abandoned children. However, although Australia positively welcomed British child immigrants at this time and in total 10,000 British children were sent to Australia between 1948 and 1967, in Scotland there were some misgivings about the migration of children of school age.[51] All authorities, including local councils, who wished to emigrate a child in their care were obliged to seek the consent of the Secretary of State who, in making a decision, adhered to a number of general principles laid down under the Children Act. One of these was that no child under the age of ten was to be allowed to emigrate on the grounds that 'he cannot be held to be of an age at which he may be expected to make a decision about emigration with any adequate appreciation of its consequences.'[52] The Scottish Office was no rubber stamp. Consent was given to the emigration of older children and when the permission of a parent had been received. It turned down a number of requests when it considered emigration was not in the interests of the child or where it was believed emigration was merely being used as a convenient and inexpensive form of child welfare. For the first time, prospective child emigrants were protected from the actions of others. A request from Wigtown County Council to emigrate under the Fairbridge Farms scheme an illegitimate boy in their care whose mother had given her consent was refused on the grounds that the boy was only 6 years old and 'it was considered that he was too young to express a proper opinion of the matter.'[53]

A large proportion of these later migrants were Roman Catholics for whom it was difficult to find foster families in Britain, although it proved just as difficult to place them with families in Australia. Many Catholic children, including a number sent by Glasgow Corporation, thus ended up in orphanages rather than being adopted.[54] Smaller numbers were sent to Rhodesia, under the auspices of the Fairbridge Farm scheme and encouraged by the Rhodesian government which positively welcomed white migrants, children included. However, children chosen for Rhodesia were selected more carefully than for other destinations. One child recalled, 'They wanted colonialists, albeit kids, but they wanted the right kind: they did not want the run-of-the-mill going out.'[55]

After the Second World War, public and eventually official response, especially to child and juvenile migration, was more critical. At a time when Britain was suffering an acute labour shortage some in government recognised that it was not sensible to 'export large numbers of young, fit and presumably fertile men and women...we cannot afford deliberately to get rid of people the age and type most likely to work and breed.'[56] In a letter to *The Scotsman* newspaper in 1955 an anonymous writer encapsulated much that was objectionable about the emigration of children. He poured cold water on 'all the romantic nonsense about a "new life for our children"'. Rather, the objective was to 'shift a burden from the British to the Australian tax payer.'

> It is quite natural that a young person should be quite ready, even keen, to emigrate overseas, for that is the season of adventure. But does it follow that the same child ten years older will be satisfied with the choice that has been made for him?...There is such a thing as natural love of a country that comes with adolescence. It is a crime to stifle that love before it gets a chance to grow, and for that reason I am opposed to child emigration except with families. And all other reasons apart, Scotland cannot afford to lose young people.[57]

Concerns like these were spreading. By 1961 the Home Office, although continuing to permit the renewal of the Empire Settlement Acts, expressed 'considerable reservation' about the emigration societies' work following a 1956 fact finding mission to Australia that was critical of the standards of child care.[58] By then it was widely recognised that Britain could offer better prospects to the homeless child and emigration from the state welfare sector dried up completely. The voluntary sector, though, continued to provide the children demanded by overseas governments and many of those sent appear to have been amongst the most deprived. Emigration continued to be a solution for the 'problem' child. Few Scottish children seem to have been included in these post-war schemes. Local authorities sent a small number and Quarrier's Homes revived its enthusiasm for emigration albeit on a limited scale. In 1960 11 boys were sent to Dhurringile Farm School in Australia under the auspices of the Church of Scotland which was an agent for the Presbyterian Church in Victoria. The Scottish Office was unhappy that permission had not been granted by the Secretary of State and noted its concern that the Commonwealth Relations Office and the Home Office had made arrangements with the voluntary emigration societies that their work would only be reviewed on an informal and purely voluntary basis.[59] It was an arrangement which permitted the emigration societies to send children away with impunity. However, the next party of five Quarriers' boys was scrutinised by the Scottish Office. All the boys were 12 years or older and all had given their consent to emigration after an interview with representatives of Australia House. Three of the boys had had no contact with their mother for some years and the other two were leaving with their mothers' consent. Reports from the party — they had sent Quarrier's Homes a tape recorded message — were positive. The boys were said to be extremely happy.[60]

There was no typical emigrant child. Boys and girls, infants and teenagers, Protestants and Catholics, the orphaned, abandoned, the homeless, even some who had surviving parents — all were regarded as suitable candidates for transportation overseas. However, boys were almost twice as likely to be selected for emigration than girls for the simple reason that girls were thought to be at greater moral risk in Canada and it was easier to find them positions at home. Boys, on the other hand, believed to be more self reliant, were in demand as cheap farm labour overseas. For this reason too, children between the ages of six and twelve were preferred and after 1897 older children who were of greatest use as workers. The majority of emigrants from Quarrier's Homes were of working age. Younger children were more likely to be adopted in their country of birth although the Whinwell Children's Home did find adoptive homes in Canada for a number of their youngest emigrants between the ages two and five years old. These were probably the lucky ones. Little William Heggie, who was sent to Canada by the Whinwell Home in 1899 at the tender age of five, was clearly much loved by his adoptive parents. The couple were heartbroken when the child died of tuberculosis five years later. In an emotional letter to Miss Croall the distress of Willie's adoptive mother is palpable:

> He was as dear to me as any child could be to a mother, he loved us as few children know how to love. I believe there seldom is as smart or bright a boy as our Willie Heggie was…he left us broken hearted. My husband says he never loved his own sons more than he loved our Willie, now we are lonely — oh so lonely and our two little girls feel the loss of him so much. I do not know what to do.[61]

While some of the little emigrants really were alone in the world, the majority were not orphans in the true sense of the word, and many of them had siblings. However, as their surviving relatives had signed away their guardianship rights upon admitting the child to an institution, the home director could send children overseas with impunity, in some cases without informing the child's family of the decision (although William Quarrier did obtain permission of a child's relatives and inform them of the impending journey). The typical case was that of the lone parent unable to care for the child who requested admission to a home, who was then obliged to accept the possibility of emigration and whose child was then emigrated. John Burnett was admitted to Quarrier's Homes at the age of ten in 1888; his father had died in an accident a year before and his mother was said to make 'a precarious living by hawking'. John had been attending a Day Industrial School but, in the absence of a secure livelihood and with no relatives prepared to help, his mother requested admission to Quarrier's Homes for her son. 'At first she hesitated about Canadian work but now says she has fully made up her mind and signs paper'. John was sent to Canada in 1891.[62]

Emigration was the most thorough and permanent means at the disposal of the voluntary organisation for separating a child from parents, especially when those parents had been deemed 'worthless' by orphanage directors. The separation of pauper children from their parents in Scotland by requiring the child to be boarded out is a precursor of this attitude. Margaret Fraser was admitted to the Whinwell Children's Home with her two younger brothers in 1912 on the grounds that she had been 'utterly neglected by mother, improperly fed, clothed and tended, education also neglected…mother and older members of the family of bad character and unfit to have charge of child.' Margaret was sent to Canada and her two brothers were transferred to Quarrier's Homes.[63] The fate of children was essentially determined by a judgement of the character of their parents. In 1903 the four Askew brothers aged between two and nine years old, were admitted to the Whinwell Children's Home at the request of the Glasgow branch of the SNSPCC who noted, 'Their mother is dead and their father is a worthless character'. The father had already been imprisoned for child neglect and was deemed to be 'of drunken habits.' 'I am sorry to say', wrote the SNSPCC superintendent,

> if they are not rescued they will be lost, which would be a great pity. They are 4 pretty children, healthy and deformed in no way. …The father has been spoken to about letting the children into a home, at first he would not consent but now sees that he cannot look after them and gives his consent now to let them go.

Miss Croall agreed to take the boys on the condition that 'the father must understand relieving him of this responsibility he must in no way interfere with them or have any after claim and that we shall have power to send them to Canada if we choose.' The two eldest sailed for Quebec in 1904, their two younger brothers following some years later.[64] Similarly, the reputation of his mother probably secured a place on a ship for John Ingram, admitted to Whinwell Home as a three year old. 'I have heard a great deal about the mother' wrote the home's director, 'and only on condition that the mother be removed from the district and a refuge found for her out of the neighbourhood would I promise to help in this case. The woman is incorrigible…'[65] It comes as no surprise to find that children were emigrated despite the wishes of relatives if home directors deemed it in the child's best interests. William Drummond was sent to Canada in 1906 after the death of his mother despite the willingness of his aunt who lived nearby to find him a position.[66] Though a parent had invariably admitted a child to a home voluntarily, child savers decided on a child's emigration by making a moral judgement on the father or mother, ignoring alternative solutions.

Children who had already been separated from their parents by death or misfortune were then often separated from perhaps the only remaining members of their close family, their brothers and sisters. A glance at the case files of siblings admitted to Quarrier's Homes and the Whinwell Home shows a cavalier attitude towards the relationships between brothers and sisters. Individuals were regularly dispatched to Canada leaving their siblings behind, the latter often following some years later when they were old enough to be found a position but with no guarantee of being reunited. The case of the four Askew brothers mentioned above is not untypical. Admitted as a family to the Whinwell Home in 1903, they all found their way onto separate ships bound for Canada. Ben and Robert left first in 1904, followed by John two years later in 1906 and William in 1909. The Home's director requested the emigrant agency 'to keep them as near to each other as possible. They are all in all to each other and Benjamin the eldest has had a fatherly care over his brothers'; but although Robert and Ben were adopted together, John appears to have been sent to a nearby farm. The four eventually went their separate ways but remarkably managed to keep in touch.[67] These boys were lucky.

Children emigrated by voluntary organisations had little choice in whether they were sent overseas and most probably had little idea of where they were going or what it entailed. Prospective emigrants were told of the great opportunities that awaited them;

being chosen for Canada was an honour. Children were kept in perpetual excitement and anticipation about joining one of the groups of up to a hundred children who left Quarrier's village two and sometimes three times a year. 'Applications to be included among the emigrants are far in excess of the number required' noted the *Narrative of Facts* in 1920.[68] Some children report being lied to — 'We were told we were going on a holiday. But that holiday never ended'.[69] But the majority appear to have been infected by the excitement. One boy, sent by William Quarrier to Canada in 1894, recalled being told 'what a wonderful place it was'. 'You can imagine the thrill, the excitement, the enthusiasm of such a prospect: to cross the mighty ocean…see new people and new lands. It was all too much for a ten year old boy to contain so I said "Yes".'[70] 'The idea of wide open spaces and cowboys and Indians inflamed my imagination' remembered another boy brought up in a coal mining town. 'I loved domestic animals and the thought of a big new country. I figured that I couldn't go wrong.'[71] But, with time, incomprehension started to mix with the anticipation. In an atmosphere of imperial pride numerous individuals and families packed their bags and sought a new life in the New World and child migration should be seen in this context of optimism, opportunity and proud colonial expansion. In these circumstances some needed little encouragement. In 1907, at the age of 15, one lad from Dundee volunteered to go to Canada to 'help open up the country.' 'Well, after reading all the books of that time about the Golden West — full of Indians, cowboys and Mounties I naturally agreed. Who wouldn't at that age?'[72] Spurred on by the popular image of empire as a land of opportunity young men in particular volunteered to emigrate, perhaps conscious of difficult family circumstances. For unstable families hit by economic crisis emigration offered a possible solution. A one-off payment for a ticket seemed a small price to pay for the chance of permanent employment in a country crying out for labour. Children were well informed about life in the colonies; in fact schools received visual material illustrating life there.[73] One young Glasgow lad recalled being visited at school by someone who asked:

> 'Who would like to go to Africa?' And I took my little pamphlet and trotted home and said 'I want to go.' And my mother and father were separated and my mother did all sorts of jobs to make ends meet

and feed us four kids...I was asthmatic, and the doctor said, 'You must get this child out of Glasgow.' Bulawayo was called 'the desert' because it's high and dry and hot. So Mother and we four children talked about it and the other three said, 'If he goes, we go.' And we went. I was ten, my brother seven, and my two sisters were twelve and six.[74]

There was no shortage of opportunities for those who wanted to leave. Being in care was not a pre-requisite. Some boys left Scotland under the auspices of the Cossar farms scheme; after five weeks training on a farm near Paisley boys were despatched to Cossar farms in Canada, Australia and New Zealand, according to one man who left age fifteen, 'as a source of cheap labour.'[75]

By the 1950s and 1960s, unlike the early years of the emigration programme when a departure was greeted with excitement and even crowds on the streets, the secrecy surrounding child emigration meant that children were virtually smuggled out of the country. Neither they nor their relatives had any idea they were being sent to Australia for good.[76] 'The nuns told us we were orphans, that we had no family and no future in Scotland' remembered one man sent to Australia from Nazareth House in Lasswade in 1951. 'They told us Australia was the Promised Land where we could ride to school on ponies.'[77] Many years later this man discovered the family he never knew he had. One child, upon being told she was to go to Australia recalled her reaction:

Blimey, I thought, have I been that bad to be sent away? Mother Superior went on to say that I had been chosen, that it was a wonderful opportunity, not some kind of punishment. But that night in bed, I cried...[78]

For some their expectations of their new home were fulfilled; for others, their new life resembled a bad dream.

On arrival in their new country children were taken direct to a reception home where they were assessed before being distributed to their new families. The process of selection could be traumatic, not unlike the experiences of boarded-out children or evacuees. 'The anxiety of the children to be among the first to get a home is very strikingly seen in the disappointment depicted on their faces if another is going before them.'[79] One young Quarrier boy who arrived in Canada in 1894 spent three days travelling from the Brockville distribution home to a farm 175 miles

A party of girls from Quarrier's Homes at 'Fairknowe', Brockville, Canada, c. 1900. The girls were looked after at the distribution home before being placed in homes across Ontario. Heatherbank Museum of Social Work.

away. Upon arrival he recalled, 'There was no tender kiss on the cheek, no kindly handshake, no enthusiasm shown in meeting this small Scottish boy. It was just a matter-of-fact meeting.'[80] Others found themselves stranded at a railway station when no-one arrived to meet them.

Once found a position it was likely that a child would be relatively isolated. Farms in rural Ontario and Quebec were scattered across huge distances connected by unpaved roads so that some were unable to get to school or even to the nearest town, especially in winter. The loneliness was difficult to conceal. 'It has taken me a little to settle down in this my new country' wrote a young girl who arrived in Canada in 1925. 'I have had a visit from my brother who has been out here eight years. I can tell you I was glad to see him.'[81] 'The first summer in Canada was a lonely experience for me' recalled another. 'There was nowhere to go and no way for me to get there if there had been.'[82]

As Joy Parr comments, the evangelical philanthropists who promoted child migration held a highly idealised view of rural Canada.[83] Not only did Canada offer these sickly children a healthy way of life, it also represented a society largely untainted by industrialisation, where class distinctions had no validity, where children might work hard and raise themselves from their working-class or pauper origins, and where they would be brought up in a religious, teetotal, moral environment. For one missionary, the advantages of Canada consisted of plentiful food 'so no temptation to steal', an absence of liquor, plenty of work and the improved self-esteem conferred by the 'value set on a boy'. Moreover, the mingling of classes 'helps to remove the feeling of being one of *lower class*, as people put it. Everyone is upper class who pays his way, and does not drink or swear.'[84] For William Quarrier Canada offered his children 'a perfectly fair start in the race of life.'

> There were homes there which would gladly open to them; there was work for their little hands to do; and there were useful and honourable careers for which they could be best prepared upon the spot. There, too, their origin would cease to be a reproach, and would only serve as a point from which they might afterwards measure the achievements of their own industry, and the blessings bestowed upon them by the Father of the fatherless.[85]

In some respects parts of Canada were regarded as an extension of the Highlands of Scotland. Knowlton, Quebec, was described by Quarrier as 'the Scotland of Canada…situated at the head of a pretty little lake, and at the mouth of a beautiful highland glen. It is a most lovely spot',[86] and he deliberately chose Brockville for the location of a reception home as it was in a district of Ontario formerly colonised by Scots. Few emigrants, most of whom would not have travelled outside their home town, seem to have noticed the resemblence. 'North Hastings is a rolling, beautiful country, but at the time of my arrival it was primitive indeed' recalled one man of his first impression in 1894.[87] The children placed in this district were received into Christian homes where, it was argued, they were treated 'as members of the family', not consigned to the servants quarters.[88] And Canada provided these children with a chance to cast off their origins, according to Quarrier's biographer:

> In Canada they were honoured and loved…But, in our land of caste, poverty throws a shadow only a little less dark than that of crime; and here the children would very probably have been surrounded by an atmosphere whose coldness and suspicion would have killed

the growth of all that makes childhood lovely, and might have developed the very vices which suspicion feared.[89]

Such an idyllic picture of Canada as a land of opportunity for these youngsters must be tempered by the reality of a hard and lonely life many experienced. It has been asserted that only around a third were well-treated while the remainder were 'exploited, neglected, defrauded or mistreated'. 'It can...be safely assumed', state Rooke and Schnell, 'that all children suffered from trans-Atlantic trauma, culture shock, and a tremendous sense of anxiety before and during their introduction to and initiation into Canadian society.'[90] The evidence for this, however, is simply too patchy. Yet for many children their introduction to Canada may be seen as a culture shock not dissimilar to that felt by children boarded out from Scotland's cities to the Highlands and Islands. A child brought up in the London slums and sent to Canada around the turn of the century commented: 'What a transplant — from the slums of London to the misery and loneliness of the backwoods. I had never seen a cow — much less a tomato or a potato plant.'[91] Cows were alien beings for city children sent to places like Tiree as well. Yet, there was a difference, especially for older children. In Canada, children under twelve years of age were adopted by families who were obliged to ensure the child received 'good clothing and schooling and to be treated as one of the family.'[92] Those aged twelve and over were indentured with an employer — usually a farmer — who was required to pay the child a regular wage, to ensure he or she attended church and Sunday school and to provide board and lodgings. There was no formal obligation upon employers to ensure their young employees continued their education as there was in Scotland and for many of the emigrants their formal education ceased upon arrival in Canada. Thus, the terms of the relationship were primarily determined by economic rather than welfare concerns. Certainly boarded-out children, as we have seen in Chapter Two, were accepted for economic reasons too. However, in Scotland they were incorporated into a crofting or farming culture which had always relied upon a degree of child labour. In Canada, the emigrant child was primarily defined as a worker; 'their work is compulsory', observed socialist critics in Manchester, 'and therefore differs entirely from that of the child who in its play hours works in its own home.'[93] It was not merely the geographical distance from Scotland that identified emigration as a radical policy, although we should not underestimate children's perception of the symbolic and actual significance of those thousands of miles. Rather, it was the enormous gap between the idealisation of what Canadian (and later Australian and southern African) rural life could offer British children and the reality of that life as conceived by the host families that marks out the emigrant experience from that of a boarded-out child in the Highlands. For some children the cultural chasm was not symbolised by the landscape, the climate or even the different accent encountered in their new home but by the treatment they received, akin to hired labourers rather than homeless children. A Barnardo boy who arrived in Canada in 1916 recalled: 'From the time we left the Home in England all kindness stopped. We were on our own.'[94]

It seems to have been widely accepted by Canadian contemporaries as well as historians that children sent to Canada from Quarrier's Homes were perceived as 'a desirable class of boys and girls' who were well-treated. Staff at Marchmont home in Belleville and Fairknowe in Brockville kept in touch with their children and the children in turn maintained contact with them and Quarrier's homes by letter. Following a personal visit to Canada in 1878 William Quarrier was reportedly delighted with the condition of the children in their new homes. 'When I saw them looking so happy and comfortable, I felt that we had great reason to praise God for His goodness…'[95] Quarrier was understandably keen to contrast the picture of the children in their Canadian homes with their former plight. 'A boy, who, when rescued, was living in a wretched hovel in Clyde Street, and was being trained as a thief by an elder brother…had grown well, was nicely dressed, and was a picture of health and happiness.'[96] It was an assessment broadly shared by J.J.Kelso, superintendent of neglected children in Ontario and instigator of the 1897 Ontario Act. Following his own detailed report into the condition of the 'Home children' Kelso, quoting Arthur Hardy, premier of Ontario, reported that 'The Scotch are well known as a most desirable class of settlers and from all we have heard of your good work…we have confidence that you would only bring the best class of children into Ontario…'[97] Quarrier, as we know, refused to accept the regulation and inspection demanded by the Ontario Act, naively confident in the belief that his children were well treated. But William Quarrier was quite wrong to be so complacent. As early as 1883 the *Glasgow Herald* had expressed some misgivings about the emigration programme in the light of disturbing reports that for some children Canada was not the land of milk and honey it was made out to be. In an editorial the newspaper questioned whether children received an adequate education, asked whether 'they are treated with ordinary fairness, not to speak of ordinary humanity?' and called upon the British government to regulate what it called the 'irresponsible deportation of the unprotected'.[98] Quarrier's children as well as those sent by the Whinwell and Aberlour orphanages were probably as open to abuse as any. Their Scots ancestry did not save them from the exploitation, mistreatment and abuse suffered by many young British immigrants.

Letters from the New World

Letters home sent by emigrant children were unwittingly used to encourage others to follow, and to satisfy charity donors. In the *Narrative of Facts*, the annual report of Quarrier's Homes, there is a mass of uplifting and overwhelmingly positive information regarding the fate of the young emigrants contained in the reprinted letters received from former home children. The letters were allegedly written by the children themselves and they give the impression of a land of opportunity, a religious, moral society, which was ready to provide any child with the chance to do well if he or she was willing to work hard. 'The farm agrees with me and I am getting fleshy' wrote one girl. 'I go to Sunday school and church regularly.'[99] From a farm near Melrose, Ontario one boy was duly grateful for the opportunity he had been given:

> If I could tell some of the boys in Glasgow what a good country Canada is, I think I could get some of them to come out here. God has been good to me, and I thank Him for His Goodness in giving me health and strength to perform the duties laid before me, and for saving me from a life of vice and misery and putting me in a way of making an honest living.[100]

The children were probably encouraged by guardians, teachers or even home inspectors to write to their benefactors in such glowing terms.[101] The pattern followed by many of them, incorporating thanks to Quarrier's Homes and to God, praise of their guardians and descriptions of their new, moral, industrious life, would have been inculcated at school and at home, informed by a Protestant evangelical discourse, often reproducing religious sentiments and idealised images of family life. 'I am very glad to say that I have got a good home' wrote one girl from Napenee in 1880; '...and ma and pa are very good to me, and I love them, but I love the Saviour better than them all...'[102] 'Really you can't imagine how happy I am and how fortunate I have been since I came to Canada' wrote one girl in 1925. 'I was adopted by a Mrs —...whom I called mother, and her husband I called father...and if I had been their own daughter they couldn't have been better to me.'[103] These letters were probably not forgeries but undoubtedly children wrote what they thought their benefactors wished to read.

Nevertheless, in the absence of any other contemporary evidence, this correspondence provides us with a tantalising glimpse of the migrant child's experience. Close readings of these letters reveal an alternative, shadowy reality characterised by loneliness, a longing for the company of brothers and sisters or friends from the orphanage and news of loved ones. 'Mr Quarrier, did you ever hear anything from my father since I came to Canada?' wrote one child in 1880.[104] Another asked, 'I would like to know very much if you have heard anything of my mother yet, as I am very anxious, and have not heard for a long time.'[105] 'As soon as you get a letter from my brother, send it as soon as you can...' was one child's plaintive request.[106] Children's desire to keep in touch with family members calls attention to one of the most serious accusations levelled at the emigration movement by its critics. The importance of family life was one of the guiding principles of the Christian-evangelical child-savers and yet emigration irrevocably severed family ties by permanently separating children from parents and siblings from one another.

An alternative perspective on children's experience is provided by adult reminiscence. Gone are the evangelical platitudes and homilies on family life and in their place are more down to earth reflections and recollections of the full range of experience: the good, bad and indifferent. These memories, as with those recorded by boarded-out children, reveal a two-dimensional picture which gives an insight into how children were regarded by the community that gave them a home as well as how the child interpreted and dealt with life in a new home in a new world.

Children had few realistic expectations of what awaited them. Stories about the Wild West had not prepared them for rural Canada or Australia, both of which struck many children as primitive. Many farms, even into the 1920s, relied on water from a hand pump, and had no electricity or flush toilets — conditions exacerbated by the freezing winters and hot, humid summers. Although conditions were probably little better and possibly worse on Scottish crofts and farms at that time, it was a far cry from the relative comfort of a children's home and especially the cottages in Quarrier's village. One lad who landed in Quebec in 1914 was shocked when he arrived to stay with a poor family who 'lived in a square frame house...and no carpets on the floors and in the winter the children ran around in their bare feet.' When after two years he was moved to a more prosperous family he recalled crying when sat down to his first meal. 'I said it was like coming out of hell into heaven.'[107] Children sent to Australia in the 1930s were confronted with similar privation. John Lane, a Barnardo's boy recalled his shock upon arrival at the Fairbridge farm school in Pinjarra in 1933 to discover girls and boys going barefoot dressed in an assortment of ill-fitting clothing. Fairbridge, with its freezing water, inadequate diet and jerry-built accommodation was 'a rough landing'.[108]

Whilst many Scottish children experienced the same sorts of conditions, it was the intensity of exploitation by farming families who acted more as employers than parents that made the emigrant child's experience so poor. Most children had no idea they were to be catapulted from childhood into semi-adulthood as soon as they were found a position. Boys in particular were sent to farms where they could be expected to rise early and work for 12 hours a day for risible wages. The work was hard manual labour. 'There were no machines until about 1905' recalled one man sent to Canada in 1894. 'The grain was cut with the grain cradle, the hay with the scythe, the hand rake was in general use, and also the hoe...'[109] 'There was always something to do on the farm':

> In the summertime we'd be up about a quarter to five before the mist had gone even, we'd be calling the cows...and then there was the regular farm work, the hay, the grain, the corn and the ploughing in the fall...It would be maybe yes possibly six months before I even

learned how to milk a cow but then as I got going I became knowledgeable enough to do a lot of chores around the farm, hoeing, gardening, cleaning the cattle...I could carry the milk in, I could strain the milk, I could wash the cows udders off...here was me a scrawny little thing and they used to tease me something awful you know...[110]

Young lads were given a great deal of responsibility. One boy told William Quarrier how he was 'learning to drive oxen, and had to hoe potatoes and beans and set turnips, and lead the horses at the plough.'[111] Despite the hardships most boys appear to have accepted their lot with resignation and some were undoubtedly very happy with their new families. 'Mr Winters sure sent me to a good place, when he sent me here', wrote one lad in 1925. 'The farmer has two cars in which he often takes me rides. He also has a wireless set and a gramophone...'[112] It is noticeable, however, that play is never mentioned in these missives home.

Emigrant girls seem to have been treated less harshly than the boys, largely because of the limited expectations of females' social and economic roles.[113] Letters of application from prospective foster parents suggest they had chosen girls to be companions or helpers around the house rather than workers. 'I teach school and my sister teaches music' wrote one woman in her letter of application; 'I have often seen the one Mrs Rutherford has, and like her, and wish to get a good smart one like her'.[114] It was a fortunate girl who pleased her master and mistress as well as this one obviously did:

> It gives me much pleasure to say we like our girl Sarah very much. We think her a very fine child. She is industrious, obedient, and kind. She has been well brought up, and piously trained...She cheers the house with very appropriate spiritual songs while about her work most of the time.[115]

But even those who landed on their feet were expected to work at appropriate tasks and domestic work was frequently the lot of the female immigrant. Winifred and Margaret Devine, who were sent to New South Wales in 1916 aged ten and nine years, were reported to be doing well in their new home:

> They have been very busy in their sewing lessons...making white frocks for Sunday wear...They have all little duties in their cottage helping with the work and they come to the house once a week in turns to learn to do little jobs like polishing silver and dusting. And

as a great treat when we have a large party for dinner one of the bigger ones comes to help wait at table.[116]

In some respects the fate of emigrant children was similar to those who were boarded out in Scotland. They were removed from familiar surroundings, separated from family and siblings, expected to make an economic contribution to the household, and often placed in isolated areas offering little contact with other children. But boarded-out children were still deemed to be children, dependents who were required to attend school. Indentured emigrant children, on the other hand, were treated by their employers as young workers, a status starkly brought home to one young boy as soon as he arrived in Canada and was placed out to work. 'When I was in the fields working I could see all the children going to school with their lunch pails. The feeling of utter loneliness would be hard to describe.' 'Actually', he continued, 'I ceased to be a child at the age of 10.'[117] 'I had no normal youth' commented another who volunteered for Canada in 1929, 'no high school days, or friends, or dances.'[118] This status of indentured worker — neither child nor adult — could be used to justify unfair treatment. Derisory wages were commonplace and education was a luxury deemed unimportant for a farm worker. One lad who emigrated to Canada in 1907 at the age of 15 was met by a farmer who told him 'that I would stay with him for one year for board and work clothes — no wages — and the next year I would get a small wage.'[119] Stories of beatings, material deprivation and sheer cruelty, although not typical are not uncommon either. Jack arrived in Ontario in 1908 from Quarrier's Home. He recalled how he was 'lonesome and cried up in the hay mow.' His loneliness was far outweighed, however, by his astonishment at his employer's parsimony:

> That year from the Christmas tree I got rubber boots, socks and mitts. I felt so happy about it. I thanked them for the gifts — I thought it was grand. Guess the answer I got. 'Oh, you're paying for everything' he said. He had to pay me once a year. In those five years I received about a dollar a year. The year I was seventeen, I got 30 cents for the year, and then they charged me 15 cents for a haircut. His wife cut it.[120]

Jack may have been unlucky but he certainly was not alone in experiencing mistreatment at the hands of his employers. Another

Quarrier's boy who emigrated to Canada in the 1920s recounted his story as follows:

> Come the wintertime and if I wasn't in at 9 o'clock at night they turned the key in the door and they wouldn't let me in and I would walk down to the barn where the farm was and sleep with the cows...and there was a Barnardo boy working for another neighbour way past the station so I was telling him about my problem, 'oh' he says 'I'll see Mr McCracken'...so Mr McCracken says 'I'll get you a job', he got me a job at this Norman McCray's well that was walking out of the frying pan right into the fire. He kicked me, punched me, broke a couple of ribs on me, the least thing I done wrong didn't know maybe what I was doing, he got me down and kicked me and give me an awful beating. I wrote Mr Winters, he was the super-intendent of the home in Brockville and I told him in the letter how I was being used, 'oh' he said 'you're lying David', he says 'they're good church people'...you know every place I went I got kicked out or shoved out or whatever you say, I had nowhere to go.[121]

Not surprisingly, the *Narrative of Facts*, published annually by Quarrier's, rarely alluded to the experiences of these children although it was grudgingly accepted that there would always be a few failures; 'It is not by any means all sunshine: there are trials and experiences that we cannot write about...'[122] It is inconceivable that Quarrier's Homes were unaware of the mistreatment and exploitation suffered by some Home children — David's experience is testimony to that. But they were loathe to admit knowledge of cruelty or to accept responsibility. 'Cruelty or unreasonable severity has had no place in our experience for many years' was the proud claim made in 1925.[123] Instead, the children themselves were blamed for any problems that arose. 'Unfortunately, as with children everywhere, we have some who bring discredit upon themselves by their wilfulness' commented Quarrier's Canadian superintendent in 1915.[124]

For some children the emotional neglect and the disdain of the community for the 'home children' was harder to bear than physical mistreatment. From the 1880s through to the 1920s there was considerable opposition within Canada to the child emigration movement. Canada, it was said, was being used as a 'dumping ground' for Britain's unwanted refuse; the children were morally and physically degenerate and thus a threat to Canadian society; and the importation of cheap labour, it was argued, threatened the jobs of Canadian citizens.[125] Hostility towards the children was publicly articulated, via the press — 'they cannot help it: it is in their blood and it will tell'[126] — and to the children's faces, or behind their backs. The farmer guardian of one boy 'always yelled at them everyday "nobody wanted you in Scotland, nobody cared about you and that's why they sent you away."'[127] Resentment and antagonism was expressed, and felt, in more subtle ways too:

> I felt ashamed. There was a kind of stigma attached to us. We were orphans, we were hired men on the farm, we were emigrants, so we felt we were lower class than a lot of the others…home children in my opinion has a connotation…you were waifs, you were abandoned children…you were kids that never knew who your father or mother was, you were the kids that they picked up off the street, it hurt.[128]

'You had to be *humiliated*' recalled a girl sent to Australia, 'you had to be *humbled*.'[129]

Punishment or Salvation?

Within the broader context of child welfare policy, emigration was not perceived as a radical or extreme solution to the problem of homeless children. In fact, from the early child-savers' point of view emigration was merely boarding out in another country. Canada and other imperial destinations were seen as an extension of home and in many respects an improvement on conditions to be found in rural Scotland. Imperial settlement policy provided the supporters of child emigration with a politically convenient justification for a programme which bore numerous similarities with boarding out: the Empire fulfilled all the conditions required by those who advocated the removal of children from their home environment, whether this was to be in Scotland or overseas. First of all it was an inexpensive means of caring for the homeless child. Secondly, it offered the probability that a child could be permanently separated from harmful influences, including the family. Moreover, the vast open spaces of Canada, Australia and South Africa appealed to the anti-urbanists who idealised rural society for its supposed healthy environment and its association with hard manual labour, religious probity, strict moral standards and temperance. In this respect little distinction was made between Highland crofters and Ontario farmers — good, honest, hardworking stock. Rural Canada especially met all the requirements. It was a Protestant farming society, devoid of the class divisions that characterised rural Scotland and yet it was populated by Scots. It was sober, moral and a land of opportunity. All of this was just a voyage across the ocean away, in countries perceived as extensions of Britain populated by 'kith and kin'. And in view of the long-standing preference for boarding out over residential care in Scotland, emigration was, at least until the 1920s, less of a radical policy leap for the Scottish child-rescue organisations than it was for the English.

However, later emigration schemes, notably the Fairbridge Farm schools and the programme run by the Catholic Church in Australia, present a different picture of children removed from one institutional setting to another. 'For seven years I was at that school' recounted a Scottish migrant to one such Australian establishment, 'being beaten, showering in cold water, doing back-breaking work on timber and log piles.'[130] This pattern of care flew in the face of British child welfare policy after World War Two which embraced care in a foster home over residential care and for this reason the programme was surrounded with greater secrecy than earlier emigration schemes. By the time the last group of emigrants departed in 1967, many of the larger orphanages in England and Scotland were in the process of closing. The majority of children who ended up in an institution overseas were granted less protection than those who had been left behind. What was for many a tough, disciplined regime was in some cases made far worse by systematic mistreatment and abuse.[131]

From the child's perspective child emigration was an extreme policy. Being packed off on a long, uncomfortable journey across the ocean, removed from family and friends, neither fully appreciating the distances involved nor the permanency of the arrangement, and placed with a new family who required a worker rather than a child, was radical in anyone's judgement. To the child, emigration meant enforced separation from cultural roots.

What are we to make of the child emigration movement? An imaginative if misguided solution to the problem of how to find homes for thousands of needy children? Or an inhumane, immoral, if not downright dangerous policy which subordinated the welfare of the child to the greater needs of the economy and the empire? Personal histories present a complex and varied picture. While some children adapted well and thrived in their new home others were exploited. Some found caring and affectionate foster families, but others moved from one placement to another or ended up in children's homes no better than the situation they had left behind in Scotland. It is not really feasible to attempt to measure the relative success or failure of the policy in any quantitative sense. Few children returned home but then opportunities to escape from an unhappy or cruel environment were limited.[132] 'Sometimes I would go upstairs and I would sit and cry' recalled one woman sent to Canada when she was fourteen; 'and I would pack my bag and think I am going to run away from here, and then I would sit down and think *where* am I going to run to. I've got nowhere to go…I used to get down on my knees every night and pray to God to get me out of there.'[133]

The cries of pain shout louder from the historical memory than the sounds of contentment, and it is easy — perhaps too easy — for the historian to act as a condemnatory judge of a practice deemed today to be beyond the pale. Yet, even taking account of the intensity of the urban problem in Scotland and the opportunities offered by overseas Dominions with their idealised Christian countryside, evangelical philanthropists used emigration schemes for almost a hundred years as an efficient means to pursue the permanent destruction of thousands of Scottish working-class families. For the majority of those who were sent away, there was no way back.

NOTES

1. Urquhart, *The Life Story of William Quarrier*, p.103.
2. *Ibid.*, pp.104–5.
3. OHS, *Narrative of Facts*, 1880.
4. OHS, *Narrative of Facts* 1874: report of departure to Canada in *North British Daily Mail*.
5. OHS, *Narrative of Facts*, 1880.
6. *Ibid.*
7. Cited in Magnusson, *The Village*, p.55.
8. OHS, *Narrative of Facts*, 1882.
9. *Ibid,* p.163.
10. OHS, *Narrative of Facts*, 1880.
11. Cited in P.Bean & J.Melville, *Lost Children of the Empire*, (London, 1989), p.2.

12. Doyle cited in Bean & Melville, *Lost Children*, p.63.
13. Twelve year old emigrant to Australia cited in Bean & Melville, *Lost Children*, p.140.
14. Twelve year old emigrant to Canada cited in Bean & Melville, *Lost Children*, p.141.
15. G.Wagner, *Children of the Empire* (London, 1982), p.xi; 'The Forgotten Children they Fed to the Empire', *The Guardian*, 6 May 1989. Around 21 million persons altogether emigrated from the United Kingdom between 1815 and 1912 although of course most of these were voluntary migrants. In addition around 50,000 convicts were forcibly emigrated to the American colonies before 1776, and thereafter 160,000 were sent to Australian colonies between 1788 and 1868; S.Constantine, 'Empire Migration and Social Reform 1880–1950' in C.G.Pooley & I.D.Whyte (eds.), *Migrants, Emigrants and Immigrants* (London, 1991), p.67 & 71.
16. See the press and public reaction to the 'revelations' in the late 1980s that 2,100 children had been sent to Australia between 1947 and 1967, for example, 'Lost Children of the Empire', *The Observer*, 19 & 26 July 1987; 'The Forgotten Children they Fed to the Empire', *The Guardian*, 6 May 1989.
17. George Cruikshank and Harriet Beecher Stowe cited in J.Parr, *Labouring Children: British Immigrant Apprentices to Canada, 1869–1924* (Toronto, 1994), p.31.
18. See, for instance, Bean and Melville, *Lost Children* which makes significant use of oral history; Phyllis Harrison, *The Home Children* (Winnipeg, 1979), a collection of oral histories of emigrants to Canada. See also Anna Magnusson's forthcoming book on emigrants from Quarrier's homes.
19. Parr, *Labouring Children*, p.xvii.
20. Parr argues that it was the child-savers' revivalist evangelicalism which emphasised the potential for individual salvation that prompted them to adopt this particular form of moral rescue. Joy Parr, '"Transplanting from Dens of Iniquity": Theology and Child Emigration', in Linda Kealey (ed), *A Not Unreasonable Claim: Women and Reform in Canada 1880–1920* (Toronto, 1979), pp.169–231.
21. See Parr, *Labouring Children*, pp.27–8; Thomas E. Jordan, '"Stay and Starve, or Go and Prosper!" Juvenile Emigration from Great Britain in the Nineteenth Century', *Social Science History*, 9 (1985), pp.145–66.
22. E.Hadley, 'Natives in a Strange Land: the Philanthropic Discourse of Juvenile Emigration in Mid-Nineteenth Century England', *Victorian Studies* 33 (1990), p. 413.
23. For details on the emigration activities of the Children's Friend Society see E.Bradlow, 'The Children's Friend Society at the Cape of Good Hope', *Victorian Studies*, 27 (1984), pp.155–77.
24. C.H.Bracebridge, 'Juvenile Emigration', *Poor Law Magazine*, IX (1866–7), p.236.

25. M.Harper, *Emigration from North-East Scotland, Vol.2,* (Aberdeen, 1998), pp.228–30.
26. 'Departure of the Innocents' (probably by Horsley), in *Our Waifs and Strays*, 1887, in Bean and Melville, *Lost Children*, pp. 59–60.
27. Bracebridge, 'Juvenile Emigration', pp.236–7.
28. OHS, *Narrative of Facts*, 1882.
29. Bean & Melville, *Lost Children*, p.78.
30. See Constantine, 'Empire Migration'.
31. Cited in Bean & Melville, *Lost Children*, p.43.
32. For a clear explanation of how Fairbridge's views on empire settlement contrasted with the evangelical motivated emigration movement see Patrick A. Dunae, 'Waifs: the Fairbridge Society in British Columbia, 1931–1951' in *Histoire Sociale/Social History,* 42 (1988), pp.224–50.
33. Cited in Harrison, *The Home Children*, p.259.
34. Dunae in 'Waifs' notes that Northcote farm school near Melbourne closed in 1958 while Molong in New South Wales remained open until 1973 and Pinjarra until 1982, fn.79, p.247. For a first-hand account of life on a Fairbridge Farm School in Australia see John Lane, *Fairbridge Kid* (South Fremantle, 1990).
35. See Linda Colley, *Britons. Forging the Nation 1707–1837* (London, 1996), especially pp.122–40.
36. M.Harper, *Emigration from North-East Scotland. Vol.1, Willing Exiles* (Aberdeen, 1988), pp.35–6 and 39–40.
37. See J.M.Mackenzie, *Propaganda and Empire. The Manipulation of British Public Opinion* (Manchester, 1986) and Mackenzie (ed), *Imperialism and Popular Culture* (Manchester, 1986).
38. Urquhart, *The Life Story of William Quarrier*, p.392.
39. B.P.P., *Report to the President of the Local Government Board by Andrew Doyle Esq., Local Government Inspector, as to the Emigration of Pauper Children to Canada,* 1875, Cmd 9.
40. *Ibid*, p.29.
41. *Ibid*, p.22.
42. *Ibid*, p.29.
43. See Constantine, 'Empire Migration', p.68. On female emigration see Harper, *Emigration from North-East Scotland*, Vol.2, chapter 6.
44. Urquhart, *The Life Story of William Quarrier*, p.394.
45. G.Wagner, *Barnardo* (London, 1979), p.237.
46. W.Quarrier cited in J.Ross, *The Power I Pledge* (Glasgow, 1971), p.59.
47. M.Harper, 'The Juvenile Immigrant: Halfway to Heaven or Hell on Earth', in C.Kerrigan (ed), *The Immigrant Experience* (Guelph, 1992), p.167.
48. B.P.P., *Report of the Oversea Settlement Committee*, 1924–5, Cmd.2383, p.8; Constantine, 'Empire Migration', p.74.
49. B.P.P., *Report of the Oversea Settlement Committee*, 1924, Cmd.2107, p.10; 1924–5, Cmd.2383, pp.10–11.
50. B.P.P., 1924, Cmd.2107, p.11.

51. See B.Coldrey, '"A Charity which has Outlived its Usefulness": the Last Phase of Catholic Child Migration, 1947–56', *History of Education*, 25 (1996), pp.373–86.
52. SRO, ED 11/410: Consent to Emigration: General Principles to be Followed, 1951.
53. *Ibid.*, 29 January 1951.
54. SRO, ED 11/410: Case 20531/N/88, 4 December 1948.
55. Cited in Bean & Melville, *Lost Children*, p.99.
56. Lord Cherwell to Churchill, 1947 cited in S.Constantine, 'Waving Goodbye? Australia, Assisted Passages and the Empire and Commonwealth Settlement Acts from 1945 to 1972', *Journal of Contemporary History* (forthcoming).
57. SRO, ED 11/384: Letter to *The Scotsman* signed 'Scotus', 13 April 1955.
58. SRO, ED 11/384: Inter-Departmental Committee on Emigration Policy, 20 November 1961.
59. SRO, ED 11/509: Emigration of Children through the auspices of the Church of Scotland, minute of 24 October 1961.
60. SRO, ED 11/509: Correspondence between Quarrier's Homes and Scottish Education Department, November 1961.
61. SAS, PD 41: Whinwell Case Files, H 38 (1895).
62. OHS, History Book 1888–89.
63. SAS, PD 41: Whinwell Case Files, F 60 (1912).
64. SAS, PD 41: Whinwell Case Files, A13 (1903).
65. SAS, PD 41: Whinwell Case Files, I 58 (1914).
66. SAS, PD 41: Whinwell Case Files, D21 (1891).
67. SAS, PD 41: Whinwell Case files, A 13 (1903).
68. OHS, *Narrative of Facts*, 1920.
69. Cited in Bean & Melville, *Lost Children*, p.110.
70. Cited in Harrison, *The Home Children*, p.37.
71. *Ibid.*, p.119.
72. *Ibid.*, p.84.
73. SRO, ED 7/1/42: Visual Information Committee, 1902–10.
74. Cited in Bean & Melville, *Lost Children*, pp.138–9.
75. Cited in Harrison, *The Home Children*, p.241.
76. See Bean & Melville, *Lost Children*, pp.110–2.
77. 'Nuns robbed me of my family', *The Scotsman*, 30 March 1998.
78. Bean and Melville, *Lost Children*, p.138.
79. OHS, *Narrative of Facts*, 1880.
80. Cited in Harrison, *The Home Children*, p.37.
81. OHS, *Narrative of Facts*, 1925.
82. Cited in Magnusson, *The Village*, p.71.
83. Parr, *Labouring Children*, p.46.
84. OHS, *Narrative of Facts*, 1880.
85. Urquhart, *The Life Story of William Quarrier*, p.101.
86. *Ibid.*, p.108.

87. Cited in Harrison, *The Home Children*, p.39.
88. Urquhart, *The Life Story of William Quarrier*, p.109.
89. *Ibid.*, p.176.
90. See P.T.Rooke and R.L.Schnell, 'The "King's Children" in English Canada: A Psychohistorical Study of Abandonment, Rejection, and Colonial Response (1869–1930)', *Journal of Psychohistory*, 8 (1981), pp.388–9. They also argue that 'probably two-thirds were exploited either brutally or with some rough equity by Canadians who took them as farm labourers or domestic servants.' p.398.
91. Cited in Harrison, *The Home Children*, p.64.
92. Magnusson, *The Village*, p.58.
93. Chorlton Board of Guardians (1910) cited in Wagner, *Children of the Empire*, p.218.
94. L.Russel in J.Stroud, *Thirteen Penny Stamps*, p.98.
95. Cited in Urquhart, *The Life Story of William Quarrier*, p.173.
96. *Ibid.*, p.174.
97. Kelso cited in K.Bagnall, *The Little Immigrants: the Orphans who came to Canada* (Toronto, 1980), p.183.
98. *Glasgow Herald*, February 1883.
99. OHS, *Narrative of Facts*, 1890.
100. OHS, *Narrative of Facts*, 1880.
101. It was not unknown for children to be made to write letters to their sending institutions to tell them how happy they were. See Bean and Melville, *Lost Children*, p.142.
102. OHS, *Narrative of Facts*, 1880.
103. OHS, *Narrative of Facts*, 1925.
104. OHS, *Narrative of Facts*, 1880.
105. OHS, *Narrative of Facts*, 1890.
106. OHS, *Narrative of Facts*, 1880.
107. Cited in Harrison, *The Home Chikdren*, p.170.
108. Lane, *Fairbridge Kid*, pp.87–9.
109. Cited in Harrison, *The Home Children*, p.39.
110. Canadian emigrant interviewed on 'The Little Emigrants', BBC Radio Scotland, 1997.
111. OHS, *Narrative of Facts*, 1880.
112. OHS, *Narrative of Facts*, 1925.
113. T.Rooke and R.L.Schnell, *Discarding the Asylum: From Child Rescue to the Welfare State in English Canada (1800–1950)* (London, 1983) however, suggest that girls were especially vulnerable and claim that 'a number of girls were indecently treated or impregnated', pp.235–6.
114. OHS, *Narrative of Facts*, 1890.
115. OHS, *Narrative of Facts*, 1880.
116. SAS, PD 41: Whinwell Case Files, D 67 (1913).
117. Cited in Harrison, *The Home Children*, p.101.
118. *Ibid.*, p.261.
119. *Ibid.*, p.85.

120. *Ibid.,* p.92.
121. Canadian emigrant speaking on 'The Little Emigrants', BBC Radio Scotland, 1997.
122. OHS, *Narrative of Facts,* 1910.
123. OHS, *Narrative of Facts,* 1925.
124. OHS, *Narrative of Facts,* 1915.
125. See P.T.Rooke and R.L.Schnell, 'Imperial Philanthropy and Colonial Response: British Juvenile Emigration to Canada, 1896–1930', *The Historian,* 46 (1983), pp.56–77; Rooke and Schnell, *Discarding the Asylum,* pp.223–69.
126. *Montreal Gazette* 1895, cited in Rooke and Schnell, *Discarding the Asylum,* p.242.
127. Interview broadcast on 'The Little Emigrants', BBC Radio Scotland, 1997.
128. Canadian emigrant interviewed on 'The Little Emigrants'. BBC Radio Scotland.
129. Cited in Bean and Melville, *Lost Children,* p.150.
130. *The Scotsman,* 30 March 1998.
131. Australian homes managed by the Roman Catholic Christian Brothers, have been at the centre of physical and sexual abuse allegations. See A.Gill, *Orphans of the Empire* (Sydney, 1997).
132. A sample of 255 children who emigrated from the Orphan Homes of Scotland between 1872 and 1931 shows that just 19 or 7 per cent returned to Scotland and one absconded. OHS, Emigration Register.
133. Cited in Bean and Melville, *Lost Children,* p.145.

CHAPTER 5

THE PROBLEM CHILD

We are not ashamed or afraid of letting readers know of some of the anxiety producing problems which confront us in coping with the maladjusted or psychopathic youngsters. Today, for example, one of our big 13-year-old loutish lads kicked over the traces, and in truculent mood, using foul and filthy language, defied his housemaster and other members of staff…We were justifiably angry and yet our hearts went out to this lad when we remembered his former home life and background.

— *Aberlour Orphanage Magazine,* 1958.

Healthy Bodies Make Healthy Minds

The *Aberlour Orphanage Magazine* reported this incident in 1958 along with several other sympathetic accounts of the activities of 'scallywag' boys and high-spirited girls found engaging in boisterous and devilish activities. The public response of the orphanage authorities was in tune with the changed attitudes of the post-Second World War era. Children who got into trouble were no longer 'dangerous' but vulnerable. Their behaviour was not wilful but a symptom of their disturbed minds and the trauma they had experienced in the past. These children demanded sympathy and support rather than punishment.

The 1950s and 1960s mark the culmination of a period of gradual but wholesale change in the way children were perceived by child welfare professionals. In the nineteenth century children, as we have seen, were predominantly defined by their physical condition; children's bodies — starved, emaciated, neglected and abused — were at the centre of professional concern. These bodies symbolised their very threat to the moral fabric of the nation and the only way to protect society was to take control of them. Thus children were 'rescued' and placed within an environment where they could be observed, disciplined and educated, or removed to far-flung rural homes in the Highlands or the Dominions. Control of the child's body was the key to dissipating the threat the homeless child represented, an attitude vividly encapsulated by the SNSPCC in 1886 which spoke of 'the numbers of neglected, bruised, maimed, *starved*, DYING children, who seek the refuge of the high windows, thick walls and strongly barred door of the Shelter, knowing that there they will find food, safety, and kindness...'[1] Of course the SNSPCC Shelter, in addition to providing a refuge, also protected society from these children until they could be placed in a more suitable environment — often an industrial school, reformatory or children's home. While the thick walls and barred doors of the refuge protected a child from harm they also ensured the child could no longer threaten society.

In the late nineteenth and early twentieth century little attention was paid to the child's emotional state. Children in Victorian society were not, and perhaps could not, be screened from horror. It is hard to imagine and almost impossible to capture the inner feelings of children who may have witnessed the death of a parent, experienced cruelty or neglect, and who were removed from their families and familiar surroundings with no explanation and no attempt to maintain contact with relatives and friends. The memories of those who went through such a crisis in their childhood tend to be blunted or blurred although some of the rawness and sense of loss and bewilderment is evident in personal reminiscences. Christine described the circumstances in which she learned she was an orphan:

> ...I remember [a cousin] coming up the stairs to me in the bedroom in the morning and saying 'you havn't got a mother or a father', I says 'I have got a mother, I haven't just got a father', 'oh but there was a policeman at the door just now and told me that your mother's died as well' and that's how I was told my mother was dead, isn't it awful...I remember seeing my mother in her coffin, two pennies on her eyes...[2]

Annie, who was taken into care at the age of eight when her mother died, was similarly reticent about the occasion of her mother's death:

> I remember when my mother died and she was only 42, you see, and I remember the day she was buried even, but er, the only thing that sticks in my mind was, er, she'd long black hair and my sister and I used to take turns at plaiting it at night.[3]

163

Other children witnessed even more dramatic domestic traumas. Dorothy Haynes in her reminiscences of Aberlour Orphanage recalled one girl who preferred not to talk about her traumatic experience:

> Joan's father drank too much, worked seldom, and bullied his wife. One day he demanded money when there was none, and Mrs Morris, at the end of her tether, drank lysol. Joan came home in time to hear her screaming, and screamed herself because the neighbours wouldn't let her go in.[4]

Bereaved, abandoned and abused children exhibited a range of symptoms. Some became withdrawn, others aggressive. Others exhibited physical manifestations of their emotional distress such as bed-wetting or eczema.

Children suddenly removed from familiar surroundings and placed with another family or in a children's home with no explanation of why this was happening to them could suffer profoundly. Until quite recently it was policy not to remind children of their parents, and foster parents usually had little knowledge of the background of their young charges. 'They never told us where they came from, they just left them with us...we were never told if they had sisters or brothers, or what sort of home they had,' recalled a former foster parent who took in two Glasgow children to her home on South Uist, one of whom was clearly disturbed. 'She came to our home and she was so fearful — easily frightened...if you lifted anything she'd take fright because she thought you were going to hit her.'[5] In many cases strenuous efforts were made to prevent contact between parents and children taken into care. It was not uncommon for children not to be told of letters and parcels sent by concerned mothers, fathers and relatives.[6] The effect of such policies on some children could be disturbing. 'I remember one boy...he ran away during the night' recalled a resident of an island in the Outer Hebrides. 'This boy had got the idea that nobody loved him or liked him and that the community didn't like him. That they didn't care what happened to him.'[7] Running away was this child's way of telling the community that he needed an outward sign that he was wanted and loved.

It was not really until the inter-war years that child welfare professionals began to define the children in their care in more than physical terms. In the 1920s and 30s they began to formulate a psycho-medical construction of childhood based on the child's consciousness or mind, augmenting and eventually superseding the idea of the child as a purely physical or bodily danger. The starved, neglected and abused child of the nineteenth century who could be nurtured back to sound physical health with plenty of fresh air and wholesome food, gradually became the nervous, maladjusted and unstable child of the twentieth century. During the 1920s and 1930s, building upon the development of educational psychology and the understanding of psychiatric illness, the Child Guidance Movement encapsulated a more holistic and child-centred approach to child welfare which prioritised non-physical treatment for common emotional disorders. The recognition of children's experiences of evacuation and the opening up of residential care institutions to public gaze after the war did more than any government committee to focus the minds of all of those involved in child welfare on the emotional as well as the physical well-being of their charges. Yet, as we shall see, children within the care system — arguably those with the most severe psychological problems — were probably the last to benefit from the attention to the root causes of emotional disturbance.

Child Guidance and the 'Maladjusted' Child

The advent of mass education from 1872 first directed attention to the extent of physical but also mental incapacity amongst the nation's children. Mass schooling permitted comprehensive medical examination and in 1908 the education authorities in Scotland were granted the power to carry out medical inspections of all children attending public schools. One survey carried out on the eve of the First World War maintained that over 40 per cent of children entering school suffered from any one of a range of 'chronic' conditions, ranging from verminous heads and skin diseases to TB and rickets.[8] In response a wide range of treatments for childhood ill-health were provided from fresh-air fortnight homes and sick children's hospitals to sun-lamp treatment specifically for rickets which was almost exclusively an urban disease.

But physical ill-health was easier to tackle than mental disturbance. For the first time teachers and other child care

Children receiving sun-lamp treatment, Cochrane Street child welfare clinic, Glasgow, c. 1920s. These children had rickets, an urban condition caused by lack of sunlight. Courtesy of Glasgow City Archives (Libraries and Archives).

professionals were confronted with a range of children including those defined as 'potentially imbecile', the 'backward' and the 'delinquent'.[9] However, at this time those who were interested in the study of children by psychological as well as medical and sociological methods were few and isolated.[10] The Child Study Association founded in 1894 and which established an Edinburgh branch in 1896, brought together a range of professionals with the aim of delivering 'methods for the direct assessment of intellectual, emotional, and moral qualities, instead of relying on indirect inferences from physical characteristics.'[11] But it was perhaps the interest in juvenile delinquency after 1918, and the investigation of the relationship between the delinquent and childhood 'maladjustment', which gave the greatest impetus to the study of a child's psychology. By this time the works of Freud were widely known. His emphasis on the subconscious and the importance of the early childhood years for the emotional development of the adult had been taken up by psychologists, and in conjunction with educationalists the belief came to be accepted that an understanding of a child's psychology was essential for a proper study of child education and development. Hence, the nineteenth-century belief that delinquency and other childhood disorders and malfunctions were inherited was gradually rejected by many professionals, and psychologists, psychiatrists and educationalists proceeded to investigate childhood behaviour against a backdrop of family circumstances, environment and childhood intelligence. Following in the footsteps of American specialists who, prior to the First World War, pioneered the treatment of delinquents, British experts (most notably Cyril Burt in London) began to interpret delinquent behaviour not as criminal activity to be punished, but as acquired behaviour within a context of the child's home, school and recreational environment.[12]

The maladjusted child, then, could be readjusted with the help of professionals who understood the requirements for satisfactory development. Children who were cared for away from their own homes needed special attention and understanding to compensate for the lack of the natural relationship with their own parents. It was recognised that children deprived of a 'normal' home life might manifest a range of symptoms such as 'insatiable demands for affection', aggression, 'attempts to snatch what they fear will be withheld', or withdrawal. It was the children's emotional needs that required attention; as one specialist put it, 'they want the stimulus of effort and mixing with the crowd outside as well as good boots and a balanced diet.'[13]

The means by which this new approach was to be delivered was via the Child Guidance team or clinic, normally consisting of an educational psychologist, a psychiatrist and a psychiatric social worker, who investigated the 'whole child'; its physical condition, intelligence and mental age, emotional stability, personality and environmental history. 'Clinics put aside most of the assumptions which had traditionally ruled adult attitudes towards children', writes Olive Sampson in her history of the Child Guidance movement, 'and substituted a flexible objectivity for moral rigidity and pedagogical formulas…to look for causes first and cures afterwards, and not to pass judgement at any stage…'[14] From 1920 the Tavistock Clinic in London pioneered this holistic approach to child maladjustment and this prototype child guidance clinic was soon emulated throughout the British Isles. In Scotland clinics were opened in 1926 at Glasgow University run by William Boyd and 1927 at Edinburgh University under the direction of James Drever, soon to be followed by the first Child Guidance Clinic to be specifically named as such — the Notre Dame Child Guidance Clinic established by Sister Marie Hilda which opened in Glasgow in 1931.

Regarded by many as a pioneer in the Scottish Child Guidance movement, Sister Marie Hilda applied her interest in psychology to the children of the Roman Catholic Notre Dame primary school, then called the Montessori School. Her research into the difficulties of children who had done well at primary school but who then did not live up to expectations later on suggested to her that they had been affected by unresolved emotional problems in their early years. She went on to open the Child Guidance Clinic as an offshoot of the Notre Dame psychology department. The clinic dealt with 'nervous/backward/delinquent and "problem" children in general without religious distinction'; it was her firm belief that:

> The child who cringes of bullies, the child who steals, the child with night terrors, the child who does not respond to ordinary treatment at home or at school or with his playmates, will grow, if not properly treated, into the bad parent, the mentally unstable adult or the habitual criminal. In one way or another the neurotic child is likely to become a liability to the state, whereas many of these children, being of superior intelligence, should be among its greatest assets.[15]

In the first 14 years of operation the staff dealt with almost 2,500 cases.[16] Sister Marie Hilda's work in establishing child guidance work, not just in Glasgow but in the rest of the British Isles, at a time when child psychology was misunderstood and distrusted by many, was universally recognised and the Notre Dame Clinic continued to be a centre for the training of child psychologists until the 1980s.[17]

In 1937 Glasgow became the first local education authority in the British Isles to support a full-time child guidance clinic at Shettleston in the East End under the direction of Catherine McCallum, who was later to become the leading clinical psychologist with Glasgow Child Guidance Service. Thereafter education authorities in Edinburgh, Ayrshire, Dunbartonshire, Fife, Lanarkshire and Aberdeen appointed child psychologists.[18] In 1945 the Glasgow clinics dealt with almost 3,000 referrals, compared with only 466 in Birmingham and 167 in Manchester.[19] By the 1950s there were 12 full-time clinics in Glasgow alone and children in rural areas were catered for by mobile educational psychologists.[20] From the beginning the Scottish child guidance service was dominated by educational psychologists, largely drawn from the ranks of practising teachers — a situation that distinguished the Scottish service from its English counterpart where child psychiatrists predominated. It was only much later, in 1951, that a psychiatric centre specifically for children was established in Scotland at the Crichton Royal Hospital in Dumfries; the educational emphasis has always dominated north of the border.[21]

The remit of the Child Guidance Service was quite broad despite the fact that so-called 'mentally deficient' children were not included in the range of clients. Indeed, the clinic:

> prefers to help with the emotional difficulties of the slightly disturbed, the nervous or over-sensitive child, who although fundamentally of sound mental health, may at times find himself in trouble or misunderstood at home or school, or even before a Juvenile Court. The child psychologist…is also frequently consulted about apparently physical conditions such as asthma, palpitations, abdominal pain, bed-wetting and even eczema, when it is suspected that hidden anxieties and fears may play a large part in their causation…[22]

Considering the range of emotional difficulties likely experienced by children in the welfare system the child guidance service seemed eminently well suited to their predicament. Yet there is little evidence that this service was utilised early on by the child care authorities responsible for placing children with foster families and certainly not by the larger residential homes who housed a high proportion of children harbouring a variety of neuroses and emotional anxieties. This was despite a recognition by some experts that there was a need within the system for some form of psychological or psychiatric assessment and treatment.

It was the Second World War, and more specifically the experience of children evacuated or cared for in wartime nurseries, that brought about a wholesale change in the way children in care were perceived by the majority of professionals in the field. The war acted as a catalyst, not only highlighting the poor physical condition of many of the children who were billeted with families in the country but also drawing attention to the effects of the separation of a child from family and home. Of course this had been happening for decades — considerable experience in these matters had been gathered by those responsible for the boarding-out system — but the war sharpened the focus on class and urban deprivation. Although the majority of children were taken into working-class households, it was the shock expressed by the middle classes who were confronted with 'slum children' for the first time which prompted widespread and often intemperate and ill-informed public debate. Moreover, the early 1940s was a moment when the professions of educational psychology and child psychiatry were establishing themselves as key players in the child care services; by then a whole lexicon of child-specific disorders had been established and evacuated children provided a wonderful opportunity for research.[23]

Evacuation, Separation and Trauma

During the month of September 1939 175,812 persons, the majority unaccompanied school children and mothers with children of pre-school age, were evacuated from designated danger areas in Scottish towns and cities. The initial evacuation areas were Glasgow, Clydebank, Rosyth, Edinburgh and Dundee but later on in the war North and South Queensferry, Greenock, Port Glasgow and Dumbarton were added.[24] The designated receiving areas ranged from Banff to Dumfries, Inverness to Wigtown.[25] Evacuation began on Friday 1st of September signalled by telegram and continued throughout the weekend. Early in the morning those who had registered to be evacuated arrived at their registration centres, usually the school, with their luggage, gas masks and packed lunches. It was reported that the 'air of the tinier children, the wide-eyed tots of the juvenile army, was that of a mass picnic' although the older evacuees were quieter indicating their realisation of the seriousness of the situation.[26] With identity labels round their necks:

> Two abreast the evacuees made their way along the streets. Songs quickened the pace. Wishes of good luck from spectators at windows were answered with ringing cheers. For most of the children evacuation was something in the nature of an adventure. Too young to realise the significance of their departure from home, they marched in buoyant spirits. The only worried people were the mothers and fathers.[27]

'A whistle sounded, the train started: the exodus had begun.'[28] The initial excitement, however, was soon replaced by exhaustion, hunger and irritability for those who spent long hours on cramped trains with few facilities. Community singing, bottles of lemonade and the countryside passing by could not sustain children's interest for long. One journey from Glasgow to Aberdeenshire took more than 12 hours. 'The journey was a positive nightmare', reported one teacher who survived this mammoth trek north.

> The evacuees were famished when they arrived, having had no food for a matter of 12 hours…The babies-in-arms kept howling for milk which was unobtainable at any station. Mothers began to grow hysterical…many children became trainsick. There was a lack of water on the train…On arrival at midnight the evacuees, teachers and helpers were so exhausted and depressed that the term 'refugees' applied to them by some of the householders seemed more appropriate than offensive.[29]

Yet, having endured uncomfortable journeys it was reported that 'most of the children were bright and cheerful' in contrast with their parents who showed most signs of anxiety.[30]

More serious problems arose when large numbers of evacuees arrived in areas ill-equipped to deal with the influx. Although billeting officers had actively sought out householders willing to take in children, the situation was often characterised by confusion and prejudice. The arrival of around 400 mothers and children at the small town of Inverary in Argyll for instance caused considerable consternation. 'And the poor wee souls were marched off the steamer' remembered a former teacher at Inverary Grammar School:

> I remember yet marching up the street with their teachers and the mothers and the babies and the helpers, and where did we take them

to but the parish church. Now if you can imagine the thunder and lightening and the rain coming down and taking the poor wee souls into the kirk! Oh it was depressing.[31]

An inadequate number of billets meant 150 had to be housed in a 'miserable, cold hall' hastily kitted out with bedding consisting of sacks of straw and mattresses purloined from the jail. Such emergency measures would not have been necessary had the Duke of Argyll permitted the use of spare rooms in the nearby 67 room Inverary Castle, although he eventually relented to allow a number of children to be housed in the castle basement.[32]

From Ayrshire to Aberdeenshire the majority of children were billeted with local householders and although many communities welcomed the evacuees such as in Campbeltown where the local newspaper commented that 'everything would be done to make the evacuees feel at home just the minute they stepped onto Kintyre ground', elsewhere the allocation of children to billets was chaotic and, for some, traumatic.[33] The scene was said to be reminiscent 'of a cross between an early Roman slave market and Selfridge's bargain basement'.[34] A system which permitted householders to select their children inevitably caused resentment and distress: 'Naturally they scanned the children and picked those of best appearance'.[35] Such scenes were similar to those experienced by children boarded out: some evacuees found they were taken on sufferance, separated from brothers and sisters, and portrayed as uncivilised, dirty slum children. True, some did arrive with head-lice, skin conditions and a variety of infectious diseases but the extent of the public outcry at the physical condition of these children only served to exaggerate the situation.[36] By 1940, following a second evacuation wave, the Secretary of State for Scotland was warned that 'the feeling of householders generally throughout the reception areas is not one of mere unwillingness but one of very strong opposition to the scheme.'[37] Rumours abounded of children who lacked the most basic toilet training and of infested children whose very presence was injurious to the health of the permanent members of the household, rumours the press did much to fuel.[38] Letters from all over Scotland were arriving in council chambers, the Scottish Office and the in-trays of newspaper editors complaining about unruly, filthy children and ungrateful, lazy mothers.[39] Just over a week after the first wave of evacuees had arrived in Perthshire from Glasgow, local feelings were running high articulated by a resident of Dunkeld in a letter to *The Scotsman*:

> People were ready and willing to help in any way possible to take in children and mothers, but not in the filthy condition a large number arrived in, with lice and scrumpox, not to mention other diseases. No self-respecting householder, and especially those with children of their own, want to have these in their homes, spreading filth and disease, nor mothers who expect everything done for them and who will not do anything to help.[40]

Britain had never before witnessed such sudden and wholesale disruption of family life. Families were torn apart as fathers and sons were called up to the services, many mothers undertook full-time work for the first time, children were evacuated and homes, shops and workplaces were bombed. In these circumstances it would not have been surprising if children suffered emotional trauma. This, at least, was the anticipation of child psychologists who carried out numerous studies into the effects of the wartime conditions and evacuation in particular. In the light of the national hysteria with regard to bed-wetting, a well-known symptom of temporary emotional disturbance, and the very high rate of return of children and their mothers to danger areas in the first weeks of the war, researchers clearly expected to find a majority of maladjusted, neurotic children as a result of evacuation. Certainly the press helped to promote the widespread impression that evacuated children were becoming 'sheer nervous wrecks'.[41]

Yet the findings of researchers should have confounded those who envisaged an army of maladjusted children returning to the cities. In his study of the incidence of neurotic symptoms among evacuated schoolchildren in three cities Cyril Burt, the leading child psychologist, concluded that 'what is most impressive is the fact that after all the mental health and moral behaviour of the children has been so little impaired.'[42] While the amount of mild emotional disturbance did increase, largely manifested by homesickness, bed-wetting and what Burt termed the 'emotional exaggeration of grievances', there was no evidence to suggest evacuation had increased the amount of serious nervous disorder.[43] In fact the opposite appeared to be the case. Amongst children who had been away for at least ten weeks and had subsequently returned home researchers found 'an appreciable improvement in socially desirable conduct and a firming up of personal character.' Evacuation had largely 'left unaffected the emotional life of the children.'[44] The majority of children in all the surveys developed reasonably good relationships with their foster-parents and for the most part those who did not settle had been placed in unsuitable homes.[45]

In fact, in explaining the drift back of evacuees to their homes, seemingly an obvious sign of children's emotional disturbance — and almost 75 per cent had done so by Christmas 1939 — researchers found parents were to blame in a high proportion of cases. Around two-thirds of Clydebank children who returned home in the first two months were brought back by their parents for a wide variety of reasons including the predictable 'parents missed child' and 'parents thought child not cared for properly' to concern about the cost of billeting. Unaccompanied Catholic children from Clydebank were the quickest to return home, possibly for financial reasons rather than due to problems associated with the billeting of these children with Protestant families.[46] It seems it was not the children, in the main, that suffered from separation from their families, but rather the parents who missed their children.

However, these research findings had little impact upon public perception. Those in Scotland personally touched by the evacuation drama — both the children and the householders — experienced something of a two-way culture shock, at least in the short term. While rural inhabitants were sometimes taken aback by the manners and habits of their urban visitors, the children and especially their mothers, were like fish out of water. Small towns like Inverary had no electricity and lighting was from oil lamps. The autumn weather on the west coast 'was not at its best' giving the evacuees a bad first impression of their temporary homes.[47] Moreover, compared with life in a city like Glasgow reception areas offered lots of fresh air but little to do. 'They soon got fed up with Southend' recalled Angus MacVicar, the minister of this village at the tip of the Kintyre peninsula.

> There was nothing to do — no cinemas, no shops, nothing at all. We'd no electricity then…How they expected Glasgow people to stay here — with the sea roaring outside and the wind howling and no shops or cinemas to go to.[48]

Owing to the legion of problems experienced by householders and evacuees, the majority of children were at home with their parents during the most serious air-raids — over 7,000 school children were still in Clydebank during the devastating air-raids in March 1941 — although after these blitz raids another 120,000 Glasgow mothers and children left their homes under the emergency conditions.[49]

Although serious psychological distress was only experienced by a minority of children as a consequence of the bombing and evacuation, the popular image of evacuees — as poor, dirty, malnourished, maladjusted and delinquent children — was more powerful than all the research papers put together. Just one or two horror stories of a child allegedly defacating in bed or committing serious damage could outweigh more measured academic analyses.[50] It was an image subsequently perpetuated in popular film and literature such as Robin Jenkins' novel published in 1956, *Guests of War* in which the evacuees are portrayed as incomprehensible, nit-infested 'slum-urchins' and which had long term implications for the care of homeless children.[51] After the war, local authorities found it increasingly difficult to recruit foster-parents; the bad press given to the evacuation experience had made them wary.[52]

However, more convincing evidence of children's emotional trauma or neuroses and strategies to deal with them was forthcoming. Studies of young children who had been cared for in wartime nurseries seemed to confirm the view already held by some child psychologists that while separation from parents — and especially the mother — was not necessarily injurious to the child's emotional health, what was likely to contribute to psychological breakdown was removal to institutional care where the child was denied adequate personal attention and affection and continuous emotional contact with the parents.[53] The observations of Dorothy Burlingham and Anna Freud of young children cared for in a London residential nursery during the war years were profoundly influential in this respect. Owing to the twin circumstances of absence of the most important instinctual need of the young child — attachment to the mother — and institutionalisation, it was found that the child's emotional development was either blunted or precociously stimulated. A variety of manifestations of this abnormal development were observed ranging from aggression towards others and excessive jealousy to the formation of strong attachments to mother figures and the development of auto-erotic habits (thumb-sucking, rocking, head-knocking and masturbation) upon being separated from the mother or mother-substitute.[54]

In Scotland, a unique experiment was carried out in order to observe and treat the small number of children demonstrating severe psychological disturbance as a consequence of evacuation and general wartime conditions. These children, said to be 'drifting in a sea of their own emotion, in a world so disrupted that their landmarks were gone', were admitted to Nerston residential clinic a few miles from Glasgow.[55] Nerston was an experimental Child Guidance Clinic run on a voluntary basis by Child Guidance staff who were keen to put into practice a number of general principles relating to the care and treatment of seriously disturbed children. It provided a unique opportunity to observe the reaction of the children under conditions of crisis, such as air raids of which there were many.[56] The Nerston regime — 'routine but no regimentation' — was based upon the recognition that such children required security, affection and discipline. Staff pioneered the progressive application of child guidance techniques, including imaginative play and group games, to cope with what they described as 'waves of delinquency', 'waves of fear, anger and exhibitionism' and 'emotional waves', providing a model for the post-war treatment of psychologically disturbed children. As Catherine McCallum concluded:

> Little crippled personalities come there, hating, fearing, distrusting, their whole view of life distorted by their unhappiness. They leave again in six, twelve or eighteen months, freer and happier individuals, grown whole again by self-knowledge, self-discipline, tolerance and sympathy for human weakness.[57]

Towards the end of the war the combination of the twin concerns brought to light by the evacuation experience — physical and psychological — was most notably foisted upon the government and the public by Lady Marjory Allen's letter to *The Times* in July 1944 on the subject of 'Children in Homes' and it was undoubtedly the war and its consequences including the destruction of families and homes which prompted her concern and the public debate which followed.[58] Lady Allen's exposure of the conditions prevalent in children's homes struck a chord with many who had been sensitised to the condition of children cared for by strangers during the war but also with child care professionals who, although confident of modern theories of child development, had suddenly come face to face with the true conditions of homeless children. Lady Allen's call for a public inquiry was timely. The immediate post-war years were ripe for public discussion between the government, local authorities, child welfare organisations, care providers and the new professions of child psychology and psychiatry. Despite the fact that few evacuees had suffered severe emotional disturbance as a result of their experiences of separation from the families, popular perception that children had indeed suffered served ironically to help the acceptance of the work of the Child Guidance Clinics in the post-war era.

The Age of the Angry Child

In 1945 17,558 Scottish children were described as being 'deprived of a normal home life', a figure which included adopted children, those placed in approved schools, remand homes and all other care situations.[59] These figures are not surprising when one remembers the social upheaval endemic in Scottish society and especially in the cities after the war. In addition to Scotland's share of war deaths, civilian casualties inflicted a heavy toll on family life. In Glasgow alone there were more than 9,000 casualties.[60] Despite a substantial increase in nuptuality (the proportion of females marrying) and fertility following World War Two, by the 1960s the Scottish family was experiencing major changes indicated by declining marriage rates, rising illegitimacy rates, and an increase in the divorce rate leading to a rapid growth in the number of lone parent families.[61] At the same time, the participation rate of women in the labour force rose quite markedly from the 1950s; whereas in 1951 32.6 per cent of adult women were employed, by 1981 this figure had increased to 42.2 per cent.[62] Much of this increase is accounted for by the rise in married women in paid work. In 1951 23.4 per cent of employed females were married while in 1981 the figure was 62 per cent.[63]

Accompanying these changes in family structure and function were considerable structural improvements in living conditions. Since the 1920s Glasgow City Corporation had been engaged in a massive slum clearance and home building programme in an attempt to ameliorate the appalling overcrowding and insanitary conditions prevalent in the 'clotted masses of slums'.[64] Between 1919 and 1955 over 100,000 houses were built in Glasgow alone, rehousing approximately 24 per cent of the population of the city after the Second World War, gradually reducing overcrowding and improving the provision of amenities such as fixed baths and WC's.[65] Nevertheless, in 1951 in Scotland as a whole 173,598 people still lived in one-roomed houses, almost 50 per cent of these in Glasgow, and 44 per cent of Glasgow's housing was still officially defined as overcrowded.[66] Thirty-seven per cent of households still had to share toilet facilities and 50 per cent did not possess a fixed bath.[67]

Slum demolition and rehousing caused immense social upheaval for families in Scotland's major cities whether the distance removed was from one side of the city to another or further afield. In addition to decanting its overspill population to the new peripheral housing estates, Glasgow Corporation also found homes for former slum dwellers in New Towns (primarily East Kilbride designated in 1947–8 and Cumbernauld in 1955) and in towns as distant as Arbroath, Kirkintilloch and North Berwick. For many families, rehousing initially meant an escape from overcrowded, run-down environments. Speaking of Springburn one woman commented that 'The conditions of living were deplorable…I just felt that I'd like to get away from it altogether.'[68] Many were happy to leave behind tenement life. Meg Henderson, rehoused from Blackhill to Drumchapel in the 1950s, recalled the country environment surrounding the scheme seemed like a paradise for children.[69] The new flats, many in high-rise blocks constructed in the early 1960s, with bathrooms, were 'like heaven' because of the spaciousness and facilities although perhaps also on account of their apparent proximity to that place.[70] In Hutchesontown, children's playgrounds were imaginatively incorporated into the overall plan. But in most of the schemes community facilities were poor or non-existent — Meg had to be bussed to school in the city and some schemes had no shops, pubs or other civic amenities such as churches and community centres. Many lamented the loss of community solidarity and neighbourliness which people remembered from their lives in the tenements. The new housing estates were often portrayed as anonymous: 'Now they're living in these big flats, nobody speaks to one another, just passing one another by.'[71] Moreover some felt that rehousing had a detrimental effect on family life and children. 'The community spirit of the tenement, the neighbourliness, was a thing that has been lost' commented a former resident of Springburn.

> Whole communities were broken up that had lived together in the tenements for years. Everybody knew everybody else...children sort of belonged to the community. They were better behaved because every neighbour took to do with you...Everybody had to do with you, and you didn't get up to so many things. And people were more tolerant of children then. You were the community's children.[72]

After rehousing 'families were broken up, the aunts and uncles no longer stayed near.'[73]

The impact of the war years and the social dislocation of the immediate post-war era certainly placed family life under tremendous strain although in Glasgow it was noted that despite all of this family relationships continued to 'exhibit a remarkable strength and adaptability.'[74] Whilst it had been acknowledged that potentially thousands of children would require some form of local authority care at the end of the war, some also began to recognise the need for a more fundamental review of child care services. It was against this background of social dislocation that the government set up a public inquiry into the condition of homeless children. At the same time, alongside the work of the Clyde Committee which reported in 1946, those who had already been championing the emotional needs of children — namely those involved with the Child Guidance Service — turned their attention to an apparently new phenomenon: the 'angry child'. The angry child was the product of the 'problem' family and thus the family, as the Clyde and Curtis Committees duly recognised, was central to the future of all children — those with and without families of their own.

> The lesson which above all else the war has taught us is the value of home. It is upon the family that our position as a nation is built, and it is to the family that in trouble and disaster each child naturally turns. It is the growing awareness of the importance of the family which has largely brought into prominence the problem of the homeless child. How then is the family to be re-created for the child who is rendered homeless?[75]

It was this attitude, that children in care had the same rights and needs as all other children in the community, which united all of those active in the children's services and which was encapsulated in the Children Act, 1948. In what has been hailed as a landmark piece of legislation the Children Act established new principles of child care; the hitherto hard line between children in care and children living with their parents was blurred. Local authorities were told to do all in their power to keep families together which meant that preventive measures took on considerable significance. In the wake of the evacuation experience and influenced by child guidance experts, especially the theories pertaining to maternal deprivation or the separation of the child from the mother popularised by John Bowlby and almost universally accepted by child welfare professionals, the new child care service was envisaged as 'first and foremost a service giving skilled help to parents, including problem parents, to enable them to provide a stable and happy family life for their children' thus reducing the chance of children being taken into care.[76] When parental care was absent, adoption and especially foster care — the traditional means of care in Scotland — were regarded as the most appropriate substitutes.

To most observers, then, it looked as if the new approach to child care had triumphed. The body of the child had largely been taken care of by provisions of the Education Act, 1944 which instructed local education authorities to extend the School Medical Service to cover school meals and milk, medical and dental inspection and a range of additional free services such as speech therapy and chiropody.[77] Certainly the physical condition of the child did gradually improve; the infant mortality rate in Scotland declined rapidly after the war; in Glasgow and Edinburgh average heights and weights improved year on year and childhood deaths from infectious diseases declined dramatically, although appalling housing conditions and poverty were still ever present in the cities and many rural areas of the country.[78] Nevertheless, the emotional needs of the child were in the ascendant, and the Child Guidance Service was now an accepted, indeed necessary, element of the child welfare web. The Children Act, 1948 made it a duty of local authorities to provide reception homes for the initial observation of the physical and mental condition of children taken into care and the 1944 Education Act obliged local authorities to provide

Child Guidance services.[79] In Glasgow alone from 1948 more than 3,000 children every year were referred to the Child Guidance Service for the treatment of maladjustment and emotional disturbance, a preventive measure in an attempt to check the development of delinquency.[80] However, the new child care service in Scotland was punctured by some large black holes meaning that certain groups of children did not benefit from all the attention being paid to emotional difficulties.

Forgotten Children

In 1945, in his evidence to the Clyde Committee, a leading Scottish child psychologist was outspoken in his belief that all children in the care of the local authority should be examined by a Child Guidance Clinic before placement on the grounds that 'I see a great deal of trouble arising in the personality of children who have had broken homes of one kind or another.'[81] The governors of the large children's homes had been noting for some time that the background of the children accepted into residential care had changed. The child in care had become the 'problem' child, the result of family breakdown. In 1945 Canon Wolfe of Aberlour was candid, recognising that homes such as his were being treated as a 'dumping ground for the weaker type of child, for the abnormal child, for the delinquent child.'[82] Local authorities may have used Aberlour and Quarrier's Homes — institutions with a renowned open-door policy — for the placement of so-called 'unboardable' children, 'the delinquent, the backward, the abnormal or degenerate child.'[83] A similar situation prevailed elsewhere. It was said that 'the great majority of boys' at a boys' home near Dumfries were 'the victims of neglect and sordid circumstance' which militated against their being absorbed into the local school.[84] Similarly at Quarrier's Homes according to the headmaster of the Orphan Homes of Scotland School in 1946:

> There are very few really destitute children in the country today...But there are many broken homes where either the parents have separated, or where they continue to live together in a state of armed neutrality, to the great spiritual and psychological harm of the children. There are many illegitimate and unwanted children who find their way into the Orphan homes...as a result there is now an overwhelming number of problem children in the orphanage, children who need, above all else, expert understanding and

> psychological help. They are not in a position to profit by the education provided, their minds being so occupied with their own problems of psychological adjustment.[85]

Yet it appears that a traditional, one might say outmoded, attitude initially prevailed at these voluntary institutions. Despite the acknowledgement amongst child care professionals of the strength of the bond between children and their natural parents and the recognition of Bowlby's theories, children were still not encouraged to maintain contact with their families. Neither were they encouraged to talk about their feelings and were told little, if anything, of the circumstances which led to them being taken into care. The warden of Aberlour 'had a poor opinion of psychologists and psychiatrists and would be unlikely to accept their guidance when it conflicted with his own judgement'.[86] 'I don't think there was any special attention for them...you were just in the orphanage, as I say I don't think the people were qualified anyway' recalled David speaking of children with emotional anxieties.[87] Canon Wolfe, while admitting that some children were found to have 'psychological complications', advocated sympathy, encouragement, lots of exercise and if all of that failed 'a sound spanking',[88] a view that may have found considerable sympathy outside the orphanage beyond professional child care circles. 'There is a craze for sending children to psychiatrists today, and I think it is absolutely wrong' remarked the Lord Chief Justice in 1951. 'I wish you could give some of them a jolly good hiding...'[89] In the minds of the orphanage management a disciplined and moral regime was quite appropriate training for disturbed children. According to Aberlour's Miss Wharton Duff speaking to the Clyde Committee in 1945, a home such as Aberlour 'does provide a solution for those that you will get no solution for...', and she elaborated:

> I think if you come down to practical politics, a Home such as ours is serving an excellent purpose, and, if I may say so, we provide in Aberlour Orphanage what I think is the only solution for this country — a sound religious training for children who need something as they get older to hold on to...I can give you instances of girls whom I have taken from the orphanage who, if they had not the bedrock of religious training, when they went out into the world would certainly have reverted to type.[90]

At Quarrier's Homes the strategies followed — religious and moral training — were similarly inadequate. It was impossible for teachers to deal with the problems of their pupils in this way.'The attempt to deal with such faults by giving good moral advice is no more likely to bring success than if the child were suffering from acute appendicitis' commented the headmaster of the Orphan Homes of Scotland school. 'The dead hand of the past lies too heavy on the homes.'[91] According to another long-serving teacher, Quarrier's management council had not kept pace with the times: 'Satisfying bodily needs and keeping cottages clean appears to be preferable to training minds and making citizens.'[92] Critics were unanimous: these homes needed to use the services of psychiatrists and child psychologists and some, to give them credit, did. The Scottish Home Department was happy to provide psychiatric help to institutions experiencing difficulties dealing with boisterous or undisciplined children and Glasgow's Child Guidance service accepted referrals of children lacking a normal family life.[93] Quarrier's Homes did begin to employ the services of an educational psychologist from the mid-1950s. That some refused to countenance such help was to the detriment of those children requiring support.

One way in which the damage of untreated emotional anxiety and disturbance could be measured was in terms of educational attainment. For some time there had been concern that both boarded-out children and those placed in residential care were not receiving an adequate education both because of limited educational provision and the fact that children were not in a condition to make the most of their abilities. In many residential care institutions, at least until the 1950s, children were not expected to rise out of their social class. 'There wasn't any incentive to do anything' recalled Arthur of his time at Aberlour in the 1920s. 'I don't think they wanted to devote time for education. They were all going to a farm anyway.'[94] Low expectations of children's academic abilities informed by a belief that intelligence was an inherited and therefore fixed trait, combined with a need to move children into employment and economic independence as soon as possible meant few, if any, made it to secondary school. In 1945 Quarrier's children were still removed from school at age 14 irrespective of their academic standard, and were thereafter employed for a year by the institution to carry out the domestic chores. The justification for this practice was, according to the school headmaster, that children should repay the homes with service.

> The theory is as unjustifiable morally as it is paralysing psychologically. There is no incentive for a boy or a girl in the Secondary department to put his heart into his school work if he knows that the next year or two of his life are going to be spent in unproductive drudgery…The policy of removing promising boys and girls from school in order to place them in blind alley jobs at the very time when their minds are most rapidly expanding cannot be too strongly deprecated.[95]

As boys were steered towards farm service, the merchant navy or the armed forces and girls found positions as domestic servants, chambermaids and housekeepers there seemed little need for education beyond elementary level. Inspection visits to children boarded out in remote areas found children's education frequently ceased at the elementary level due to low expectations on the part of the guardians combined with the hope that the child would begin to contribute financially to the household as soon as possible, or owing to the distance away of the nearest secondary school. Peter, boarded out in a village on the Moray Firth Coast enjoyed school and had regularly been top of the class. He sat the qualifying examination to progress to secondary school:

> but no word, nobody came to say you'd passed or you hadnae passed so we were actually back at…Ardersier public school lining up waiting to go back after the summer holidays and a teacher came out and said 'you shouldn't be here, you passed your qualifying, you should be at Inverness Royal Academy.' So I don't know whether my foster parents had been told and chose to ignore it because they didn't want me going to Inverness, it was ten mile away you know…I can only assume that was the reason for it…[96]

Peter did eventually attend Inverness Academy but did not do as well as expected. 'It was nine hours away [from a miserable and cruel foster home] but the release I think for getting away from there my schooling fell right down.'[97] Few boarded-out children appear to have been given the opportunity to pursue their own career ambitions. Betty left school on Tiree when she was 15 recalling, 'I think I would've liked to have gone on in school, I would've liked to have been a nurse…There was no money. I mean once you was 15 that was Glasgow Corporation put you out to work.'[98] Certainly the majority of children in care in the 1940s and 1950s left school as soon as possible after their fifteenth birthday. In Thomas Ferguson's study of 205 children placed in care by Glasgow local authority only 34 children attended senior secondary schools and only three continued their education until the age of 18.[99] However, some children did benefit from a more progressive policy whereby the local authority financed a training course: 'They bought all my books' remembered Frances who attended a nursing course after leaving school, 'my train fare backwards and forwards every day...they supplied all my clothes...a starting up kit really.'[100] In fact as a result of this help Frances was able to pursue her choice of career unlike the natural children of her foster parents who were more restricted in their opportunities owing to financial constraints.

Frances' experience may have been unusual. Certainly contemporaries were unanimous in the opinion that boarded-out children were 'below average intelligence' and 'backward' in terms of educational attainment. Glasgow's Director of Welfare in 1947 attributed this state of affairs to the hereditary principle, 'the fact that 90 per cent of the children were taken from neglectful parents', although it was more likely due to children having missed schooling in their early years.[101] However, one anonymous Scottish Education Department civil servant commented, 'I doubt if that fact can account for what is alleged to be the backwardness of boarded-out children as a class.'[102] The educational attainment levels of orphanage children caused even greater concern. It was widely accepted that although 'intelligence' was largely hereditary, attainment was affected by external factors, emotional difficulties being one of them. The child psychologist Dr MacCalman acknowledged that it was 'a well known fact' that children in residential care were 'backward':

> A child is not free to learn if he is inhibited emotionally. It is quite usual to find a child with a mental age of ten who has got an educational age of eight in these institutions for children, because they have not got the emotional drive or the emotional freedom to learn.[103]

This point of view was wholeheartedly endorsed by the headmaster of the Orphan Homes of Scotland School who was clearly frustrated at the failure of the management to address the difficulties experienced by many of the children. The best efforts of the teaching staff were hampered by the lack of facilities, the expectation of management that all children would complete domestic chores before and after school, the failure to attend to the development of children during the pre-school years and the social isolation of the children. It was said that very young children who had been in residential care since infancy were slow to develop and indeed invented their own language, a phenomenon also noticed amongst young institutionalised children during the war.[104] Once in school children's development was retarded by their lack of experience in the outside world as Mr Gellatly explained:

> One great difficulty the Home teacher has is setting subjects for composition. There are three or four centres of interest, the church, the school, the cottage and football. Apart from these the child's hold on the ordinary things of life which everyone takes for granted, is slender in the extreme. For instance, the very ordinary idea of a *shop* hardly ever occurs in a composition. The children rarely enter a shop, some of them perhaps never...Simple facts are taught one day and are forgotten the next because the facts are unrelated to the child's experience.[105]

The attitude of Quarrier's Homes was contrasted with the different approach adopted by Barnardo's in at least some of their homes. These were located in cities thereby combating the children's sense of isolation from the real world and not all Scottish children's homes so obdurately restricted the opportunities of those in their care. By 1945 Smyllum Orphanage could boast that children were encouraged to continue their education beyond junior secondary and a number had already successfully gained places to train as teachers, nurses and secretaries.[106] By the 1960s though, there were attempts to broaden the experience of children in the larger residential homes. Quarrier's Homes, for instance, was fortunate to benefit from the services of a music teacher who held quite progressive ideas about the therapeutic role of music for children with emotional difficulties. A child who learned to play an instrument or who sang in the choir found a means of self-expression and also often a sense of achievement and self-confidence. Many took 'O' grade music and progressed through piano examinations. Music also helped to introduce children to the world outside the orphanage; choirs from the home were entered in the Greenock festival competitions (and were successful despite the disparaging comments of some other competitors) and children attended the opera and classical concerts in Glasgow.[107]

The concerns expressed by Mr Gellatly remained however. During the 1950s, educational assessment in the form of the IQ test became popular. One such test carried out at the Orphan Homes of Scotland School on 124 children in 1950 suggested that 60 per cent of pupils could be classified 'borderline defective and dull' compared with 24 per cent in the school population in general. In one special class for 38 'backward' children the average amount of retardation in reading was 6.5 years, in spelling 6 years and arithmetic also 6 years. It was noted that 'As a result of years of failure and frustration the pupils of this class are restless and distractible.'[108] The report seemed to confirm what many — including the Scottish Council for Research in Education — had suspected for some time; that not only were institutionalised children worse off educationally than their boarded-out counterparts but that long-term residential care had a 'detrimental effect on intelligence.'[109] One report on Quarrier's Homes commented that 'many of the children there seem to become duller and their general alertness and powers of observation reduced as their stay in the home lengthens.'[110] 'It is rather a shocker', commented one civil servant on the report, 'although one knew in a general way that children in institutional homes were somewhat retarded.'[111] However, having established the unsatisfactory nature of educational provision in children's homes little was done to improve matters. Although the Scottish Council for Research in Education was asked by the Education Department to conduct an investigation into the effects of long-term residential care on educational development at the larger homes including Aberlour and Smyllum Orphanages, it was never carried out due to a lack of funding. The one positive result of the report was that selected children were to be allowed to attend a psychological clinic conducted at the homes once a week.[112] This was a small step in the right direction.

One of the reasons to account for the limited attention paid to the psychiatric needs of children in foster care and residential homes was the fact that they had not been classified as 'problem' children. Although many children within the care sector may have had emotional problems, very few had been assessed in a reception centre or Child Guidance Clinic prior to placement. The 'maladjusted' or 'delinquent' child on the other hand, was immediately identified and placed in a special school, the successors of the former reformatories and industrial schools. These institutions were established under the Children and Young Persons (Scotland) Act 1932 for the education and training of children who had already been convicted in the juvenile court or who had been identified as pre-delinquent or beyond parental control.[113] Although the disciplinary regime in these institutions was far stricter than in most children's homes, at least by the post-Second World War period there was a recognition that some of the children would benefit from psychiatric treatment by a trained child psychiatrist.[114] There was little point in releasing delinquent or potentially delinquent children back into the community if their fundamental difficulties had not been resolved or treated. Statistics repeatedly showed that convictions amongst former reformatory and industrial school residents were higher than amongst the general population.[115] By the 1950s all Scottish Approved schools (List 'D' schools) made use of outside clinics although there existed no uniform system of recognition and treatment for the 'less seriously maladjusted', demonstrating the need for a classifying and guidance centre for the assessment of children prior to placement and continuous treatment thereafter.[116]

Anecdotal evidence points to the long term harm inflicted on some young people who were ill-equipped for life after care. A far from unbiased observer made the point in 1945 that boarded-out children, especially those found homes in remote rural areas, were no better prepared for life than their counterparts in residential care. 'They have to sink or swim unaided, and they generally sink back to the slums and become the flotsam and jetsam of humanity.'[117] Those who had been boarded out on the islands were often forced to return to the mainland to find work at the age of 15 or 16, leaving behind the only family they had ever known. One foster parent remembered, 'They had to leave at 15. Well there was no work for them: they had just left school. They had to go away...After that they didn't do so well, despite everything.'[118] One girl who had spent most of her childhood on Tiree was removed from her foster home by Glasgow Corporation and sent back to the city. 'They told us we were going to be sent to be trained and to work. Anyway, that wasn't how it happened. They sent us to a Salvation Army Home.' The support of her foster family helped her through this time and she eventually returned to the island to work on the croft.[119] David, whose years at Aberlour coincided with the time when that home was said to have contained a high proportion of children with severe difficulties, commented:

> A lot of them went to prison of course…They all strayed off the path I think. I think it's to do with your upbringing, having no mother…it must have been harder for older boys coming in to it. I think it sort of imbalances them some way along the way, because they came out of the orphanage and they more or less go on the street…they just make their own way, probably no advice, no sense or whatever. I've heard a lot of them are in prison.[120]

Thomas Ferguson's findings prompted him to comment that 'it would indeed have been surprising if more than a fair share…had not contrived to run foul of the law.'[121] In fact 32 per cent of the boys in his study of the Glasgow care system were convicted in the courts before the age of 20, the majority for theft, significantly higher than the 16 per cent conviction rate amongst boys attending ordinary schools.[122]

By the early 1960s — more than 30 years after the establishment of child guidance clinics in Scotland — there was greater social and professional acceptance of the value of child guidance work. Emotional disturbance in children was taken seriously and regarded as a legitimate reason for children's failure to achieve in school or to attain satisfactory social adjustment. In 1961 the Glasgow Child Guidance Service operated four main clinics and another eleven district clinics, mostly serving the new housing estates on Glasgow's periphery.[123] More than 5,000 cases — around 3,000 of them boys — had been seen in 1961–2 by a team of 41 consisting chiefly of psychologists and speech therapists, compared with just 245 cases in 1937–8. By far the most common symptom prompting referral was bed-wetting but a wide range of symptoms were treated from asthma and constipation, tics and spasms, shyness and food difficulties to temper and unruliness, viciousness, theft, truancy and sex offenses.[124] Indeed, it was noted that certain so-called 'reactive' symptoms — such as aggression, attention seeking, theft and so on — had seen a significant increase prompting the principal psychologist to dub the 1960s as 'the age of the angry child'.[125] Yet by the early 1970s the remit of the service had expanded to take on board remedial teaching and help for children with specific reading disabilities and the number of such cases soon overtook those defined as emotional or behavioural.[126] However, despite the range of emotional and behavioural difficulties tackled by the child guidance clinics, there is still no evidence that children in care who required it were provided with any special help. The majority of referrals were made by schools, including a small number by Approved Schools, and parents although some children in the care of the local authority may have been referred prior to placement.

It took until the 1960s then for the child welfare service to complete a fundamental idealogical shft. Concern with the body or physicality of the child receded or at least was allayed as a new understanding of childhood developed which placed greater emphasis on the mind and the relationship between environment and emotional stability or distress. By the post-Second World War era it was no longer adequate to simply provide for the homeless child in a material and physical way; rather the child deprived of a normal home life required what George Bernard Shaw called 'maternal massage'.[127] The new psychologists pioneered this approach and their work was given a boost by the popular reaction to wartime evacuation. The war had demonstrated in Scotland, as elsewhere in the British Isles, that while children separated from their parents and placed with a caring foster family suffered little serious emotional disturbance, those who had been cared for in wartime nurseries and residential institutions suffered considerable psychological trauma. The Clyde Committee and subsequent legislation accepted the need for attention to be paid to children's psychological well-being which augured well for childen in care. Yet there is irony in the fact that although Scotland pioneered the child guidance clinic she then failed to apply the understanding of children's emotional development to the most vulnerable children in the community, those in care. The management of Scotland's largest voluntary children's homes refused to acknowledge their children could be helped by professionals and stubbornly stood by the tried and tested disciplinary regimes. Major advances in the understanding of the child's needs which had benefited children in mainstream society passed by those in care. At the same time other children, notably those classified as 'problem' children or 'potential delinquents' were referred to child guidance specialists in an attempt to readjust such children to society.

One of the unforeseen consequences of the post-war emphasis on the 'problem' or 'angry' child was the renewed definition of children as potential threats. Children who were not re-adjusted, whose emotional difficulties were not diagnosed and treated, were in danger of progressing to full-blown delinquency and rendered less capable of constructing stable families of their own. However, so much effort was expended on restoring or shoring up families, avoiding the separation of children from parents, or else placing children with substitute foster parents that the rights and needs of children in residential care were, to some extent, sidelined. But in these circumstances children could still be victims, not at the hands of neglectful parents or as the result of poverty but in the hands of those entrusted with their care. The discovery of widespread physical and sexual abuse of children in residential care is a reminder that both the bodies and minds of homeless children require sensitivity, sympathy and 'maternal massage'.

NOTES

1. SRO, GD 409/5/1: SNSPCC Annual Report, 1886, p.10.
2. Interview with Christine.
3. Interview with Annie.
4. Haynes, *Haste Ye Back*, p.77.
5. Hannah NicAsgaill (South Uist foster parent), *Air Fasdadh*.
6. A very moving example of this was recounted on *Barnardo's Children*, BBC 1, broadcast 12 and 14 August 1997.
7. Aonghas MacCulmhein, *Air Fasdadh*,
8. Mackenzie, *Scottish Mothers and Children*, p.238.
9. See G.Keir, 'A History of Child Guidance', *British Journal of Educational Psychology*, 22 (1952), p.8.
10. The socialist Margaret McMillan was one of the pioneers who grounded her work on child education in the 1890s in a belief that the child's mind was a creation of the body. She accepted the idea of the unconscious human mind following European thought and, although accepting that the bodies of working-class children had to be cured before attending to the mind she advocated the stimulus of the child's senses through free and imaginative play. 'The point of an ameliorative educational system was to provide the body with food

and the mind with impressions, so that a rich mental life could be created within a formerly stagnant body.' See C.Steedman, *Childhood, Culture and Class in Britain: Margaret McMillan 1860–1931* (London, 1990), p.208.

11. Keir, 'A History of Child Guidance', p.10.
12. See D.R.MacCalman, 'The General Management of Maladjustment in Children' in R.G.Gordon (ed), *A Survey of Child Psychiatry* (London, 1939), pp.257–8.
13. SRO, ED 15/137: Provisional National Council for Mental Health, 'The care of Children brought up away from their own Homes.' October 1944.
14. O.Sampson, *Child Guidance: its History, Provenance and Future* (Manchester, 1980), p.8.
15. Sister Jude (Maureen McAleer), *Freedom to Grow: Sister Marie Hilda's Vision of Child Guidance* (Glasgow, 1981), p.30.
16. *Ibid*, p.43.
17. See *Rediscovery of the Family and Other Lectures: Sister Marie Hilda Memorial Lectures 1945–73* (Aberdeen, 1981).
18. See C.M.McCallum, 'Child Guidance in Scotland', British Journal of Educational Psychology, 22 (1952), pp.79–88.
19. Sampson, *Child Guidance*, p.48. It has been estimated that in England between 3,000 and 4,000 children a year were seen by all the clinics put together in the late 1930s; D.Thom, 'Wishes, Anxieties, Play, and Gestures: Child Guidance in Inter-War England', in R.Cooter (ed), *In the Name of the Child* (London, 1992), p.215.
20. By 1952 only one Highland county — Ross and Cromarty — had appointed an educational psychologist.
21. McCallum, 'Child Guidance in Scotland', pp.80–3. Child psychiatric services were offered by three other clinics, the Edinburgh Sick Children's Hospital, the Notre Dame Child Guidance Clinic in Glasgow and the Child Psychiatric Clinic in Kirkcaldy.
22. Cited in Sampson, *Child Guidance*, p.53.
23. One psychologist noted, 'the unusual conditions of the war have provided a kind of unplanned experiment on the influence of certain changes on the early development of young children.' E.M.John, 'A Study of the Effects of Evacuation and Air Raids on Children of Pre-School Age', *British Journal of Educational Psychology*, XI (1941), p.174.
24. Another 1.5 million persons, including more than 800,000 school children were evacuated in an identical process in England and Wales. See J.Macnicol, 'The Evacuation of Schoolchildren', in H.L.Smith (ed), *War and Social Change* (London, 1986), pp.3-31.
25. Edinburgh evacuees were scattered all over the eastern side of the country; Rosyth evacuees were concentrated in Fife, those from Clydebank were received in Argyll and Dumbarton, Dundee evacuees were found billets in Angus and Kincardine, and Glasgow evacuees were sent to places between Aberdeen and Dumfries.

26. *The Scotsman*, 2 September 1939.
27. W.Boyd (ed), *Evacuation in Scotland: A Record of Events and Experiments*, (London, 1944), p.39.
28. *Ibid.*, p.39.
29. *Ibid.*, p.56.
30. *Ibid.*, p.57.
31. Mr Donald McKechnie cited in *Evacuation: A Collection of Sources* (Strathclyde Museum Education Service), pp.93–4.
32. See House of Commons Debates, 5th series, Vol.351, 14 September 1939; records of the Billeting Officer, Inverary cited in *Evacuation: A Collection of Sources*, pp.6–7.
33. *The Campbeltown Courier*, 9 September 1939, cited in *Evacuation: A Collection of Sources*, p.30.
34. Macnicol, 'The Evacuation of Schoolchildren', p.13.
35. Boyd, *Evacuation*, p.60.
36. In fact despite reports that 100 per cent were unclean, an examination of adults and children in Stirling showed that only 11 % of the children were infected with vermin, 11% with septic sores and just 1.5% with scabies although 19% were found to have dirty clothing. Boyd, *Evacuation*, pp.62–3.
37. SRO, ED 24/7: Memorandum to the Secretary of State for Scotland from the Convention of the Royal Burghs of Scotland, 21 May 1940.
38. SRO, ED 24/7: Advisory Committee on Evacuation, Minutes of 10th Meeting, 22 September 1939.
39. See, for example, the letters from Rothesay in *Evacuation: A Collection of Sources*, pp.33–5.
40. *The Scotsman*, 12 September 1939.
41. Cited in C.Burt, 'The Incidence of Neurotic Symptoms among Evacuated School Children', *British Journal of Educational Psychology*, X:1 (1940), p.10.
42. Burt, 'The Incidence of Neurotic Symptoms', p.12.
43. *Ibid*, p.9.
44. W.Boyd, 'The Effects of Evacuation on the Children', *British Journal of Educational Psychology*, XI (1941), pp.120–6. Bed-wetting was usually a temporary reaction to excitement, nervousness and 'the cold of country houses'; Boyd, *Evacuation*, pp.65–6.
45. In the Cambridge survey only 25 or 8 per cent of 304 children surveyed seemed to have developed an unsatisfactory relationship with their carers although the results may have been skewed by only surveying those children who stayed in Cambridge. A.Straker and R.H.Thouless, 'Preliminary Results of Cambridge Survey of Evacuated Children', *British Journal of Educational Psychology*, X (1940), p.99. Similarly a London study found just 17 out of 100 cases of unsatisfactory relationships between children and foster parents. M.A.Davidson and I.M.Slade, 'Results of a Survey of Senior School Evacuees', *British Journal of Educational Psychology*, X (1940),

p.187. See also John, 'A Study of the Effects of Evacuation and Air Raids', p.175.

46. Boyd, *Evacuation*, p.84 and 116. He also notes that Catholic families were less willing to allow their children to be evacuated in the first place.

47. *The Campeltown Courier*, 30 September 1939 in *Evacuation: A Collection of Sources*, p.67.

48. Interview with Mr Angus MacVicar in *Evacuation: A Collection of Sources*, p.91. Boyd also notes that town dwellers were bored with the country; they missed their friends and neighbours and city amusements. Boyd, *Evacuation*, p.71.

49. Boyd, *Evacuation*, p.30 and p.120.

50. Boyd notes that the number of serious cases was very small but does comment on the higher degree of incompatibility — on grounds of social class, language and religion which caused the breakdown of billeting arrangements; *Evacuation*, pp.67–8.

51. Robin Jenkins, *Guests of War* (Edinburgh, 1997).

52. SRO, ED 11/267: Ayr Social Welfare Committee, evidence to Clyde Committee, 5 July 1945. There were other reasons to account for this however; greater prosperity in the postwar years meant taking in a child was no longer a financial necessity but cultural attitudes also played a part.

53. John, 'A Study of the Effects of Evacuation', p.175.

54. Burlingham and Freud, *Infants without Families* (London, 1944).

55. 196 children were admitted between 1940 and 1943 suffering from a range of neuroses. Catherine McCallum, 'Nerston Residential Clinic' in Boyd, *Evacuation*, p.189.

56. It was discovered that 'provided the adults remain calm the children are not emotionally disturbed to any great extent.' McCallum, 'Nerston Residential Clinic' in Boyd, *Evacuation*, pp.182 and 186.

57. McCallum, 'Nerston Residential Clinic', p.189.

58. *The Times*, 15 July 1944.

59. SRO, ED 11/155: Committee on Homeless Children, 11 June 1945.

60. *Third Statistical Account: Glasgow*, p.59.

61. For a detailed analysis of these changes see M.Anderson, 'Population and Family Life' in A.Dickson & J.H.Treble (eds.), *People and Society in Scotland, Vol.III, 1914–1990* (Edinburgh, 1992), pp.12–47.

62. A.McIvor, 'Women and Work in Twentieth Century Scotland', p.139.

63. *Ibid.*, p.142.

64. *Third Statistical Account: Glasgow*, p.449.

65. This figure is based upon a calculation multiplying the number of applicants for municipal housing accommodated between 1945 and 1955 (51,879) by average family size (5).

66. J.Butt, 'Working Class Housing in the Scottish Cities 1900–1950' in G.Gordon and B.Dicks (eds.), *Scottish Urban History* (Aberdeen, 1983), p.260.

67. *Third Statistical Account: Glasgow*, pp.873–4.

68. Kirkintilloch W.E.A. Retirement Class, *Two Communities: Springburn and Kirkintilloch. A Chronicle of Glasgow Overspill* (1983), p.30.

69. Henderson, *Finding Peggy*.

70. *Two Communities: Springburn and Kirkintilloch*, p.32.

71. Jean Faley, *Up Oor Close: Memories of Domestic Life in Glasgow Tenements, 1910–1945* (Oxon, 1991), p.166.

72. *Ibid.*, p.169.

73. *Ibid.*, p.171.

74. *Third Statistical Account: Glasgow*, p.766.

75. *B.P.P., Report of the Committee on Homeless Children (Scotland)*, 1946, Cmd.6911, p.14.

76. Hendrick, *Child Welfare*, p.219.

77. *Ibid.*, pp.200–2.

78. *Third Statistical Account: Glasgow*, p. 509 and p.896; D.Keir, *The Third Statistical Account for Scotland: The City of Edinburgh* (Glasgow, 1966), p.358.

79. Stroud, *An Introduction to the Child Care Service*, pp.132–5. Glasgow Corporation did operate a reception centre which worked closely with the child guidance service; SRO, ED 11/294: Notes of discussion with Glasgow Director of Welfare, 20 December 1947.

80. *Third Statistical Account: Glasgow*, p.668.

81. SRO, ED 11/266: Dr D.R.MacCalman evidence to Clyde Committee, 1945.

82. SRO, ED 11/266: Evidence of Canon Wolfe and Miss Wharton Duff to Clyde Committee, 1945.

83. See Haynes, *Haste ye Back*, p.179 and *Aberlour Orphanage Magazine* Vol.LXX, Jan–Feb 1951.

84. SRO, ED 11/154: Letter from headmaster, Noblehill School Dumfries to Clyde Committee, 19 June 1945.

85. SRO, ED 11/161: Mr C.H.Galletly to Clyde Committee, 15 January 1946.

86. SRO, ED 11/443: Aberlour Orphanage Annual Returns, Minute of 24 December 1948.

87. Interview with David.

88. *Aberlour Orphanage Magazine*, Vol.LXX, Jan–Feb 1951.

89. SRO, ED 15/137: *The Scotsman*, 23 April 1951.

90. SRO, ED 11/266: Evidence of Canon Wolfe and Miss Wharton Duff to Clyde Committee, 1945.

91. SRO, ED 11/161: Mr C.H.Galletly to Clyde Committee, 1946.

92. SRO, ED 11/269: Headmaster of Orphan Homes of Scotland School to Clyde Committee, 1945.

93. SRO, ED 11/155: Miss H.R.Harrison, Scottish Home Department, evidence to Clyde Committee, 1945; *Third Statistical Account: Glasgow*, p.702.

94. Interview with Arthur.

95. SRO, ED 11/269: Mr Gellatly to Clyde Committee, 1945. Aberlour Orphanage operated an identical policy.
96. Interview with Peter.
97. *Ibid.*
98. Interview with Betty.
99. T.Ferguson, *Children in Care and After* (London, 1966), p.59.
100. Interview with Frances.
101. SRO, ED 11/294: Inspection of boarded-out children. Notes of discussion with Mr Ford, 20 December 1947.
102. SRO, ED 11/294: Minute of 5 December 1947.
103. SRO, ED 11/266: Dr D.R.MacCalman to Clyde Committee, 1945.
104. This observation has subsequently been confirmed by independent studies. See, for example, B.Tizard and A.Joseph, 'Cognitive Development of Young Children in Residential Care', *Journal of Child Psychology and Psychiatry*, 11 (1970). For a discussion of research on social retardation in residential care see R.Dinnage and M.L.Kellmer Pringle, *Residential Child Care: Facts and Fallacies* (London, 1967), pp.8–18.
105. SRO, ED 11/161: Mr Gellatly to Clyde Committee, 15 January 1946.
106. SRO, ED 11/158: Questionnaire completed by Smyllum Orphanage, 1945.
107. Conversation with former music teacher at Quarrier's Homes.
108. SRO, ED 11/288: Psychological tests of children in Voluntary Homes, 1950–54.
109. *Ibid.*
110. SRO, ED 11/288: Memorandum from W.N.Smith, 19 February 1951.
111. SRO, ED 11/161: Minute of 19 March 1951.
112. SRO, ED 11/288: unidentified newspaper cutting, 31 January 1952.
113. See Collin, 'The Treatment of Delinquent and Potentially Delinquent Children', especially chapter 4.
114. By the 1960s it was commonly accepted that psychiatrists with no experience with children could do more harm than good. 'A psychiatrist with a mental hospital background might be as useful with non-psychotic adolescents as the average Maths specialist if asked to teach Greek' commented one HMI in 1961. SRO, ED 15/167: Memo from HMI McPherson, 12 July 1961.
115. Collin, 'Treatment of Delinquent Children', pp.298–302.
116. SRO, ED 15/137: Scottish Advisory Council for the Treatment and Rehabilitation of Offenders; statement on provision of treatment for maladjusted children, January 1949; Report on Approved Schools, 1951.
117. SRO, ED 11/266: Evidence of Governor of Dumbarton Townend Hospital to Clyde Committee, 1945.
118. Hannah NicAsgaill (South Uist), *Air Fasdadh*.
119. Sine NicCaluim (Tiree), *Air Fasdadh*.
120. Interview with David.

121. Ferguson, *Children in Care and After*, p.115.
122. *Ibid.*, p.134.
123. GCA, D-ED 9/1/16/1: *Report on the Child Guidance Service*, 1961–62.
124. *Ibid.*
125. GCA, D-ED 9/1/16/2: *Report on the Child Guidance Service* 1964–5.
126. GCA, D ED 9/1/16/3: *Report on the Child Guidance Service*, 1970–71.
127. *The Times*, 21 July 1944.

CHAPTER 6
THE CHILD IN DANGER

Fortunately, Scotland, as in most matters connected to the education and welfare of children, is much in advance of England, and there is little reason to fear that such things as have been called attention to in England could happen on this side of the border.

— *Glasgow Herald*, 7 March 1945.

A Shocking Case of Cruelty

This pious claim to Scottish superiority in child welfare dates from 1945, shortly after the conviction and sentencing of English foster parents for the neglect and manslaughter of a child placed in their care by Newport local authority. Less than a year later newspaper editors were forced to eat their words as the Walton case hit the headlines. In July 1945 John and Margaret Walton from Dysart in Fife appeared in the High Court in Dundee charged with ill-treatment towards the two boarded-out boys in their care, Norman and Harry Wilson aged 12 and 10 years. The indictment against the couple alleged that:

> they wilfully assaulted and ill-treated them in such a manner likely to cause them unnecessary suffering and injury to their health. They were also charged with having beaten and thrashed them with a wooden spoon or spurtle or similar instrument, and with a cane and electric cable, knocked them to the ground and kicked them, pulled their lips with a pair of pliers, tied Harry Wilson to a chair and thrashed him with an electric cable and cane, placed him on the crossbar of a pulley, raised him to the ceiling and caused him to fall from the crossbar to the ground, tied him to the seat of a lavatory, placed his feet against a wringer and frightened him by placing him in a dark cupboard contrary to the Children and Young Persons (Scotland) Act 1937, Section 12.[1]

The condition of the two young boys shocked all those who came into contact with the case. Harry's headmaster, upon seeing the young lad's body, commented that 'it would have been impossible to put a two-shilling piece on a white part of his body so badly discoloured was it',[2] an opinion graphically confirmed by the local doctor:

198

This boy, small for his age, was crying and in a state of great fear. He was trembling from head to foot and obviously suffering from shock. He was on the verge of collapse. He looked as if he had been badly beaten about the face and head...Examination of the body when stripped of clothing revealed a ghastly state of affairs. The trunk was a mass of weals and bruises...

'I am of the opinion' stated the doctor in unequivocal terms, 'that this boy has been grossly maltreated and that he will take years to fully recover from the injuries and mental shock resulting from these injuries.'[3] It was by far the worst case seen by the RSSPCC inspector in his 28 years experience of child welfare work.[4] John and Margaret Walton were found guilty of wilful assault and ill-treatment of Harry Wilson and received prison sentences of just nine and twelve months respectively.

Despite the obvious cruelty meted out to the boys in the Walton case, attributions of innocence and guilt were more complex than one might have expected. Until the late twentieth century, cases of child abuse rarely reached the public domain. A few cases like that of the Waltons hit the headlines in the late 1940s but there was so little public or judicial comprehension of the very existence of abuse that it became the practice to place at least some of the blame on the children. Norman and Harry Wilson were described as 'difficult'.[5] They had spent some time in a remand home before being boarded out, the implication being that these two lads were unmanageable and implicitly deserving a good hiding now and again, a point used to some effect by the Waltons' defence. The court heard that the boys had been 'running around wild' and stealing before being placed in care and defence witnesses accused the boys of dishonesty.[6] The boys' foster mother, on the other hand, was said to be 'very fond of children' and tried to pin the blame for Harry's condition on his brother.[7] This discourse on childhood culpability had also been in evidence a few months earlier south of the border during the trial of another couple, Reginald and Esther Gough, following the death of one of two brothers boarded out with the couple in Shropshire. Although incontrovertible evidence proved that thirteen-year-old Dennis O'Neill died from acute cardiac failure after being beaten on the chest and back while in a state of under-nourishment, attempts were made in court to portray the boy and his ten-year-old brother Terence, who was cross-examined for two hours until he burst into tears, as disobedient, unruly boys who were capable of barbarous cruelty to the animals on the Goughs' farm.[8] These boys, like Norman and Harry Wilson, were no angels; none of them had had a very fortunate childhood, but in the words of the prosecution at the Gough trial, 'No possible naughtiness on the part of the child could excuse a person beating him with a stick until the blood comes.'[9] Lord Russell, sentencing John and Margaret Walton reiterated this sentiment, condemning the attempt of the defence counsel to plead the case of the accused on the grounds of provocation. 'It would be a sorry day for this country if assault upon and ill-treatment of young persons could be justified on the ground that they were provoking and had been guilty of petty pilfering. Provocation could never justify cruelty to a child.'[10] The care of children, he continued, was an issue 'close to the public conscience'.

The war and its consequences, the scandal of residential care highlighted by Lady Allen, and then the Gough case, had all pushed child welfare to the front of the political and social agenda. The Walton case raised the profile of the issue in Scotland and led the judge to condemn John and Margaret Walton who had failed the test of a caring post-war society:

> it is obvious that the charges of which you have been convicted show that there was a callous and cruel lack of the elementary humanitarian feelings which ought to be in the breasts of everyone who comes into contact with children, however difficult, unruly and problematic they may be.[11]

The press attention paid to these two cases provoked a public debate unheard of before in England and in Scotland.[12] The judge in the Gough case told Reginald Gough that his behaviour had 'shocked the world.'[13] According to one observer:

> This case has awakened a healthy anger in the public, but it is a tragic commentary on our social organisation that before the public interest could be effectively aroused on behalf of the hundred thousand children in the care of the State or of Charitable Institutions, this helpless child had to lie in a dark, cold room, sick and bruised, crying out in pain, and with no-one in the world to whom he could turn for help in those last terrible moments of his life…[14]

These comments were acutely observed. Even a cursory survey of the press and government papers highlights the relative absence of child abuse in public consciousness throughout much of the nineteenth and twentieth centuries. Indeed, with the exception of two brief periods of concern, from the 1880s to the outbreak of World War One, and from 1945 to 1948, child abuse — physical, emotional or sexual — was absent from view until the 1970s when the public inquiry into the death of Maria Colwell at the hands of her step-father unleashed a groundswell of official and popular interest in the treatment of children. Thereafter, a succession of high profile and controversial cases of alleged mass child abuse in Rochdale, Cleveland, Orkney, Ayrshire and North Wales exposed the vulnerability of children in modern society. Hardly a week goes by in the 1990s without child abuse in the news headlines, ranging from parental neglect or cruelty to physical or sexual abuse in children's homes and the threat to children from paedophiles in the community. In fact, public awareness of the potential or actual threat to children from adults has probably never been greater. Society's tolerance of the physical mistreatment of children is now much lower, and there are many more safeguards in place to protect children, especially those in care, from harm. The risk to children from external threats, however, is perceived to be greater than ever. Ever since the Moors murders in the late 1960s, parents have had cause for panic. More recently the shooting of 16 primary school children in Dunblane in 1996 and the murder of a young boy in Aberdeen by a paedophile in 1997 have given rise to the widespread perception that the state is not fulfilling its obligations to protect children. As a result, parents are taking direct action. In working-class neighbourhoods they are taking to the streets to hound out paedophiles.[15] The middle classes simply permit their children far less freedom by escorting them to school and accompanying them to the playpark.[16] In the 1990s it is perceived that children are more at risk from harm than they were 100 years earlier.

The acid test for any humane society is whether it is able to ensure the safety of its most vulnerable members. Children believed or found to be at risk of mistreatment or neglect at the hands of their carers are entitled to protection. Since the late nineteenth century the state has attempted to provide this protection, combining support for the birth family with the ultimate safeguard, the removal of the child to a place of safety. Yet, despite all the safeguards, children were still abused, in their own homes and in places of safety. And despite all the statements to the contrary, the Scottish record appears to be no better than anywhere else.

The issue of child abuse forces the historian to tread carefully. Cruelty towards children arouses strong emotions and may prompt hasty judgements of individuals and organisations. It is all too simple from our late twentieth century viewpoint to condemn those in the past who treated children with less respect than would be acceptable today. Such present-mindedness contributes little to any fair understanding of child care practices in the past. While child abuse is a constant in history, it does not occur in a moral vacuum but is constructed and informed by any number of cultural beliefs and practices. The changing attitude towards corporal punishment of children is an example of how the treatment of children must be understood within a broader context. The physical chastisement of a child by a parent or schoolteacher was widely seen as acceptable within rather undefined limits until very recently, A survey in 1977 found the tawse was used on 10,000 occasions in Edinburgh schools in one term alone.[17] Yet, by the early 1980s institutional violence against children was coming under increasing attack from parents, children, teachers and not least from the European Court of Human Rights which eventually shocked the government into its abolition in state schools in 1986. Many of those who suffered abuse as children only come to a realisation of the unacceptable nature of their treatment in adulthood in the light of more modern standards of child care. Recalling the actions of a children's home housemaster one respondent told me that 'at the time I didn't think it was abuse but then thinking about it now I suppose it was abuse...'[18]

As this man's testimony highlights, the concept of child abuse is a fairly modern phenomenon which has only found its way into everyday usage in the last 30 years or so. The concept was originally used to refer to a more specific form of physical mistreatment, what came to be called 'battered baby syndrome' in the 1960s; but it appears that the term entered public consciousness in the early 1970s particularly following the events surrounding the death of Maria Colwell in 1973.[19] Since then, abuse has become a generic term encompassing a wide range of emotional, physical and especially sexual mistreatment of children. Although legal definitions of child neglect and cruelty are always fairly rigid, the concept of child abuse has always been fluid.

Research into the history of child abuse is hampered by the silence of the victims and the opaqueness of the sources. With the exception of the testimony of some brave individuals who have spoken of the cruelty they suffered in the past at the hands of the adults entrusted with their care, we are mostly reliant upon official reports and materials produced by adults. The words of children are rarely heard and just as rarely believed. The cross-examination of Norman Wilson and Terence O'Neill in their respective court cases in an attempt to undermine their statements despite incontrovertible medical evidence, demonstrates a privileging of adult testimony. Harry Wilson was accused of lying and making up stories. Yet, witnesses attested that his physical condition had been so poor he had been unable to sleep owing to the pain in his head and unable to dress himself because his hands were too swollen.[20] The issue of adult versus child testimony is an issue still unresolved in cases of physical and sexual abuse today. Although significant steps have been made to listen to children more, their voices are still not always believed.

The Discovery of Child Abuse

The history of child abuse has conventionally been written with the children left out. It is a history of the state's recognition of abuse and its attempts to legislate to protect the victims and punish the perpetrators. The history of child abuse, then, is essentially a history of public awareness of the phenomenon focusing on two distinct periods. The first period coincides with the founding of the NSPCC in England and the SNSPCC in Scotland in the 1880s and the legislative barrage between the 1889 Prevention of Cruelty to Children Act and the 1908 Children Act. The second period commences with the discovery of battered baby syndrome in the 1960s and has proceeded with little respite until the 1990s, encompassing physical cruelty but more specifically focusing on sexual abuse. But cruelty was not absent before the SNSPCC rooted it out and did not stop in the intervening period; to paraphrase Harry Hendrick writing about England, 'abusing' adults are ever present.[21] Neglected, mistreated and abused children are ever present too. Although the public gaze was turned away from the plight of children for much of the twentieth century, abuse in all its forms continued to be experienced by children within their own families and within the child care system in Scotland. Parents continued to be prosecuted, families split up and children placed in care.

The formation of branches of the Society for the Prevention of Cruelty to Children in Glasgow and Edinburgh in 1884 helped to focus attention in Scotland on the plight of neglected and mistreated children in general. The Scottish National Society (SNSPCC) as it became in 1889 (it changed its name to the Royal Scottish Society or RSSPCC in 1922) quickly established itself as the key agency responsible for the surveillance of families and the enforcement of child protection legislation.[22] Indeed in 1913 the Local Government Board for Scotland admitted that but for the SNSPCC 'we have some reason to think that, in Scotland at least, these clauses [of the Children Act 1908 dealing with offences against children] would be practically inoperative.'[23] By 1900 local committees had been established the length and breadth of Scotland, from Inverness to Wigtownshire; the Society's power over the community was immense.[24] The figures speak for themselves. On the eve of the First World War, across the whole of Scotland almost 130,000 complaints had been dealt with in 30 years, affecting around 360,000 children, more than 10,000 Scottish children per year. More than 10,000 persons had been convicted and 24,000 children had been removed from their homes and placed in industrial schools, children's homes and poorhouses.[25] After the wartime slump in the Society's activities, investigations soon picked up again and as Figure 6.1 shows, the number of complaints followed up averaged almost 7,500 each year.[26]

The problem appeared to be growing. In fact quantitative assessments of the extent of cruelty to children only provide a mere indication of the effectiveness of surveillance, investigations and prosecutions, not of abuse itself. The gradual expansion of the SNSPCC's activities ensured that the number of cases investigated would inevitably increase. The Society's inspectors were vigorous in rooting out neglect, acting on tip-offs from neighbours and initiating visits to 'problem' families. The targetting of working-class areas where neglect was easier to find inflated the figures. The neglect, mistreatment and abuse had always been there; the Society just provided the impetus for the expression of public concern about the treatment of children in society in general. In 1908, for example, the Edinburgh Committee of the Society not only made around 200 visits to families each week

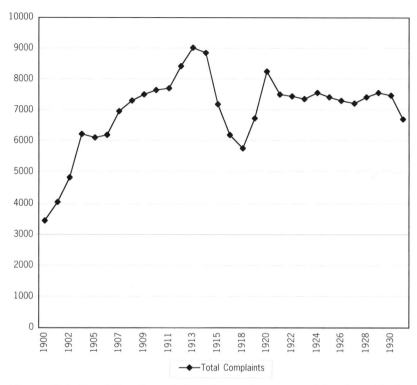

Figure 6.1. Total Number of Complaints Investigated by the RSSPCC, Scotland 1900–1941
Source: GCU, RSSPCC Archive: Annual Reports, 1900–1941.

but also acted in response to public concern about babies attached in their cradles to barrel organs, the condition of children in the Senegal village at the Edinburgh exhibition and the clothing of Somali children in the Marine Gardens.[27]

'The cruelty', as the Society's officers were commonly known, were both respected and feared. They possessed the powers to protect children but also to remove them from their homes despite the Society's avowed intention not to 'relieve parents of their responsibilities' but to impress and enforce responsibility upon parents.[28] In the words of the Glasgow Society, 'Parents who show a desire to do what is right are encouraged to persevere, and those who are lax and not making proper supervision are warned and made to feel that matters cannot continue without some improvement being shown.'[29] This attention to parental responsibility is reflected in the nature of the cases the Society

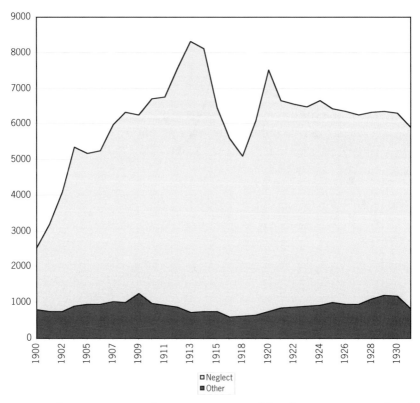

9000

8000

7000

6000

5000

4000

3000

2000

1000

0

1900 1902 1905 1907 1909 1911 1913 1915 1918 1920 1922 1924 1926 1928 1930

□ Neglect
■ Other

Figure 6.2. Categories of Cases Investigated by the RSSPCC, Scotland 1900–1941

Note: Other reasons includes, ill-treatment, abandonment, exposure, begging, singing and selling, indecent assault, immoral surroundings and other wrongs.

Source: GCU, RSSPCC Archive: Annual Reports, 1900–1941.

undertook to investigate throughout a century of child protection work. Cases defined as neglect and starvation consistently dominated officers' case loads. In 1900, at the peak of public concern about child welfare, the Society's officers investigated 3,449 complaints across Scotland involving over 9,000 children and more than 4,000 offenders. Of these 2,535, or 76 per cent, were identified as cases of neglect and starvation, 101 as ill-treatment or assault and more than 400 were cases involving children begging, selling and singing on the streets.[30] As Figure 6.2 shows, this was a trend that was to continue through the Depression up until the Second World War and beyond.

The nature of the Society's work and especially the increasing acceptance of intervention in the family was influenced by the broadening of definitions of neglect, cruelty and abuse in a series of legislative impulses which permitted the Society a wider remit. In Scotland, under Scottish common law, 'the wilful and culpable neglect of a child...or cruel treatment' was already a crime punishable by imprisonment, but the Prevention of Cruelty to and Protection of Children Act, 1889 — dubbed the Children's Charter — gave child cruelty a higher public profile.[31] Subsequent legislation spelled out responsibilities of parents more clearly and established the principle that neglect need not be intentional for a prosecution to be brought. The Children Act, 1908, consolidated all previous legislation and in addition criminalised incest. Successive legislation widened the definition of cruelty to include neglect, a development that inevitably resulted in a rise in the number of complaints to and prosecutions by the SNSPCC. Neglect was a more widespread problem; more often than not it was a consequence of poverty, easier to detect than cruelty and superficially easier to deal with.

The legislative momentum from the 1880s up to the Second World War progressively emphasised the independent rights of the child to be protected from neglect, ill-treatment and cruelty, and to be safeguarded by the state. The inevitable consequence of this approach to child protection — despite the protestations of the SNSPCC — was the downgrading of the birth family and an emphasis on the rehabilitation of the child in an alternative environment. In the wake of wartime experience and the Clyde and Curtis Reports of 1946, the 1948 Children Act reflected a new ethos in child protection policy which, through the 1950s and 1960s, focused upon family-oriented support work and the improvement of conditions in care.[32] Local authorities were required to 'make use of facilities and services available to children in the care of their parents.'[33] They were urged to coordinate child protection services in order that all possible assistance from statutory services was made available to support families.[34] Preventive work was now in the ascendant; the natural family was to be given help and encouragement in order to fulfil the requirements of parental responsibility. Notwithstanding a period in the 1960s when concern about juvenile delinquency dominated the child welfare agenda, the dominant trend in the late twentieth century has been to support the family.

'A Nation's Peril'. Children rescued by the NSPCC, c. *1907. The NSPCC and the SNSPCC arranged many such before and after photographs in order to publicise their work and attract support.* Heatherbank Museum of Social Work.

Successive legislative reform in the child protection arena represented, as Jose Harris has argued, 'a major restructuring of the legal relations between husbands and wives, parents and children, the family and the state'.[35] Child protection legislation and practice from the mid-nineteenth century to the present has been characterised by a series of unequal power struggles. Primarily these struggles have been played out between child-welfare professionals and parents, the state and the family, the middle classes and working classes, men and women and, at the centre, adults and children. The actions by voluntary organisations, child welfare charities, local authorities and carers — birth parents,

'A Nation's Hope'. The same children at Quarrier's Homes following their 'rescue', c. 1907. Heatherbank Museum of Social Work.

foster parents, residential care staff — have also brought about shifts in the way the power relationship between children and adults was perceived and experienced. That power relationship was exercised primarily in class terms but it was also influenced by gender stereotypes.

Poverty, Class and Neglect

For just over a century the SNSPCC played a key role in the policing of parental behaviour. The Society was concerned with more than just the protection of children. As Hendrick states for England, 'the NSPCC was of vital importance in reshaping public opinion away from the view that the family was inviolate, towards a view which recognised that if the ideal of the family were to be realised, then a certain amount of interference by outside bodies was essential...'[36] This violation of the working-class family was not new. Poor families had long had to live with the threat of intervention from Poor Law officers and when their powers were increased under the Children Act, 1908, prosecutions for neglect in the sheriff courts were a regular occurrence.[37] The SNSPCC inspector was merely added to the list of officials empowered to discipline the family although unlike the police and the parish inspectors 'the cruelty man' was usually perceived as a more independent figure who could be trusted to give the family a chance. The reshaping of public opinion, then, occurred not so much amongst the poorer sections of the working class but amongst the 'respectable' working class and the middle classes who condoned the new interventionism of the state and its ciphers since it was hardly likely to affect them. Neglect and starvation — which accounted for around three quarters of all cases in Scotland before the First World War — signified the failure of the poor to fulfil their responsibilities towards their children; the middle classes could rest easy in the knowledge that they were unlikely to be accused of such a crime.[38] Few questioned conditions within more wealthy families although the Catholic Archbishop Maguire of Glasgow, in an address to the annual meeting of the Glasgow branch of the Society in 1915, in a veiled reference to the religious dimension of poverty in Glasgow, 'wished the Society had the right to investigate the homes of the better classes as well as the homes of the poor, as they might often find cases which surprise them very much.'[39]

This was a perceptive comment. Child cruelty and neglect was widely perceived as a problem of the working classes. Although the RSSPCC tacitly acknowledged that cruelty was also to be found amongst the rich, it admitted that 'unfortunately the Society had no means of bringing [these] cases to light.'[40] The reporting of cases in 'respectable' middle-class homes was infrequent. One such was the sad case in 1892 of little Peter Gow, adopted by 'a very respectable Christian woman' in Edinburgh who 'showed great affection *outwardly* for the child...took him to church and meetings, had him christened George Kenneth Gow after her fancy.' Attempts by the woman's housemaid to draw attention to the plight of the child had so far been fruitless but she persevered:

The servant reported that it was a common thing for the mistress to tie the child to its bed and she herself go to a Gospel meeting. On such an occasion the maid managed to convey a message to the officer and he along with Dr Littlejohn…appeared at the front door…receiving no answer…they got a ladder and gained entrance to the house through a back window and found the child as the servant girl had said tied to his little bed and her mistress away to the NOON DAY PRAYER MEETING.[41]

Poverty, ignorance, incompetence and bad habits such as drinking and gambling were believed to be primarily to blame for child neglect, and interventions in middle-class households were few and far between. It was lower-class families that bore the brunt of the Society's investigative patrols. Careless, 'savage' parents were easy to identify in the city slums, especially as they were already likely to be known by the parish authorities. In an emotive report from 1910 the Society drew attention to the pervasiveness of neglect and starvation amongst Scotland's poorest:

The passer-by little thinks of the long-drawn-out tragedy being enacted behind the stone walls of the house that looks so commonplace and is so familiar. And yet behind such walls there are children crying out their little hearts when there ought to be nothing but joy and laughter. They are hungry, for there is no food. They are cold, for there is no fire. They are in rags, filth and vermin. They are lonely and miserable, for there is no-one to comfort and care for them. They may have a drunken mother. Possibly their father is lazy and heedless of them. The passerby sees none of this. He knows it not. Yet, there it is — in the great cities, the country town, even in villages and rural districts.[42]

Although the great majority of cases dealt with were in the cities — more than 50 per cent of children investigated by the Society in the years up to 1915 were in Glasgow, Edinburgh and Aberdeen — the rural lower classes had their fair share of cases. The endemic poverty in parts of the Highlands was a sure sign of child neglect in the eyes of the Society's visitor to those parts. On a rare visit to the Hebrides and Western Isles in 1906 the Dingwall inspector professed to have found cases in Stornaway 'as bad as several I have seen in the slums of Glasgow.' 'The most of the houses in Lewis are really shocking' he continued, 'they are rarely cleaned and smell of manure, fish entrails and all kinds of rubbish.' In South Uist:

> In one of the houses I visited I found the cattle in the living room. The children were poorly clothed and dirty and they had to lie upon the bare flooring of the bed as what straw they used to have under them had to be given to the cattle and this was all due to the father being a lazy, drunken character.[43]

By the 1930s there was perhaps a better understanding of the economic causes of general child neglect in the Highlands, yet Society officers continued to adopt a condescending attitude toward rural inhabitants in the remoter regions of the country. They commented that 'Quite a third of the parents dealt with are the feckless, thriftless type, with a slum complex and hereditary handicap, who breed prolifically.'[44] The presence of dirt was still regarded as an indication of neglect and ill-treatment, epitomised by the Russell family, ejected from the island of Canna to nearby Muck 'because they would not conform to the required standard of cleanliness' on that island. 'Their gravitation to Muck', remarked the inspector attempting to inject an element of sarcastic humour into his report, 'seems to me a coincidence in retrograde motion.'[45]

The Society regarded those least willing to open themselves to the judgemental gaze of the inspectors as the most reprehensible; they evidently had something to hide. 'The people are so strange and will not tell on one another' remarked an inspector of the inhabitants of the Hebridean islands,[46] implicitly contrasting this secrecy with the relative openness of respectable working-class communities who regarded 'the cruelty' as an important check on parents who went beyond the bounds of reason in the treatment of their children. Families who so obviously failed to conform to the Society's ideal encompassing parental responsibility, cleanliness and thrift were easy prey. Travellers, hawkers and tinkers, who were fairly common in urban and rural parts of Scotland, were regarded as marginal characters whose primitive living conditions — in tents and caves — and nomadic habits, marked them out as a group unable to provide materially or morally for their children.[47] In 1912 the Society took steps to 'protect' and 'rescue' the children of vagrants since they were being brought up 'in ignorance and idleness' to 'live the parasite life.'[48] The McPhee family, discovered by Stirling's SNSPCC inspector, camped in the hills outside the town was typical. The unmarried couple and their two illegitimate children were already well known to the Society.

212

Traveller's children, c. 1930s. The fact that such children were dirty and lacked a permanent shelter meant they were targeted by the child-savers who sought to place them in residential care. Scottish Life Archive, National Museums of Scotland.

> The couple are vagrants of no fixed place of abode, and have never had a home, and are of drunken, indolent, and other bad habits, and of the class who move from place to place putting up of a night under an old canvas erection on a bare space of ground.

Having apprehended the family, the inspector found 'the 2 children were dirty, verminous, raggedly and thinly clothed but they appeared to be healthy.' Nevertheless, in view of the conditions in which they lived and the fact that three children of the same family had allegedly died in infancy 'probably due to exposure and the life they were living', the two youngsters were removed and placed temporarily in Whinwell Children's Home. Just a few months later they sailed to Australia with an emigration party.[49]

Although the RSSPCC paid lip-service to the notion that abuse was classless, their actions spoke louder than words. Officers patrolled working-class districts looking for neglect and misuse and invariably found it in the primitive black houses of the Highlands and in the overcrowded tenements of the cities. In the midst of the Depression the Motherwell and Wishaw branch noted that 'it is in the industrial area where the most of the complaints arise and "failing to provide" is the most numerous.' The reason was not, according to this inspector, unemployment and insufficient dole money but rather 'gambling fever which is making such havoc among so many families at present.'[50] The presence of gambling schools was testament to the selfishness of parents whose children were kept hungry as a result. It was amongst the 'dangerous classes' above all, addicted to drink and gambling, living in squalor, that children were most prone to neglect; environment, it was believed, was a guide to character and behaviour.

Through the 1930s and 1940s there was no easing off in the RSSPCC's activities. The Society continued to investigate around 7,000 complaints across Scotland each year concerning more than 20,000 children. Neglect continued to account for the vast majority of cases and this was still the case after the Second World War despite growing prosperity. By the 1960s and 70s, although the annual number of cases had declined, the nature and severity of them appears to have hardly changed at all. The majority of complaints and investigations were still centred on urban areas, especially Strathclyde Region (encompassing Glasgow) which accounted for almost a quarter of the case load.[51] A clear picture of the Society's activities and the situation of its clients is provided by an analysis of over 6,000 cases from the West of Scotland, predominantly Glasgow, between 1969 and 1985.[52] The fact that 70 per cent of cases investigated in this period were classified by the RSSPCC as 'neglect' — just 415 ill-treatment cases were identified — conceals the multiplicity of factors conspiring against families struggling to bring up children. Overcrowding, appalling housing conditions, high rates of residential mobility, rent arrears, the constant threat of eviction, inadequate furnishings and bedding, unemployment, poverty and sickness characterised the lives of many working-class families in Glasgow well into the 1970s. Financial and marital problems were present in more than half of all cases investigated, alcohol abuse was a factor in more than 35 per cent of families and a quarter experienced housing problems as Figure 6.3 demonstrates.

More than half of all families investigated lived in council accommodation, another 28 per cent were in rented housing and

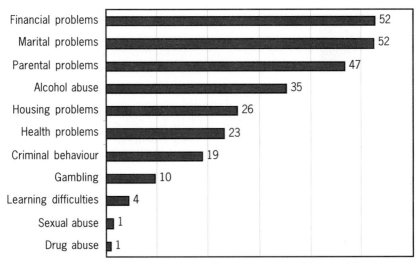

Percentage of cases with each family problem

Figure 6.3. Problems Present in Families under Investigation by the RSSPCC, Glasgow Area 1969–1985.
Source: GCU, RSSPCC Archive.

91 families were still living in condemned premises. A large proportion of families — 63 per cent — lived in accommodation comprising three rooms or less and almost 30 per cent had five children or more with 50 families comprising more than ten children. In addition, more than a quarter of fathers were unemployed. This shows that working-class families were still the focus of the Society's investigations, both in the traditional working-class districts of the city such as the Gorbals, Parkhead, Bridgeton, Dennistoun, Springburn and Maryhill and in the new housing schemes, notably Blackhill, Drumchapel, Easterhouse and Ruchazie. In Easterhouse the Society's Women Visitors even established a caravan as a focus for their activities on that estate. Roman Catholic families were the subject of 31 per cent of investigations, exactly proportionate to the estimated Catholic population of Glasgow.[53] In contrast with the nineteenth century when the stability of families was threatened by long-term illness or the death of a parent, in the late twentieth century family fracture was more likely to be the result of severe financial and housing problems which in turn caused marital tensions and breakdown. Although very few of the families investigated in this period were officially headed by single mothers, 40 per cent of

215

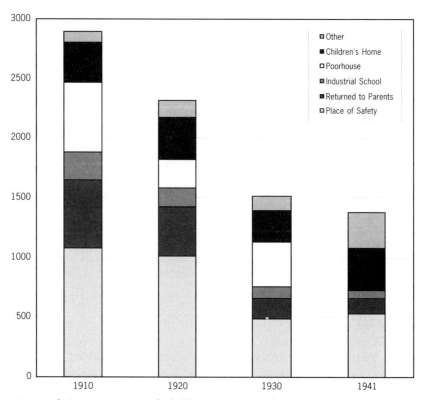

Figure 6.4. Destination of Children Removed from Families by RSSPCC, Scotland 1910–1941
Source: GCU, RSSPCC Archive: Annual Reports.

parents were either separated or divorced and many women were coping alone. In these circumstances the Society's officers and women visitors (introduced to assist the work of inspectors in 1948) complemented the role of the social work department. Whilst social workers had statutory obligations and inevitably had no choice but to adopt a punitive role in some cases, Society inspectors saw themselves and were seen by their clients as impartial. Their role was not only to detect neglect and cruelty but to advise and support families and for this reason they were trusted as independent arbiters, at least until the Orkney affair in 1991.

By the second half of the twentieth century it became the role of the Society to come to the aid of families in order to prevent children being taken into care. As Figure 6.4 shows, since the early decades of the century, the proportion of children removed from families by the Society had steadily declined. This trend continued after the war. More than 80 per cent of children in cases dealt with in Glasgow between 1969 and 1985 remained with their parents. Officers liaised with the social work department, the housing authorities, factors and the police; they helped parents obtain furniture and bedding and delivered food parcels when necessary. They also gave 'advice', especially to 'careless' and 'feckless' mothers such as this lone mother, cohabiting in a council house with her 'paramour' and her three children: 'Advised the mother not to marry as is not dependable and there is a strong possibility that he will continue to be unfaithful when he tires of married life.'[54] The result of these tactics was that fewer children were taken to places of safety, fewer parents were prosecuted and the Society spent most of its time and resources on supervision visits.

The Society knew that children in middle-class homes were also subject to physical and emotional cruelty but it was rarely disclosed. While material neglect is usually evident — in malnourished and diseased bodies and dirty and ragged clothing — physical and especially emotional abuse has always been easier to conceal. The surveillance of working-class families had a long history but the middle classes were, and still are, more resistant to interference in the private sphere of parent-child relations.

Unnatural Mothers and Cruel Men

The Society's emphasis on child neglect as opposed to physical cruelty underlined a central tenet of child protection practice. Not only was child abuse predominantly a working-class phenomenon, it was also gendered.[55] Women and men were not regarded as equally responsible for either children's protection or their abuse. Women, as primary care providers, were rendered responsible for child care and thus were also blamed for neglect. Men, on the other hand, were not seen to be intimately associated with the domestic sphere; male abuse of a child was thus frequently located outside the home and took the form of physical cruelty. The consequences of these gendered constructions of the perpetrators were to be far-reaching.

The first public exposure of alleged wilful child-neglect on a large scale — the so-called 'baby-farming' scandal of the 1870s —

focused attention on the relationship between parents — especially mothers — and the state. Baby-farming was said to be as prevalent in Scottish cities as it was in London. Both the press and the SNSPCC periodically stoked public interest in the practice, the former discovering 'prison like' conditions in the poorest streets containing neglected, starved infants, lying on bare boards and drugged with opium.[56] The SNSPCC was similarly animated by the issue, using emotive descriptions of infant victims such as this one from 1890 to evoke sympathy and support for their investigative work.

> They were put in little chairs in corners of the room, where they had bottleless teats put in their mouths…the nurse children were seldom fed at all…In the day two were always in their wooden chairs. Their thighs became raw by their position and the filth they sat in…Untended, hungry, thirsty, crying, so they lay, day by day, suffering from measles, until one was taken up to be 'laid out' and the other to be removed to kindlier care, where it speedily died. Both children were insured, each for £4.[57]

No doubt some of these establishments were run by unscrupulous persons for financial gain; no doubt children were dying and mothers were being cruelly exploited at a time of great vulnerability as the *Glasgow Herald* acknowledged in 1910 when it referred to a system — baby-farming — which 'fastens parasitically on the frailty of women and the helplessness of their offspring'.[58]

The baby-farming scandal was a red-herring. From the perspective of child protection only a change of attitude towards single mothers, enabling them to remain in employment while caring for their babies, would get rid of the necessity for such dangerous forms of child care. Women like Mary Hood, in service in Helensburgh, who had been forced to place her daughter in the care of another woman in order to hold onto her position had no alternative.[59] Mothers were desperate, not immoral and unnatural. Yet, the debate about baby-farming had a wider resonance and longer term significance in two respects. Firstly, the assumption by all concerned that women, that is mothers, were primarily responsible for children's welfare and thus should be excoriated when the quality of care they provided was deemed unacceptable was expressed repeatedly in a number of contexts into the twentieth century. Secondly, state intervention in the family and especially in the relationship between mother and child was now legitimised. Some mothers, apparently, were unfit to take responsibility for their children.

The SNSPCC, along with all other child welfare agencies, adhered to the implicit belief in the mother's prime responsibility for the welfare of her child despite its talk of encouraging parental responsibility and in particular enforcing fathers' commitment to the financial upkeep of their children by means of the 1908 Children Act. In fact, parental responsibility was a euphemism for the mother's responsibility.[60] At a time when the physical needs of the child were deemed most important, when the majority of SNSPCC cases were defined as 'neglect and starvation', the role of the mother — in providing food, clothing, warmth and acceptable, clean accommodation — was placed under the spotlight. The neglectful and cruel mother was an object of vilification. 'There is something so alien to human nature in *cruelty to children*' commented the director of the Whinwell Children's Home in Stirling in 1895:

> That a woman should forget her child is admitted as a bare possibility…but that a woman should starve her child, should ill-treat it, should even torture it, — is this a thing to be believed? Yes, and in a lovely, highly privileged Christian town like Stirling…[61]

The town of Stirling and its environs appeared to contain many of these unnatural 'anti-mothers', seemingly selfish individuals who showed little affection for vulnerable children.'The bairn is dying at any rate, and what's the use botherin' trying to keep life in' was the response of one mother to the SNSPCC's attempts to help.[62] Drunken, incompetent, ignorant, immoral mothers not deserving custody of their children pervade the histories of children accepted into children's homes as this selection of comments drawn from Whinwell Children's Home and Aberlour Orphanage case files illustrates:

> I have heard a great deal about the mother and only on condition the mother be removed from the district…would I promise to help in this case. The woman is incorrigible.[63]
>
> Owing to her drunken, indolent and other bad habits and her persistent neglect, by failing to keep her clean or have her educated, I removed her from the custody of this woman…[64]
>
> His mother *will not* give up her bad ways tho (sic) all kindness and help has been shown her…[65]

> Child utterly neglected by mother, improperly fed, clothed and tended...mother and older members of the family of bad character and unfit to have charge of child.[66]
>
> [Mother] had been living in one of the lowest lodging houses in town, associating with the worst characters and her two children painfully exposed to all kinds of vice and immorality. The woman...with her mother hawked together and of bad character.[67]

And what of the fathers? In the presence of a bad mother, fathers could not be expected to take over the nurturing duties. The father of two young sons admitted to Aberlour Orphanage in 1899 was described as 'an industrious hard working man...kept poor in consequence of the drunken habits of his wife.' The children 'are having a melancholy example and upbringing owing to their mother's conduct and neglect.'[68] Similarly, widowed or deserted husbands were portrayed as feckless, irresponsible, and understandably unable to care for their children in the absence of their mother. Whinwell's Miss Croall echoed the sentiments of child welfare workers everywhere when she noted that 'a widower is perfectly helpless with children. He cannot mother the bairns and be the breadwinner too; while he tries to do a *father's part*, the children miss their *mother*.'[69] Without a woman there could be no family. Children needed a mother but so did husbands it seemed.

Child neglect, as opposed to deliberate cruelty, was more often than not portrayed as a consequence of a mother's negligence, a theme brought into sharper focus during the First World War. Women, it was said, were taking advantage of their husbands' absence to enjoy themselves with the consequence that children were suffering. The increasing number of cases of child neglect brought against mothers in the Edinburgh sheriff court appeared to confirm the trend. While in 1910 23 out of 50 cases involved the mother alone or both parents, in 1915 46 cases out of 54 were brought against 'drunken' or 'immoral' mothers such as Catherine Gilroy, '35, a soldier's wife...charged of neglecting her children aged 15, 10, 8, 7, 3 and 1 year. She pled guilty.'[70] The trend for prosecuting 'drunken mothers' continued throughout the war years. In 1917 the Edinburgh District Committee of the SNSPCC commented on:

> a determination amongst a large number of women to go their own way and live as they like in the absence of their husbands...The

moral surroundings in these homes is as bad as it can be and the children's minds are being poisoned by the atmosphere in which they live...The inspectors find that the question of morals is becoming more acute than that of drink.[71]

Moreover, it was noticed that children were being left alone for long periods while women spent time in public houses and cinemas. 'A common practice is for women to lock children in and take the key away so that the Inspectors cannot get access to the children.'[72] It was alleged women were spending their separation allowance on drink and entertainment and attempts were made to withdraw the payments from those judged to have given way to intemperance.[73] However, the inebriate mother scare was a temporary phenomenon which abated as men returned from the war.[74] It was a pattern repeated during World War Two, not suprising perhaps when women were left alone to care for young children or were working full time without any significant child care support.

The conviction that mothers bore prime responsibility for the care of their children never receded in the minds of policy makers and child protection workers, even during the Depression when severe economic privation made the job almost impossible at times. In 1931 'carelessness in the management of the house on the part of the wife, her disregard for economy, and a habit of buying on credit' was blamed for the suffering and neglect of children.[75] But not all were quite so condemnatory. The circumstances of the Depression persuaded many that mothers were not necessarily individually responsible. Rather, more often than not, they were victims of social and economic circumstances — poverty, poor housing, lack of help — and needed support rather than criticism. When the Women's Group on Public Welfare carried out a study of three groups of mothers and children in 1946–7 they concluded that:

Thousands of women bring up families in extremely adverse circumstances. Indeed, the remarkable feature which impresses anyone who examines the problem is not the fact that some women neglect their children in difficult circumstances, but that so many mothers in unpropitious surroundings manage not only to rear a family but to make a real home...In looking at these families there emerges one dominating feature — the capacity of the mother...It is her calibre that matters.[76]

221

Although it was recognised that mothers were usually doing their best in trying circumstances, they were not let off the hook altogether. Old attitudes died hard and nowhere more so than within the ranks of the RSSPCC. Despite the greater emphasis in the post World War Two period on supporting parents and keeping families together, mothers were still in the front line against child abuse. Now though they were judged by the unrealistic standards of the Society's women visitors whose attitudes towards poverty paralleled those of the housing and health visitors (the 'sanny folk') who tyrannised working-class housewives in the new housing schemes.[77] A dirty, untidy house immediately gave a bad impression of a woman's child care abilities. 'Mother appears to be a typical Blackhill mother' commented the visitor to a family of seven in 1970. 'Mother is obviously a careless type...I feel she will require constant supervision.'[78] The fact that many mothers were struggling to keep their children housed, clothed and fed without the financial support of a partner was recognised but it did not justify slatternly habits.

Middle-class concern about working-class motherhood has continuously coloured child protection policy and practice. In the coded language used by the RSSPCC and the majority of child welfare workers, parental responsibility implied maternal responsibility. Thus women who paid other women to take care of their children were as unnatural as those who made a living from 'baby-farming'; women who failed to nurture their children in the approved way were not fulfilling their natural role. Drunken mothers, dirty mothers, immoral mothers, all forfeited their right to custody of their children. Neglect was female.[79]

Cruelty, on the hand, was male, or so it came to be constructed. Contrasted with the well-meaning but feckless and therefore blameless lone father, unable to look after his children alone, was the image of the working-class brute who drank and gambled his earnings, beat his wife and terrified his children. Cruelty was portrayed as the result of callous behaviour that even an unnatural mother would be incapable of unless she were coerced. Harry Hendrick in his study of child welfare policy in England suggests that cruelty was a problem for the child-savers. Accounting for less than four per cent of all cases dealt with by the RSSPCC in Scotland before 1930 and still only 6 per cent in the Glasgow area between 1969 and 1985, physical mistreatment or assault of a child was a hidden crime.[80] Any attempt to deal with cruelty in a more public way would have entailed questioning not just the behaviour of the poor — a legitimate pastime in Victorian Britain — but the more private power relations within all families, including those of the middle classes.[81] While neglect was a working-class phenomenon, cruelty was classless. It was relatively easy to chastise poor mothers for their inadequate child-care skills. It was quite another thing for inspectors — the majority of whom were men until the First World War — to challenge the authority of fathers in their own homes. As a result, the amount of cruelty discovered and prosecuted by the Society was undoubtedly a small proportion of that which occurred.

The Society's reluctance to see cruelty in relation to either the middle classes or women meant that almost certainly serious cases remained undiscovered as Peter's experience demonstrates. Peter was boarded out to an Inverness-shire village in 1938. He described how 'hammerings were daily, everyday without fail you got a belt. She had a big leather belt with two thongs which she kept in the kitchen drawer and you got belted everyday.' The beatings were not discovered by the Glasgow Corporation inspector since 'we were all lined up the day beforehand and warned when the inspector asks you whether you like it here you'll tell him yes or you'll get another hammering...' with the result that both Peter and his brother suffered serious injuries at the hands of their foster 'mother'.[82]

The conviction that women were incapable of wilful cruelty to a child also meant the actions of women employed as residential carers was overlooked. In 1998 allegations of physical and mental cruelty against a number of female religious orders in Scotland going back 30 years highlighted the danger of accepting the woman as nurturer ideal. 'People think of nuns as angels' commented one former resident of a Catholic children's home in Scotland, 'but I think of them as ogres.'[83] 'The fact that they were women, these nuns, somehow makes it worse in my heart' said another. 'They didn't have any kindness in them. I find that shocking.'[84] As a result of the enforced silence of children and the inability of the child welfare services to look beyond their own horizons, only certain shocking instances came to light which conformed to the stereotypes of brutish male perpetrators.

One means by which men could be legitimately policed in their relations with children was in respect of sexual abuse. We are accustomed to thinking about sexual abuse as a very recent discovery, yet child welfare professionals were very conscious of the sexual threat to children, especially young girls, from the late nineteenth century. In response to a sensationalist press campaign centred upon juvenile prostitution or the so-called 'white slave trade', the Criminal Law Amendment Act passed in 1885 raised the age of consent for girls to 16 and made it an offence to procure a girl for sexual purposes under the age of 21.[85] In 1908, a long campaign by child savers, women's organisations and the police succeeded in achieving the Punishment of Incest Act. However, this legislation had more to do with the control of public morality and the disciplining of single women than it did with the protection of children. There continued to be a public taboo around the sexual abuse of children evidenced by the remarkably few cases of sexual assault recorded as such by the SNSPCC — just 47 cases in the whole of Scotland were defined as 'indecent and criminal assault' before 1915.[86] It is more likely, as Louise Jackson has shown for London, that communities dealt with indecent assault of children themselves by discovering incidents and reporting them to the police.[87] There was no need for intermediary child-savers. Even after the war when sexual assault was an issue discussed more widely in the public domain, it does not seem to have been uncovered or acknowledged by the SNSPCC who recorded only 3 cases out of a total of 1,997 investigated in Glasgow in 1931.[88] On the other hand, child savers were intensely concerned with the sexuality of working-class girls, and to a much lesser extent boys, reflected in the number of children 'rescued' from so-called immoral surroundings.[89] The belief that girls assaulted as children grew up to be 'dissolute women', that is prostitutes, guided the policy of organisations such as the National Vigilance Association, the Scottish Council for Women's Trades and the National Council of Women, as well as the SNSPCC.

In order to address the issue of sexual abuse of children, campaigners shifted it outside the home and thus away from the immediate family. This permitted discussion of a taboo subject within safe and familiar boundaries.[90] The family remained inviolate. The male perpetrators became 'moral degenerates', mothers once again were cast as the protectors of their (female) children, and the children themselves were portrayed as delinquents or, at the very least, sexually precocious. The Victorian image of the family therefore remained intact.[91] The taboo word 'incest' never need be uttered. This discourse on the family denied the existence of sexual abuse within the idealised family unit. If it occurred at all it was because of the immoral and degraded living conditions of the lower classes. All of these arguments, based around class and gender, were fully rehearsed in Scotland in 1924–25 in the evidence presented to a Government Committee inquiring into the subject of sexual offenses against children. Between 1921 and 1924 more than 2,000 cases of assault or other indecent offenses had been reported to the police in Scotland involving 2,680 children under the age of 16 although proceedings were instituted in only 1,050 of these.[92] These statistics almost certainly represented a tiny proportion of all sexual offenses against children. In Glasgow's western police division alone between 1921 and 1925, 197 cases were recorded involving more than 300 children with offences ranging from indecent exposure to rape and incest. In 104 cases the perpetrator was not traced.[93] Representatives of a wide range of interested parties, including the police, local authorities, voluntary organisations and members of the legal profession presented evidence which, although it demonstrated a heightened awareness of the extent of sexual assault against children, tended to confirm a series of long-standing prejudices which did little either to protect the children or to bring the perpetrators to justice. The 'evil of the overcrowded home' was one such belief repeatedly blamed for such offenses, not simply owing to the sleeping arrangements in one or two room apartments but, according to one witness, because 'the sensitiveness of the child to indecency and immorality is blunted.' 'Where families live in single rooms the children see much that is undesirable', making them 'more easy prey to attack'.[94] In addition it was believed that tenement housing positively encouraged attacks on children in common closets, stairs, closes and back courts, often unlit and deserted. Almost 50 per cent of reported cases in Glasgow's Western Division occurred in these areas and young girls appeared to be most at risk as this typical example from Stirling demonstrated.[95] According to the five year old victim:

> I was playing along with my little sister C. in the back court where we live and near to Mr H's (the accused) house. We were playing alone. While we were playing there…Mr H. came out of his house.

He was drunk. He came over to us and gave us each a penny…He then took hold of us by the hand and took us into his house. On going inside he shut the door and took us into the kitchen…When he came into the bed beside me he took down my knickers and lay on top of me and hurt my stomach. He also touched my 'Bobby' with his 'Dickie' and his hand and hurt me…he then put C. and I out of the house. We went up the back stair…and through the lobby into the street and along to Marriott's sweetie shop where we spent our pennies on sweets.[96]

Cases such as this one reinforced the view that young girls were at risk in overcrowded, working-class areas of towns and cities. Here, there were plenty of opportunities for an assault, not just in the closes and courts but in places of entertainment frequented by young people such as darkened cinemas, ice-cream parlours and fried-fish shops with partitions. But also the girls, brought up in the depraved conditions of their own homes, crammed together with fathers, brothers and lodgers were, so it was said, on the cusp of depravity themselves, and often quite ready to offer themselves to men 'for pennies'.[97] According to an Edinburgh park keeper there were 'young girls who appear ready or willing to go to isolated places with strange men.'[98] Freudian psychoanalytic theory may have influenced this interpretation of the pattern of sexual abuse. The belief that children were sexual beings and that young girls in particular could be culpable in seducing men helps to explain why there was a general reluctance to accept that children could be the wholly innocent victims of sexual abuse.

Sexual abuse or assault, then, was professionally constructed primarily as a working-class phenomenon.[99] It was also portrayed as a crime committed against young girls by men. Yet only certain men could commit such an offence, namely 'moral degenerates' and 'men of low moral and weak intellect';[100] 'fiendish brutes that go prowling about luring innocent children';[101] 'lurking men beside schools and in gardens near swings, ponds where little girls bathe and wade';[102] men 'of a poor mental capacity with morbid ideas';[103] and those men who continued to believe that 'intercourse with a pirrie young girl cures men of the [venereal] disease'.[104] Child abusers were stereotyped as abnormal men, sex pests or beasts, marginal characters who had no place in the family, in any family, and hence child abuse was removed from the home and placed on the street, in the park, in the cinema and more unlikely, in the ice-cream parlour. Sexual assault was something that happened to girls when they wandered to a dangerous place and encountered a strange man.[105] Men in general and fathers in particular were largely absolved from this crime. The family remained intact. This was a peculiarly middle-class perception. Some 70 years later, the popular discourse on the sexual threat to children is still shaped by similar misconceptions. Although child-care professionals recognise that so-called 'stranger-danger' has been exaggerated and that 'most abuse is committed by people children have most reason to trust', the popular press continue to perpetuate the myth that strangers in the community are responsible for the majority of sexual attacks on children.[106]

Women in general, on the other hand, were seen to constitute the front line against sexual abuse. Mothers in particular were once again made to feel responsible for the protection of their daughters. While they were to shield them from premature sexual awakening, they were also implored to explain to them the facts of life. 'Much harm is done by distorted knowledge gained from other children.' Furthermore children should be more explicitly warned of the dangers: 'many mothers have said to me, that they could not understand how the child let the man do such things to her, as they had always warned her if she went with a man he would cut off her head.'[107] If mothers were to be responsible for the education and control of their daughters, women in general could play an important role in preventing sex crimes and aiding in the prosecution of offenders. A regiment of women — policewomen, female doctors, women court attendants, women park attendants, female teachers of sex education — were recommended to stem the tide. Little has changed in the 1980s and 90s. It is generally accepted that men form the vast majority of abusers but women have still been held responsible for knowing what was happening and failing to stop it. This attitude fails to recognise the gendered power relations within dysfunctional families which often render a woman powerless to prevent harm occurring.

In the inter-war years, therefore, the issue of child abuse in the guise of sexual assault was displaced away from the home allowing the child savers to retain their ideal image of the family more or less intact. One of the consequences of this shift in the abuse agenda was that children within the family were left at potential risk. The construction of the male sex offender as a pervert essentially let fathers (and all women) off the hook. And the labelling of abused children as sexually precocious and potentially delinquent perpetuated an image of the victim as threat. Such children — the unruly and wild and the abuse victims — had to be disciplined, placed in institutions such as industrial schools and reformatories where they would receive the moral education their mothers had failed to provide.[108]

There was no significant repudiation of this attitude until the 1960s when the discovery of 'battered baby syndrome' alerted child care workers to the incidence of long-term ill-treatment — albeit physical cruelty — within the family.[109] By this time doctors and child protection workers were certainly more aware of the problem and were less likely to believe parents' excuses for childrens' injuries as in the case of this child, admitted to a Glasgow hospital in 1966 with multiple fractures and bruising. The doctor informed the RSSPCC officer that X-Rays revealed the child had suffered similarly in the past but when questioned

> the mother informed me that the child had fallen off the toilet pan and struck her head on the bath. When I asked the mother how she accounted for the child's other injuries, she stated that Jane was one of these type of children who were always receiving bruises and bumps and falling all over the place...[110]

But although society now accepts that children are in danger of physical injury and sexual abuse within the family, such cases are still notoriously difficult to uncover and prosecute. In the Glasgow area between 1969 and 1985, although few cases of indecent assault were officially recorded by the RSSPCC, sexual abuse was an issue in 57 cases — though still only a tiny proportion, not even one per cent, of the total investigated.[111] Cruel men and women were more likely to escape detection and punishment than 'neglectful' mothers whose actions towards their children were placed under constant surveillance. As a result, neglected children were discovered and their families supported whilst child victims of cruel and abusive treatment were often left in danger.

A Place of Safety

Since the very beginning of child welfare and protection services in the modern sense, children perceived to be at risk — from neglect, physical abuse or sexual abuse — have been removed from their birth families and transferred to a place of safety, be it a temporary shelter, a foster home or some kind of residential care institution. In all cases a child was entitled to expect a guaranteed minimum quality of care in the substitute home, and certainly protection from the risks to which he or she had been exposed within the birth family. We now know that for many children this did not happen. For some, the physical, emotional and sexual abuse they received at the hands of foster parents, residential care workers or other child residents was far worse than anything they had suffered at home. Until quite recently, in contrast with the plethora of voluntary child saving organisations who aimed to rescue children from abusive families, there was no equivalent independent authority to intervene between children in care and their carers.[112] A child could not be rescued twice. As a result, children like Harry Wilson who suffered appalling injuries at the hands of his foster parents in 1945 and possibly hundreds in children's homes across Scotland were subjected to treatment ranging from the insensitive and cruel to the inhumane. Neither the discovery of child abuse in the late nineteenth century nor the rediscovery in the 1960s and 1970s paid any attention to the condition of children in care. In the 1990s however, there is a general acceptance that the abuse of children in residential care homes throughout the British Isles since the Second World War was endemic. In 1996, the Report of the National Commission of Inquiry into the Prevention of Child Abuse noted:

> The catalogue of abuse in residential institutions is appalling. It includes physical assault and sexual abuse; emotional abuse; unacceptable deprivation of rights and privileges; inhumane treatment; poor health care and education. This is especially disturbing because many of the children in residential institutions have already been deeply harmed.[113]

One way of approaching the history of abuse of children in the welfare system is by analysing the prevailing culture of care. The treatment of children in any society is dependent upon a combination of economic, social and political factors. Any analysis of child abuse, rather than emphasising the individual pathology of the perpetrator, must pay attention to the economic and social position of the family, or the substitute family, and the relationship between the family and the state.[114] The discussion of boarding out and residential care in previous chapters has already shown that at least until the Second World War what we would define as abuse today — over-work, corporal punishment, an absence of affection and so on — was commonplace, if not entirely acceptable for all of the previous century and much of the present one. The culture of the boarding-out system in Scotland, whereby children were not infrequently 'dumped' on foster families and treated as an economic resource, may have accentuated a family atmosphere characterised by an absence of affection. The affective family, some would argue, was late arriving in presbyterian Scotland. Children were treated like farm servants, expected to contribute to the household economy; they were not regarded as full and equal members of the family. In the 1940s the death of Dennis O'Neill and the severe injuries suffered by Harry Wilson forced the authorities to look at the system which placed these children with such unsuitable foster families, but there was no recognition that child abuse was a wider social problem as one response to the O'Neill tragedy noted:

> It is very easy (and very proper) to blame the bully, the brute, the sadist for the death of this child. It is easy too (and proper) to blame the authorities responsible for leaving the child with unsuitable people. But the responsibility does not end there. We, the general public, by our moral laziness, by our lack of critical attention to the problem of these children, have contributed indirectly to his death. The crime against Danny O'Neill is one in which the whole nation must take its share of guilt...[115]

Harry Wilson and Dennis O'Neill were seen as unfortunate victims of a care system gone wrong. They had been wrongly placed with aberrant guardians — inherently cruel individuals who could not be regarded as symptomatic of a wider problem. The government inquiry into the circumstances surrounding the O'Neill case restricted its remit to the failures of social work practice.[116] In both cases the care system was seen as being at fault rather than any fundamental attitude towards the protection of vulnerable children. Moreover, children like these who had already spent some years in foster or residential care, were portrayed as 'problem' or 'difficult' children and thus not representative of children in general. The implicit assumption here is that society needed protecting from such children.

These cases failed to ignite any significant long-term public concern surrounding the wider issue of child protection and child abuse, and neither did the little known case of Richard Clark who suffered a cerebral haemorrhage resulting in severe brain damage at the hands of private foster parents in Perth in 1974. At the age of three, Richard had been placed in the care of a couple who already had a criminal record for cruelty to their own daughters. Social workers did express some concerns about the ability of the foster mother to cope with Richard, but the private foster arrangement was nevertheless sanctioned by the local authority. Anxiety that Richard was being mistreated was expressed by the boy's father, grandmother and the health visitor, all of whom observed evidence of bruising on his face and body, yet nothing was done to remove the child from danger until his condition deteriorated necessitating immediate admission to hospital. Here it was found that Richard had multiple bruising inflicted over a period of time as well as injuries perpetrated that day causing the haemorrhage and irreversible brain damage. The committee of inquiry concluded that 'a major error of judgement was made' in allowing Richard to remain with the family when evidence suggested he had been at risk for some time.[117]

The Richard Clark case demonstrated that foster care, and especially private fostering arrangements, offered no guarantee of protection from harm. There had been widespread concern at Richard's condition, yet outside intervention in the form of frequent visits by social workers and health visitors failed to protect him. If children being cared for within the community, by their birth parents or foster families, cannot be protected, arguably children in residential care, isolated within homes which operated as islands, are equally at risk from abuse.[118] A total institution such as a children's home had a tendency to develop its own standards of behaviour, its own culture of care which may have deviated significantly from acceptable societal norms. Owing to limited outside intervention in the running of these homes the culture of care altered remarkably little until the 1960s. As a result we must remain sceptical as to whether children were placed in a secure and safe environment.[119]

It is clear that in some children's homes, especially the larger voluntary homes, a disciplinary regime run on a system of rewards and punishments was regarded as the only way of maintaining control over hundreds of potentially unruly youngsters. 'You *must* smack children of that age often' were the reported words of a nurse in a home for young children in 1945, 'how else can you keep 30 small children of that age quiet all the time?…You have to smack pretty hard because they soon get used to it and then it doesn't hurt any more.'[120] However, allegations of abuse suffered by former residents of a number of Catholic-run children's homes from the 1930s through to the 1980s suggests that a smack was the least of their worries. Allegations of physical and mental abuse range from degrading treatment to callous disregard and physical mistreatment. Bed-wetters, it has been claimed, were made to parade around wearing their wet sheets and a sign on their backs; children were allegedly forced to eat their own vomit and beatings were commonplace.[121] 'They crucified us, they simply crucified us' recalled one man of his experiences in the 1930s.[122] Others have claimed that menstruating girls were forced to take baths containing disinfectant and were not provided with sanitary towels.[123] 'We didn't complain because we didn't know any different' is a common refrain.[124] So ingrained was the abusive treatment of children that the victims, many of whom had spent most of their lives within the welfare system, were unaware they were entitled to better standards of care.

There can be no doubt that most of the abuse of children within residential care occurred within a culture of dangerously unequal power relations, silence and complicity. Staff suspected of what was euphemistically called 'unorthodox' behaviour were quietly dismissed.[125] Parents who complained about the treatment meted out to their children were pushed aside. The father of four children formerly in Duncarse home in Dundee and transferred to Aberlour Orphanage, notified the police when he suspected they were being battered but 'as usual no notice was taken of my complaints'. 'My bairns haven't done anything wrong. They're only homeless. Could something not be done to expose my complaint and get my bairns home?' he implored in a desperate letter to the Clyde Committee.[126] Children were also denied a voice, they were unable to complain about any treatment they perceived as unfair since, as one woman recalled, 'the victim had no-one to appeal to as there was no-one but the mother in the house.'[127] In homes where discipline was instilled by fear, children were unable to alert anyone to the abuse they were suffering. If bruises were discovered on their bodies they were told to lie; recalled one woman, 'you'd no opportunity anyway to tell your visitors exactly what happened because it was like a prison visit. They stood next to you and listened to every word you were saying.'[128] And in any case, the word of a child was invariably treated as unreliable. When complaints were made about one of Barnardo's homes in Scotland in 1945 the management response revealed an alarming lack of respect for the children in their care:

> ...it would appear that most of your criticisms are based on remarks made by the boys themselves. We have found by experience that their statements are not always reliable, for it is not unnatural that boys should sometimes be tempted to encourage interest in or sympathy with themselves by stating facts which are out of focus with the truth.[129]

It seems that this reluctance to believe the words of a child was commonplace until very recently. 'I told them what he had done to me. I got called a liar' recalled one woman who complained she was being sexually abused by a care worker in an Edinburgh children's home in the late 1970s.[130] In a climate of disbelief children were put at great risk, unable to repel unwanted sexual attention from adults. 'He took me into a van and sexually interfered with me under my pants' recalled a former resident of an Aberdeen children's home in the 1960s and 70s, 'but what can you do? You can't tell anybody.'[131] Following the conviction of two former children's home workers in Edinburgh in 1997 for a catalogue of sexual crimes against girls and boys, *The Scotsman* leader articulated a widespread sense of anger but also *déja vu:*

> Yet again, children living in fear were simply not taken seriously...Yet again, it seems, there was a culture of secrecy among the people who ought to have known better. And yet again, in blind, brutal complicity, small children were left entirely defenceless at the mercy of evil individuals paid...to 'care' for them.[132]

And even today there are some who dismiss claims of abuse against residential care workers as fantasy. Responding to the allegations recently laid at the feet of the Poor Sisters of Nazareth in their Scottish children's homes, the Bishop of Aberdeen, the Rt.Rev. Mario Conti, defended the Church:

> There are some people who clearly have got bad memories. Some people whose lives are not as happy as they ought to be are looking

for reasons why and they're looking into their past…I am simply saying that some people have been making fantastical allegations about the Sisters.[133]

The defensive posture adopted by the Catholic Church in Scotland stands out as anachronistic at a time when there is far greater emphasis on listening to the child's voice. Children's rights stand at the forefront of the child welfare service today. The Children Act, 1989, requires all agencies providing care for children to have a complaints procedure and has at its heart the principle that 'each child has the right to express his or her views freely and those views should be given due weight.'[134]

The Orkney Affair

Since 1987 British society has been stunned by a cascade of furores over child abuse: Cleveland, Rochdale, Orkney, Ayrshire, North Wales and Edinburgh. Indeed, there is almost no part of the country unaffected. The 1980s and 1990s have seen sexual abuse claim the political limelight and, in Hendrick's words, 'open up a boulevard of concern' around the treatment of children in modern society.[135] Just one year after the government officially acknowledged the existence of sexual abuse in 1986,[136] the Cleveland crisis and subsequent child abuse cases, most notably in Orkney, acted as metaphors for a national crisis or moral panic surrounding the rights and responsibilities of parents, children and an array of professionals. '"Cleveland" was rendered a symbol of the powerful ambivalences surrounding child abuse', writes Harry Ferguson, 'over whose construction of "abuse" holds truth, and over the power of class, gender, national and local cultures in the determination of appropriate policies and practices.'[137] In 1995–6, sexual abuse accounted for 17 per cent of cases of children referred to Social Work Departments in Scotland, while 31 per cent were recorded as physical injury cases and 15 per cent as physical neglect.[138] In the United Kingdom as a whole it has been estimated that up to 100,000 children each year have a potentially harmful sexual experience.[139]

In February 1991 a remote part of Scotland became the focus for the public fascination with child sexual abuse when nine children from four families were removed from their homes on the island of South Ronaldsay in Orkney and flown to the mainland. Their disclosures had led social workers to believe they were at risk from organised ritual abuse involving a number of adults on the island including the local Church of Scotland minister. The Orkney affair occurred in the wake of a series of high profile sexual abuse scandals south of the border, but here the media labelling of the alleged abuse as 'satanic' lent the whole affair a bizarre and for many, an unbelievable, twist. Moreover, Orkney appeared to many to be such an unlikely location for child abuse on such a scale. Whereas in Cleveland the majority of those suspected of abusing their children were from working-class communities, Orkney was geographically and conceptually a long way away from Cleveland in public imagination. Orkney was represented as a traditional, innocent community which had been 'raped' by interfering social workers. 'We are talking about the bureaucratic rape of a community here' commented a friend of one of the families involved.[140] For many observers it was difficult to believe that the abuse of a child could occur in such a close-knit community. 'The certainty that nothing like the ritual abuse alleged ever took place stems from a simple fact. This is an observed community, one where binoculars have pride of place by croft house windows' wrote a local journalist in the midst of the affair.[141] Orkney came to symbolise a power struggle between the state represented by social workers, the police and the RSSPCC who were said to have engaged in a 'witch hunt', and parents who were universally presented in the media as innocent victims. The social workers were variously compared to the Gestapo, Saddam Hussein and 'satan busters',[142] while parents were represented as trapped and powerless to prevent further incursions into their homes. 'We all dread the thought of a stranger breaking into our homes at night and kidnapping our children, and that's exactly what happened', remarked *The Sun* in its sensationalist style.[143] The community saw itself as besieged and defenceless; parents were asking '"Is my child safe? Whose child will be snatched next?"'[144] The children, on the other hand, who had been placed with foster families on the mainland, some in Strathclyde, most in Highland region, had no voice. The parents, those accused of abuse, were accepted unquestioningly by the press as advocates on the children's behalf.

In the midst of the furore the Orkney sheriff dismissed the application of the social work department for place of safety orders for the nine children and announced that in his view 'the children were safer at home.'[145] The children were returned to their parents on 4 April, the court case was abandoned and a public inquiry was set up to conduct an investigation into the actions of all the agencies involved. The inquiry did not address the issue of the original allegations of abuse. In Orkney, as in Cleveland and Rochdale, those with the media on their side — the parents — won the day, appealing to the widespread and popular belief that ordinary, hardworking and respected parents do not abuse their children.[146]

In Orkney there was no evidence — medical or otherwise — that proved abuse had occurred. The actions of all the agencies involved were shown to be seriously flawed and the Clyde Report on the affair was highly critical of them. The social workers were roundly criticised for their handling of almost all aspects of the affair including the dawn raids on the children's homes, the swiftness with which they were removed to the mainland, and the unprofessional way in which the children were subsequently interviewed. The consequences of the Orkney affair for child protection policy and practise in Scotland and the rest of the country have been profound.[147] It was largely responsible for the winding up of the RSSPCC as an investigative organisation owing to the criticism that its officers had failed to act impartially. The result of this is that Scotland now lacks an impartial organisation which can mediate between families and agencies with statutory obligations. Moreover, the Orkney saga has forced child protection workers to tread much more carefully in respect of children's allegations of abuse. One of the main recommendations of the Clyde Report stated that although allegations made by a child regarding sexual abuse should be taken seriously, they 'should not necessarily be accepted as true, but should be thoroughly examined and tested before any action is taken.'[148] Some have argued that ironically, post-Orkney, children are possibly at greater risk owing to the reluctance of social workers to believe children's allegations and owing to the absence of any independent child protection organisation.[149] Child welfare workers are well aware of the dangers. In the midst of the Orkney saga child protection workers in Scotland were warned that 'a significant number' of child sex abusers were escaping prosecution in spite of the fact that 'very few allegations of child sexual abuse actually occur where there is no substance to the allegation.'[150] As Beatrix

Campbell has observed, the media created 'a climate of opinion that clouded our consciousness' and which has had a long term impact upon child protection work throughout the British Isles.[151] On the other hand, there is little evidence for the existence of ritual or so-called satanic abuse in the British Isles.[152]

There is no doubt that a great wrong was perpetrated against children and their parents in Orkney. But the long term consequences of the affair have cast a shadow over child protection practise in this country and more especially have harmed the relationship between child protection workers and parents. Social workers are no longer trusted. Orkney has come to symbolise the interfering state and the powerlessness of parents. This is vividly demonstrated in one woman's reaction in 1994 to a letter she received from her social worker: 'When I got the letter I was very shocked. I said "Ah-ah...what's happening with the social worker! What have I done? Are they coming to take my children away?" I was scared. I hoped that what happened to the Orkneys isn't going to happen to me now...'[153]

Why has sexual abuse become the obsession of the late twentieth century? Despite evidence that sexual abuse within the family was recognised in the nineteenth century, the labelling of such abuse as incest and the attempt to shift responsibility for other forms of sexual assault outside the home, placing the blame on 'monsters', meant that child welfare professionals perpetuated an atmosphere of denial which protected the perpetrators and silenced the victims.[154] Part of the explanation for the contemporary obsession with sexual abuse undoubtedly lies in a greater willingness of victims, many of them now adults, to speak out about the abuse they suffered in the past.[155] Media coverage of the issue has rekindled memories of time spent in care and prompted a reassessment of the care received. 'You hear a lot more about child abuse now than you ever did' commented one former children's home resident who recalled a number of incidents ranging from inappropriate touching and fondling to the singling out of boys for personal attention, perceived as harmless or merely odd at the time but which today might be interpreted as abuse.[156] However, despite evidence that a child is more at risk from abuse by relatives and friends within the home than from strangers, the popular construction of sexual abuse continues to deny this fact. The revelations centred upon children's homes, the popular media campaign to name and shame paedophiles which has prompted a regulatory response from government, and the Orkney fiasco tend to shield the family from suspicion. This is not to argue that sexual abuse is endemic in Scottish society; rather, it suggests there is still a tendency by those outside the child protection agencies to deny intra-familial abuse (not only perpetrated by adults but also by siblings) by focusing on the traditional scapegoats: perverts and bogey-men.

In 1989, Prime Minister Margaret Thatcher summarised the underlying principles of what was to become the Children Act: 'Children are entitled to protection from harm and abuse, and innocent families from unnecessary intervention by the state.'[157] For more than a century of child protection practise those in the business of rescuing children from abuse have walked a tightrope between the rights of the family and the safety of the child. Various parties have been blamed for the harm inflicted upon children — working-class parents, neglectful mothers, cruel men, wicked paedophiles — but few listened to the voices of the children themselves. Harry Wilson, Richard Clark and the victims of abuse in residential homes were left to suffer in silence. 'When I think about it now you read about cases of child care and abuse' commented Peter; 'I think we were treated worse than that and nobody said boo and we didnae say anything. You can appreciate the cases you hear on television people reporting 30, 40 years… you can see why it can come out.'[158]

NOTES

1. *Glasgow Herald*, 23 July 1945.
2. *Glasgow Herald*, 2 August 1945.
3. SRO, JC 26/1738: High Court (Northern Circuit) Processes.
4. *Ibid.*
5. *Glasgow Herald*, 4 August 1945.
6. *The Scotsman*, 2 and 3 August 1945.
7. *The Scotsman*, 3 August 1945.
8. *The Times*, 15 February and 17 March 1945.
9. *The Times*, 16 March 1945.
10 *The Scotsman*, 4 August 1945.
11. *The Scotsman*, 4 August 1945.
12. There was subsequently an official inquiry into the Gough case; see *B.P.P., Report by Sir Walter Monckton on the circumstances which led*

to the boarding out of Dennis and Terence O'Neill at Bank Farm, Minsterley and the steps taken to supervise their welfare, 1945, Cmd.6636. There was no inquiry into the Walton case.

13. *The Scotsman*, 16 March 1945.
14. SRO, ED 11/154: C.A.Kersh evidence to Clyde Committee, 1945.
15. This has occurred already in Stirling and in Inverness. See 'Community in fear after paedophile returns home', *Scotland on Sunday*, 22 March 1998.
16. 'Minded out of their Minds', *The Observer*, 29 March 1998.
17. H.Hendrick, *Children, Childhood and English Society 1880–1990* (Cambridge, 1997), p.78.
18. Interview with David.
19. See N.Parton, *The Politics of Child Abuse* (Basingstoke, 1985), pp.48–99.
20. *The Scotsman*, 2 August 1945.
21. Hendrick's exact words are '"abusing" parents are ever present' but I would extend this definition to include adults responsible for the care of children. *Child Welfare*, p.242.
22. Between 1889 and 1894 the Scottish Society for the Prevention of Cruelty to Children existed as an independent organisation. In 1894 the SNSPCC affiliated with the NSPCC in England to become the NSPCC Scottish branch. In 1922 it received the Royal Charter and was renamed the Royal Scottish Society for the Prevention of Cruelty to Children (RSSPCC). In 1992 the name was changed to Children 1st and the organisation ceased its investigative work.
23. Mackenzie, *Scottish Mothers and Children*, p.186.
24. SRO, GD 409/5/15: Edinburgh Committee Annual Report, 1900.
25. Mackenzie, *Scottish Mothers and Children*, pp.188–9. The comparable figures for NSPCC investigations in England are as follows for the period 1884–1914: 812,682 cases investigated involving 2,260,292 children. There were 55,292 prosecutions. Ferguson, 'Cleveland in History', p.149.
26. GCU, RSSPCC Archive: Annual Reports 1919–1930.
27. SRO, GD 409/3/1: NSPCC Case Committee Minute Book, 1907–1910 (Edinburgh Committee).
28. SRO, GD 409/57/3: unidentified newspaper cutting, 1914.
29. Mackenzie, *Scottish Mothers and Children*, p.198.
30. SRO, GD 409/5/15: Number of cases investigated in Scotland during the year 1900.
31. For a full discussion of the debates surrounding the introduction of the Bill see G.K.Behlmer, *Child Abuse and Moral Reform in England, 1870–1908* (Satnford, Ca., 1982), chapter 4.
32. L.Fox-Harding, *Perspectives in Child Care Policy* (London, 1991).
33. Hendrick, *Child Welfare*, p.218.
34. SRO, ED 11/403: Working Party on Children Neglected in their Own Homes, 23 December 1949. This working party was set up to

address the problem of prevention of cruelty to children, an issue not within the remit of the Clyde and Curtis Committees.

35. J.Harris, *Private Lives, Public Spirit: Britain 1870–1914* (Oxford, 1993), p.75.
36. Hendrick, *Child Welfare*, p.59.
37. See GCA, D-HEW 27/3: Parish of Govan Combination, Intimations and Prosecutions, 1911–16.
38. Mackenzie, *Scottish Mothers and Children*, p.188.
39. SRO, GD 409/57/3: unidentified newspaper report, 1915.
40. SRO, GD' 409/19/4: *The Scotsman*, 19 April 1934.
41. SAS, PD 41: Whinwell Case Files, K 83 (1892).
42. Extract from SNSPCC Annual Report, 1910 in B.Ashley, *A Stone on the Mantlepiece* (Edinburgh, 1985), pp.87–8.
43. In Ashley, *A Stone on the Mantlepiece*, pp.77–8.
44. Report to the Executive Committee of the SNSPCC, 1932 in Ashley, *A Stone on the Mantlepiece*, p.115.
45. SRO, GD 409/29/4/4: Inspector's Report on visit to North West (undated).
46. SRO, GD 409/29/4/1: General Reports by Inspectors of the RSSPCC on Condition of Children in the North West, Hebrides and Shetland, 1906.
47. See Mackenzie, *Scottish Mothers and Children*, chapter 46, 'The Caithness Tinkers'.
48. Cited in Ashley, *A Stone on the Mantlepiece*, p.96.
49. SAS, PD 41: Whinwell Case Files, M 45a (1903).
50. SNSPCC Executive Committee, Motherwell and Wishaw branch, 1932 in Ashley, *A Stone on the Mantlepiece*, p.118.
51. GCU, RSSPCC Archive: Annual Report, 1977.
52. GCU, RSSPCC Archive: Case records database. The database contains anonymised details of 6635 cases.
53. Estimated percentage of Catholics in Glasgow in 1984 = 31%. Calculated from figures on church membership in P.Brierley and F.Macdonald, *Prospects for Scotland: Report of the 1984 Census of the Churches* (Edinburgh, 1985), p.90.
54. GCU, RSSPCC Archive: Case L64/158.
55. For an excellent analysis of the subjective practice of the NSPCC see H.Ferguson, 'Rethinking Child Protection Practices' in The Violence Against Children Study Group (eds.), *Taking Child Abuse Seriously* (London, 1990), pp.121–42.
56. Dunbar, 'Philanthropy in Twentieth Century Glasgow', MPhil, 1997, p.82.
57. SRO, GD 409/5/5: Report of the Work in the Eastern District, 1890.
58. 'The Traffic in Infants', *Glasgow Herald*, 5 January 1908.
59. SAS, PD 41: Whinwell Case Files, H 45 (1903).
60. Little appears to have changed, despite studies which show that although woman are the majority of emotional abusers, physical and especially sexual abuse is a predominantly male phenomenon. In 1987 the mother was found to be the perpetrator in only one per

cent of sexual abuse cases. See C.Parton, 'Women, Gender Oppression and Child Abuse' in *Taking Child Abuse Seriously*, p.43.

61. SAS, PD 41/1/1: Whinwell Children's Home Annual Report, 1895.
62. SAS, PD 41/4/5: *Fifty Years on a Scottish Battlefield, 1873–1923*, p.33.
63. SAS, PD 41: Whinwell Case Files, I 58 (1914).
64. *Ibid.*, F 52 (1920).
65. Aberlour Orphanage Case Files, schedule 1123.
66. SAS, PD 41: Whinwell Case Files, F 60 (1912).
67. *Ibid.*, M 29 a (1893).
68. Aberlour Orphanage Case Files, schedule 209.
69. SAS, PD 41/1/1: Whinwell Children's Home Annual Report, 1907.
70. SRO, GD 409/6/1: Conviction Book 1902–34, case 38.34.
71. SRO, GD 409/1/5: Edinburgh District Committee Minute Book, 1912–22.
72. *Ibid.*
73. Ashley, *A Stone on the Mantlepiece*, p.108.
74. 1916: 40 cases, 21 drunken mothers; 1917: 25/21; 1918: 21/17; 1920: 39/12. SRO, GD 409/6/1: Conviction Book 1902–34.
75. SRO, GD 409/19/4: *The Scotsman*, 12 November 1931.
76. Women's Group on Public Welfare, *The Neglected Child and His Welfare: A Study made in 1946–7* (London, 1948), p.22. Their studies showed that cases of severe neglect and wilful cruelty were few and far between. Only 36 cases of serious neglect were found amongst 2,256 cases of widows receiving supplementary pensions and amongst 234 cases of children admitted to Dr Barnardo's homes, only 8% were as a result of wilful neglect while 59% were categorised as arising from misfortune.
77. On the supervision of women in Blackhill see A.McGuckin, 'Moving Stories: Working-Class Women' in Breitenbach and Gordon (eds.), *Out of Bounds*, pp.197–220.
78. GCU, RSSPCC Archive: Case H 848.
79. See L.Gordon, *Heroes of their Own Lives: the Politics and History of Family Violence, Boston 1880–1960* (London, 1989), p.4.
80. Mackenzie, *Scottish Mothers and Children,* p.188. GCU, RSSPCC Archive database.
81. Hendrick, *Child Welfare*, pp.57–8.
82. Interview with Peter.
83. *The Scotsman*, 20 November 1997.
84. Recorded interview,'Woman's Hour', BBC Radio 4, 19 December 1997.
85. See J.Walkowitz, *City of Dreadful Delight: Narratives of Sexual Danger in Victorian Britain* (London, 1992). In Scotland, along with the SNSPCC and the NVA, the Free Church and the United Presbyterian Church had agitated for reform of the age of consent and the repeal of the Contagious Diseases Acts. See K.M.Boyd, *Scottish Church Attitudes to Sex, Marriage and the Family 1850–1914* (Edinburgh, 1980), pp.210–1.

86. Mackenzie, *Scottish Mothers and Children*, p.188. Mahood notes that various child protection agencies before 1920 made only indirect references to incest or sexual abuse and preferred the charge of 'wandering' which indicated a girl was too frightened to return home. Mahood, *Policing Gender, Class and Family*, p.107.
87. Louise A.Jackson, '"For the Sake of the Children": Policing Sexual Abuse in London 1870–1914', unpublished paper, 1996.
88. SRO, GD 409/57/2: RSSPCC, Report by Executive Committee for 1931. This low figure for indecent or sexual assault is possibly explained by the separate crime of incest but may also reflect the secrecy of this crime.
89. Mackenzie, *Scottish Mothers and Children*, p.188. The SNSPCC recorded 1,577 such cases between 1885 and 1915.
90. See Gordon, *Heroes of their Own Lives*.
91. See parallel developments in the United States described in Gordon, *Heroes of their own Lives*, pp.22–3.
92. SRO, ED 11/447: Number of cases of assault or other sexual or indecent offenses reported to the police in Scotland, 31 July 1921–31 July 1924.
93. SRO, ED 11/447: Miss Helen Blair, policewoman, Western Division Glasgow evidence to Departmental Committee.
94. SRO, ED 11/447: Headmaster, Bristol Public School, Edinburgh evidence to Departmental Committee.
95. SRO, ED 11/447: Miss Helen Blair to Departmental Committee.
96. SRO, ED 11/447: Paper 30: child assault case heard at Stirling Burgh Police Court, 1925. Names have been anonymised.
97. SRO, ED 11/447: National Vigilance Association of Scotland, evidence to Departmental Committee.
98. SRO, ED 11/447: Park-keeper Gray, Kings Park Edinburgh evidence to Departmental Committee.
99. Only one witness giving evidence to the committee admitted that 'even males of education and good standing have figured conspicuously in the offenses'. SRO, ED 11/447: W.Grassick, Superintendent Dumbarton.
100. SRO, ED 11/447: W.Grassick, superintendent Dumbarton.
101. SRO, ED 11/447: Stirling Burgh Police Court, child assault case.
102. SRO, ED 11/447: Mrs I.Nisbett, Inspector in Women's Auxiliary Service, evidence to Departmental Committee.
103. SRO, ED 11/447: Park-keeper Gray, evidence to Departmental Committee.
104. SRO, ED 11/447: D.Macphater, City of Glasgow Police.
105. See Mahood, *Policing Gender, Class and Family*, pp.107–9 on 'wandering girls'.
106. Kent, *Children's Safeguards Review*, p.88. Only 10 per cent of abusers in a recent study (1994) were strangers to the child, (Kent p.9). See also C.Parton, 'Women, gender oppression and child abuse', p.43. Citing a 1987 study she shows that 31 per cent of

sexual abuse in England and Wales was committed by the biological father, 26% by a father substitute and 35% by another male relative, neighbour or friend.

107. SRO, ED 11/447: Policewoman Helen Blair, Glasgow Western Division.

108. See Mahood, *Policing Gender, Class and Family*, pp.124–32.

109. However, even today the discourse of the knowing female child who invites or invents abuse is still present. See the London High Court case, February 1998 involving the prosecution and acquittal of several very young boys for the alleged rape and indecent assault of a young girl.

110. GCU, RSSPCC Archive: case H 922.

111. GCU, RSSPCC Archive database.

112. Today in Scotland children's homes are subject to inspections by the local authority, HMI when education is supplied on the premises, the Social Work Services Inspectorate and the Mental Welfare Trust. Some Scottish local authorities employ Children's Rights Officers. Children in care also have access to ChildLine, an independent telephone helpline. Kent, *Children's Safeguards Review*, p.65 & 81.

113. Williams of Mostyn, *Childhood Matters: Report of the National Commission of Inquiry into the Prevention of Child Abuse* (London, HMSO, 1996), p.19.

114. This approach was pioneered by Nigel Parton in *The Politics of Child Abuse.*

115. SRO, ED 11/154: 'Letter to Nobody', evidence submitted to Clyde Committee.

116. *B.P.P., Report on the Circumstances which led to the boarding out of Dennis and Terence O'Neill*, 1945, Cmd.6636.

117. *Report of the Committee of Inquiry into the consideration given and steps taken towards securing the welfare of Richard Clark by Perth Town Council and other bodies or persons concerned*, (HMSO, Edinburgh, 1975).

118. This is not to say that foster care is safer than children's homes. ChildLine has received a high percentage of calls from children in foster care telling about abuse. *The Guardian*, 20 November 1997.

119. One of the eight fundamental principles underpinning residential care in Scotland as laid down in the Skinner Report (1993) states: 'Young people should feel safe and secure in any residential home or school'; cited in Kent, *Children's Safeguards Review*, p.7.

120. SRO, ED 11/158: National Vigilance Association of Scotland, evidence to Clyde Committee.

121. Interview with former resident, *The Guardian*, 8 November 1997.

122. 'A Time for Penance', *Frontline Scotland*, BBC Scotland, 10 February 1998.

123. *The Guardian*, 8 November 1997; *Scotland on Sunday*, 25 January 1998; *The Scotsman*, 26 January 1998. See also Aberdeen *Evening Times*, 10, 11, 12 June 1997.

124. *The Guardian*, 8 November 1997.
125. See the case of a housemaster at Aberlour Orphanage whose violent and unorthodox treatment of the boys was reported by another member of staff resulting in the dismissal of both men. SRO, ED 11/154, correspondence, January 1947.
126. SRO, ED 11/154: Robert McVeigh to Clyde Committee, 1945.
127. SRO, ED 11/154: anonymous letter, evidence to Clyde Committee, 1945.
128. Recorded interview, 'Woman's Hour', BBC Radio 4, 19 December 1997.
129. SRO, ED 11/154: Dr Barnardo to Sgt Young, North Berwick regarding Redholm Home, 2 January 1945.
130. 'Childhood's Betrayed', *The Scotsman*, 5 December 1997.
131. 'A Time for Penance', BBC Scotland. Broadcast 10 February 1998. Similar stories were recounted by girls held in Ireland's magdalene homes during the same period. See 'Sex in a Cold Climate', Channel 4, broadcast 16 March 1998.
132. *The Scotsman*, 5 December 1997.
133. 'A Time for Penance', BBC Scotland.
134. Kent. *Children's Safeguards Review*, p.91.
135. Hendrick, *Child Welfare*, p.254.
136. According to the Joint Steering Group for Child Protection in Scotland (1992), sexual abuse is defined as follows: 'any child below the age of 16 may be deemed to have been sexually abused when any person(s), by design or neglect, exploits the child, directly or indirectly, in any activity intended to lead to the sexual arousal or other forms of gratification of that person or any other person(s) including organised networks. This definition holds whether or not there has been genital contact and whether or not the child is said to have initiated the behaviour.'
137. Ferguson, 'Cleveland in History', p.147.
138. *Statistical Bulletin: Social Work Series* (Scottish Office, October 1997), p.19.
139. Williams of Mostyn, *Childhood Matters*, p.9.
140. *The Scotsman*, 4 March 1991.
141. *The Scotsman*, 4 March 1991.
142. D.H.S.Reid, *Suffer the Little Children. The Orkney Child Abuse Scandal* (St.Andrews, 1992), p.11; *The Scotsman*, 5 March 1991; K.Winter, *The Day They Took Away our Children* (Norwich, 1992), pp.16–17.
143. Cited in Winter, *The Day*, p.22.
144. *The Scotsman*, 2 March 1991.
145. *Ibid.*
146. Indeed, the Inquiry report noted that '...the campaign mounted to support the parents in seeking the return of the children did not assist towards constructive dialogue...' *The Report of the Inquiry into*

the Removal of Children from Orkney in February 1991 (HMSO, Edinburgh, 1992), p.352.

147. See S.Asquith (ed), *Protecting Children. Cleveland to Orkney: More Lessons to Learn?* (Edinburgh, 1993).

148. *Report of the Inquiry into the Removal of Children from Orkney* (1992).

149. This argument has been strongly argued by Liz Kelly who talks about 'creating a child abusers' charter'. *The Death of Childhood*, BBC 1, broadcast May 1997.

150. *The Scotsman*, 22 March 1991.

151. B.Campbell, 'Questions of Cleveland Will Not Go Away', *The Scotsman*, 3 June 1997.

152. *Child Protection: Messages from Research*, (London, 1995), p.74.

153. *Child Protection: Messages from Research*, p.27.

154. See L.de Mause's controversial article, 'The Universality of Incest' in *The Journal of Psychohistory*, 19 (1991), pp.123–64.

155. In a survey carried out on behalf of the National Commission of Inquiry into the Prevention of Child Abuse in 1996, 1,121 letters were received from people who had suffered from abuse and other interested parties. 80% of writers referred to experiences of sexual abuse, rape or molestation. C.Wattam and C.Woodward, '"And do I abuse my children?...No!"', in *Childhood Matters*, Vol.2.

156. Interview with David.

157. Cited in Fox-Harding, *Perspectives in Child Care Policy*, p.234.

158. Interview with Peter.

CHAPTER 7
THE VOICE OF THE CHILD

It wasn't a life when you look back, for any girl...I didn't let it affect me, I just made the best of life as I could...

— Annie: Bethany Home, Aberdeen 1914-21

Scotland — a Caring Nation?

The humanity and progress of any society may be judged by how it treats its children and particularly those children denied a normal home life. In Scotland the challenge was pressing owing to the ongoing and persistent crises from the early nineteenth century. The Scottish family, both in urban and rural parts of the country, has been constantly under strain from overcrowded, inadequate housing, a low wage economy, high rates of geographical mobility and waves of urban regeneration. Community support networks could never hope to provide a wholly adequate safety-net for children whose parents could not provide for them. Although children were absorbed into substitute families at times of pressing need, these measures were generally short term. Within this context, a distinctive Scottish child welfare policy developed with roots that lay in the kirk's poor relief system and in religious charitable provision. Boarding out was the most distinctive element of a Scottish approach to the care of pauper children which involved separating children from parents and relatives judged unfit to take responsibility for their welfare and placing them in a moral environment. Scotland's rural areas, and especially the crofting counties, were judged ideal for the moral and spiritual re-education of these urban waifs. At the same time, religious charities and voluntary initiatives inspired by evangelical missionaries were wholeheartedly encouraged as a necessary adjunct to local authority welfare provision. By the First World War the map of Scottish child welfare was both institutionally and ideologically characterised by a morality derived from charity and the church.

The primary role of the child welfare system in Scotland from the mid-nineteenth century to the present day was to act as a crutch for families in crisis. Most families did not require a permanent child care solution, but a temporary period of respite. Voluntary homes helped families to survive. Parents used the system, often to their own advantage. Yet, until the Second World War, there was a fundamental mismatch between parents' expectations of the child welfare system and the aims of the child savers. It would not be an exaggeration to say that child welfare workers have used the solutions at their disposal — boarding out, emigration, residential care — as a form of social engineering. Separating children from their parents, severing all contacts with their cultural roots, instilling children with the values of the church, and physically removing them to underpopulated parts of Scotland and the colonies thereby creating new families, were all strategic responses to a fear of urban degeneration and hereditary pauperism. The image of the rural crofting or farming family — independent, hardworking, moral, sober and untainted by urban vice — dominated Scottish child welfare policy and practice right up until World War Two.

However, it would be misleading to make too strong a case for the distinctiveness of the Scottish system. Boarding out aside — and even this was increasingly favoured by English authorities from the turn of the century — there is little to distinguish children's experience of care in Scotland from their counterparts elsewhere. Scotland contained two of the largest children's homes in the British Isles despite her pretence of rejecting institutionalisation; child emigration was as enthusiastically promoted in Scotland as it was in England; and despite Scotland being in the vanguard of child guidance work in the inter-war period, children in care drew little benefit from this progressive ideology until the 1950s. Neither has the Scottish child welfare system been immune to accusations of abuse. Yet the popular and, until recently, official perception was that a homeless child in Scotland could expect a better standard of care and greater protection from mistreatment than his or her counterpart in England.

Until the Orkney crisis in 1991 the Scottish child welfare system had never before excited such public interest and concern. It is unfortunate that the rights of children have not, until now, prompted such an outcry in Scotland. While the death of Dennis O'Neill in England in 1945 did induce some soul searching south of the border, the Scottish reaction was to complacently perpetuate the popular fallacy of the supremacy of the Scottish system. Less than six months later the reaction of the Scottish press to the trial of the Waltons in Dundee for the abuse of Harry Wilson was muted. The leader writer in the *Glasgow Herald* spoke of the problems of dealing with 'difficult' children and blamed the breakdown of the boarding-out system on 'the general disruption of life' in the immediate post-war period.[1] Once again, in 1946 following the publication of the Clyde Report, *The Scotsman* proudly opined that 'the whole tenor of the report issued today…is in keeping with the highest traditions of social reform in this country.'[2] In 1974 the inquiry into the abuse of Richard Clark by private foster parents in Perth aroused little more than a murmur in contrast with the Maria Colwell inquiry in England some months earlier. Even today, the belief that the Scottish welfare system has, in the main, served its children well is perpetuated by ill-informed eulogies to well known Scottish institutions. Although not the worst children's home by any means it is surely naive to state that 'Quarrier's basic philosophy of clean air and solid teaching seemed to work', and to proclaim that 'there were few failures'.[3] As revelations about the abuse of children in Edinburgh children's homes over a number of years and allegations of a catalogue of emotional, physical and sexual abuse in institutions run by Catholic religious orders seeps into the public consciousness in Scotland, a more realistic, practical and effective strategy for the protection of children which involves listening to children's needs and acting upon them is surely a positive step.[4]

Adult Power and Children's Rights

The history of child welfare and protection is partly the history of the fluctuating power of child welfare workers over the family. Parents have seen their authority wane as philanthropists, child-savers and, more recently, social workers have taken decisions about children's future. As a result, children were transferred from a family environment which may have been characterised by a complex mixture of relations based on affection, economic reciprocity and so on, to a non-negotiable situation in which the child had few rights and the guardian possessed more absolute and uncomplicated power than a parent. That power relationship, which has remained largely unchanged until quite recently, is at the heart of this study. Granted the responsibility to protect and care for the most vulnerable children in our society, adults have used this power in their own interests. These interests do not always coincide with the interests of the child. This dissociation of the interests of adults and children is most starkly illustrated by the child emigration programme. Economic considerations, moral concerns, imperial ambitions and missionary zeal — all were used to justify a policy which severed children from their families, friends and cultural roots. No-one sought to elicit the views of the children themselves. Those who enthusiastically volunteered to go had little understanding of what emigration entailed and no-one disabused them of the belief that they were embarking upon an adventure. In other parts of the system decisions were made to remove children from parents, and especially lone mothers, purportedly in the children's interests. Children were driven to remote parts of the country and dumped on guardians who agreed to look after them for payment. At no time were the children themselves asked what they wanted to happen to them. It was not until the 1980s that children within the care system were accepted as possessing an audible voice and independent rights to influence their destiny.

Too often adults used their power carelessly and sometimes callously. Although the deliberate abuse of power has been rare, the systematic oppression of children for adult purposes was symptomatic of a welfare system founded upon charity. In orphanages children were subjected to a disciplinary regime which served the interests of the carers. In many cases it was a regime that tried to sap the spirit of the young inmates. Strong doses of religion, a banal and pappy diet, a complex system of rewards and punishments, a limited education and little time for play rendered children docile and malleable. Annie remembered the girls in her orphanage were sent to bed at 6 o'clock every night, were dressed in uniforms and taught to observe an arcane routine so that life 'was just an existence from morning to night.' 'You see we was frightened to do anything wrong you see. The religion wouldn't let us do that.'[5] Continual observation, day and night, instilled fear in those who had done nothing wrong. Children in one Catholic orphanage were regularly checked through the night to ensure they slept with their arms crossed over their chests; failure to adopt this holy sleeping position resulted in being woken by a thrashing.[6] What is so depressing about the history of child welfare in Scotland as elsewhere is the fact that although adults entrusted with the care of children had the power of enablement and enhancement, more often than not they created a repressive system which stifled children's exuberance and restricted their choices. Adult reminiscences, informed by late twentieth century notions of childhood defined as dependence, ignorance, freedom from economic responsibility and the desirability of play, sometimes define their own childhood years as a lost childhood. Refused comics and sweets, games and toys, subjected to continual beatings and sent out to work during school holidays, Peter described his 12 years with a foster family as 'a lost childhood, completely lost.'[7] Few were able to subvert the system although challenging the dress code, sneaking out to steal apples or buy sweets were small but not insignificant signs of children's independence. Running away was probably the most direct means of challenging the system. Few succeeded — they had nowhere and nobody to run to — but some did manage to escape. Eight year old Hugh, partially disabled and living with his adoptive mother, a miner father on strike and nine children in a three-roomed house near Stirling in the 1930s, was sent away to a home in St Andrews by 'the cruelty'. On only his second day there, Hugh recalled:

> we were out walking and I was in the rear, when we passed a bus just leaving…and it was going to Stirling so I jumped on and told the conductress I was being met at Stirling, when we got to Stirling I got off when the bus stopped to let someone off, and I bolted and made my way home…and my mother decided I could stay.[8]

Sadly, the callous and deliberate abuse of power by those entrusted with children's care in the community has been widespread and profoundly damaging. And the refusal of adults to take responsibility for their actions, both at the time and in retrospect, indicates a continuous history of the oppression of children in the welfare system. The attitude that all children in care must, by definition, deserve some degree of punishment dies hard. In a recent interview a representative of the Catholic Church in Scotland stated that it would be very surprising if children, 'many of whom were from poor homes in the sense of broken homes, who nowadays subsequently would have been approved school children, did not need some sort of discipline reaction.'[9] Poor children, children of broken homes, children who ended up in care through no fault of their own, children often already emotionally damaged and thus extremely vulnerable, were mistreated by the very adults entrusted with their care. And until recently these children had no rights.

The end of the twentieth century has witnessed a profound shift in the power relationship between adults and children. For the first time the powerlessness of children is being redressed as children have begun to acquire rights of their own. The 1989 United Nations Convention on the Rights of the Child provides for the child's right to be heard in any decision that may affect his or her life, a principle that clearly has significant impact on children in the care system. In Scotland the UN principles have been incorporated in the 1995 Children (Scotland) Act which confers each child with the right to be treated as an individual; each child has the right to protection from all forms of abuse, neglect or exploitation; and every child has the right to express his or her views freely and those views should be given due weight.[10] Moreover, the Act places considerable emphasis on the requirement of all of those entrusted with child care to have regard to the views of the child, representing not simply a policy change but a fundamental attitudinal shift too.[11]

Identity and Belonging

One of the most striking features of personal narratives of childhood in care is the issue of identity. In Western culture the concept of the family is closely identified with the blood tie despite evidence suggesting that families in past times were open, flexible institutions which freely accepted new members. 'If history has a lesson for us' writes John Gillis, 'it is that no one family form has ever been able to satisfy the human need for love, comfort and security.' 'We must recognize' he continues, 'that families are worlds of our own making.'[12] Nowhere was this more true than in Scotland where several waves of urban transformation and rural poverty caused a high degree of family dislocation and reconstitution. Yet despite the evident elasticity and adaptability of the modern family, those who were forcibly separated from kin express a need to locate their identity in that lost blood family. Ever since the Poor Law which tried to separate children from dissolute parents, child care authorities deliberately severed children's ties with their blood relatives, both by physically removing the child and placing him or her at a considerable distance from family roots and by denying the child contact with or knowledge about surviving family members. Thus, throughout most of the period there was a conscious attempt to deny and even destroy the previous identity of the child. In the nineteenth century this policy of substituting nurture for nature was justified on the grounds that it would help bring an end to hereditary pauperism. In the twentieth century children were to be given a fresh start without the inconvenience of interference from family members, an attitude plainly acknowledged by a representative of Glasgow Corporation in 1945: 'Obviously blood is thicker than water...The fact remains that if the children are a good distance apart from their original upbringing, obviously the opportunities of intervention by parents are lessened.'[13] It was widely believed that continued contact with the birth family would prejudice the child's adaptation to the foster family. Both child and foster parents were kept in the dark about the child's background. Few ascribed to the alternative view, now almost universally held, expressed here in 1945 by the Educational Institute of Scotland:

> If the Homeless child is not to indulge in unhealthy fantasy, or become a prey to the first unfortunate suggestion regarding his parentage, he should be told the truth about his origin, however unpleasant it may be. If the child is to grow up with any regard for truth and any trust in those who have nurtured him, he should be answered kindly and gently but truthfully, when he asks about his parentage.[14]

Secrecy by the authorities and ignorance on the part of carers meant some children were left in limbo, denied knowledge about their natural family but never really accepted as an equal member of the foster family either. 'We were never treated as one of the family; no no you knew exactly what you were' commented Peter.[15] In many respects boarding out left children in a no-man's land. A child with two surnames was immediately identifiable as a 'boarded-out', as was a child with distinctive clothing or one who was unable to speak Gaelic. For many, whether they were well or ill-treated, researching their birth family and the circumstances in which they were taken into care has helped them to come to terms with childhood experiences. Betty spent a happy, almost idyllic childhood on Tiree with a loving couple but she still felt driven to find out why she had been sent there. 'I was accepted by that family…That is my family, and I've got my own family but they're there as well but to my dying day I'll not forget them and all the kindness they showed me.'[16]

For increasingly large numbers of former boarded-out children and residents of children's homes, discovering the truth about the circumstances in which they were taken into care, including the identity of their parents and siblings, has enabled them to recover some elements of a lost identity. Fortunately, this quest has been made easier by the fact that the larger children's homes like Quarrier's and Aberlour have retained original admission records and local authorities, especially Glasgow Corporation, kept meticulous records. For some the physical resemblance of blood family members establishes a link with a family they never knew. As Betty told me, 'I can see it in the pictures, I'm very like my mother'[17] Frances admitted to curiosity about her birth family when she had had her own children, commenting, 'I'd think I wonder where that one takes, my family…the looks…to hold your baby and say "Oh that's uncle's this and this and that"'.[18] Frances, who was boarded-out as a baby, had always been told by her foster mother that her natural mother 'was only 16 and her mother wouldn't have her'. She subsequently discovered the story was untrue, that unknown to her foster parents her mother had been a 20 year-old, single Jewish woman in Glasgow, whose parents had disowned her when she became pregnant by a Glasgow Protestant man. For Frances, the search for her mother was given added significance. 'When I found out I was Jewish I thought now I should've had a chance to follow my culture…because reading up you'll never be a Jew.'[19]

Since the Second World War there has been far greater awareness by the child care profession of the strength of the bonds between children and their natural parents. One result of this has been the emphasis on support for the family, initiatives to restore children to their birth parents whenever possible, and legislation to permit children placed in care to trace their birth parents and gain access to information held by local authorities and voluntary organisations on their care history. Most child care organisations such as Barnardo's, Quarrier's Homes and Aberlour Child Care

Trust, employ people to respond to enquiries from former residents of children's homes and those who were boarded out, in an attempt to reconstruct an identity from fragmentary information. Addresses of these organisations are contained in the Appendix to this book. For some, the process of discovering roots has been revelatory and satisfying. 'Having just made contact with my two brothers, I know I had a far better upbringing and they were brought up by their natural parents' wrote one woman with a very happy experience as a boarded-out child.[20] For others, such as this man boarded out on South Uist, the process of discovery is unnecessary.'The upbringing which I got in this home has made me what I am. There's nothing surer than that, nothing surer.'[21]

The child care system leaves an indelible mark on all those who experience it. For some the mark is visible to others. 'There's a stain on you, a stain and I don't ken anything in this world that would leave a stain so much', reflected one former orphanage boy.[22] For others the mark is personal, something not readily revealed to others. What is undeniable is that an individual's childhood experience has long term effects which may reverberate for generations. As one respondent said to me, 'I spoil my kids rotten...in fact they're living my childhood you know.'[23]

At the close of the twentieth century child welfare is constantly at the forefront of the public agenda. This was not always so as we have seen from the last 150 years of child welfare policy and practice. The challenge for policy-makers and practitioners in the twenty-first century will be to continue listening to children in order to learn lessons from those who experienced pain and happiness, sadness and love.

NOTES

1. *Glasgow Herald*, 4 August 1945.
2. SRO, ED 11/162: Press Cuttings, *The Scotsman*, 8 October 1946.
3. *Glasgow Herald*, 4 February 1998.
4. See the recommendations contained in Kent, *Children's Safeguards Review*.
5. Interview with Annie.
6. 'A Time for Penance', BBC *Frontline Scotland*, broadcast 10 February 1998.
7. Interview with Peter.

8. Correspondence with Hugh.
9. Bishop of Aberdeen, Rt.Rev. Mario Conti, speaking on 'A Time for Penance', *Frontline Scotland*, BBC Television, 10 February 1998.
10. Kent, *Children's Safeguards Review*, p.91.
11. Kent, p.91.
12. John R.Gillis, *A World of their own Making. A History of Myth and Ritual in Family Life* (Oxford, 1997), p.240.
13. SRO, ED 11/266: Evidence of Councillor Brown to Clyde Committee, 1945.
14. SRO, ED 11/159: Memorandum from Educational Institute of Scotland to Clyde Committee, November 1945.
15. Interview with Peter.
16. Interview with Betty.
17. Interview with Betty.
18. Interview with Frances.
19. Interview with Frances.
20. Eleanor, questionnaire.
21. Pol MacCaluim (South Uist), *Air Fasdadh*.
22. Interview with Arthur.
23. Interview with David.

APPENDIX

Useful Addresses and Information

Children's Homes

Aberlour Child Care Trust
Head Office, 36 Park Terrace, Stirling FK8 2JR
Tel: 01786 450335

Quarrier's Homes
Quarrier's Village, Bridge of Weir, Renfrewshire, PA11 3SX
Tel: 01505 612224
Internet: http://www.quarriers.org.uk

Smyllum Orphanage
Daughters of Charity of St.Vincent de Paul
Provincial House, The Ridgeway, Mill Hill, London, NW7 1EH

Boarding Out & Adoption

Barnardos
Scottish Adoption Advice Service, 16 Sandyford Place, Glasgow
G3 7NB
Tel: 0141 339 0772

Glasgow City Archive (for Glasgow Corporation records)
Mitchell Library, Charing Cross, Glasgow, G3 7DN.
Tel: 0141 287 9999
email: archives@gcl.glasgow.gov

Emigration

Barnardo's
After Care Section
Tanners Lane, Barkingside, Ilford, Essex 1G6 IOG

Child Migrants' Trust
8 Kingston Road, West Bridgford, Nottingham, NG2 7AQ

Help & Advice

ChildLine (24 Hour helpline service)
Freephone 0800 1111

BIBLIOGRAPHY

A. Unpublished Documentary Sources

Scottish Record Office

Education Department Papers (ED)
Royal Scottish Society for the Prevention of Cruelty to Children (GD 409)
High Court Papers (JC)

Glasgow City Archives

Glasgow Parochial Board Children's Committee Papers (D-CH)
Glasgow City Health and Welfare Papers (D-HEW)
Glasgow School Records (SR)
Glasgow Parish Council Miscellaneous Prints (T-PAR)
Archive General Notes (AGN)

Stirling Archive Services

Stirling Parish Poor Law Records (SB 11)
Whinwell Children's Home Papers (PD 41)

Quarrier's Homes, Bridge of Weir

Orphan Homes of Scotland History Books Vols 1–59, 1872–1938
Canadian Register, 1872–1931
Case Files on Children Admitted to Orphan Homes of Scotland
Narrative of Facts, 1880–1960

Aberlour Child Care Trust Headquarters, Stirling

Aberlour Orphanage Case Files
Register of Admissions

Glasgow Caledonian University

Royal Scottish Society for the Prevention of Cruelty to Children Archive and database.
Glasgow Papers (G)
National Papers (N)

B. Oral History Sources and Correspondence

Interviews

Annie. b.1907 Aberdeen. 1914–21 Bethany House Children's Home, Aberdeen.

Betty. b.1937 Glasgow. 1937–43 boarded out to Cullen, Aberdeenshire. 1943–56 boarded out to Tiree.

Christine b.1920 Moray. 1928–35 Aberlour Orphanage.

Frances b.1936 Glasgow. 1936–54 boarded out to Aberdeenshire.

Arthur b.1911 Aberdeen. 1920–24 Aberlour Orphanage

Robert b.1934 Glasgow. 1937–48 boarded out to Banffshire.

Peter b.1934 Glasgow. 1938–48 boarded out to Invernessshire

David b.1951 Rossshire. 1955–67 Aberlour Orphanage

Tom d.o.b.unknown. 1960s teacher at Quarrier's Homes, Bridge of Weir

Correspondence

Evelyn b.1949 Rossshire. 1955–1964 Aberlour Orphanage

Eleanor b.1933 Glasgow. 1943–48 boarded out to Aberdeenshire.

Helen b.1938 Aberdeenshire. 1945–53 Aberlour Orphanage

Jean b.1935 Paisley. 1942–3 Barrholme Children's Home, Largs.

Frank b.1938 Glasgow. 1939–53 boarded out Aberdeenshire

Hugh b.1927 Stirling. 1935 Children's Home in St.Andrews

Ernest d.o.b. unknown. 1960s Aberlour Orphanage.

Other Oral History Sources

Air Fasdadh (Boarded Out). BBC Scotland, broadcast 16 and 23 January 1997. Interviews with 14 people boarded out by Glasgow Corporation to the Gaelic-speaking islands (Tiree, Eriskay, Barra and South Uist) in the 1950s and 1960s, along with residents of the islands and a representative of Glasgow Corporation.

Childhood Days at Aberlour Orphanage. Video produced by Speyside High School, 1991. Interviews with former residents and staff of Aberlour Orphanage, Aberlour, Speyside.

Woman's Hour, BBC Radio 4, broadcast 19 December 1997. Interviews with former residents of Scottish Roman Catholic Children's Homes.

The Little Emigrants, BBC Radio Scotland, broadcast 1997. Interviews with people emigrated to Canada by Quarrier's Homes and their relatives.

A Time for Penance, Frontline Scotland, BBC 2 Scotland, braodcast 10 Febuary 1998. Interviews with former residents of Scottish Roman Catholic Children's Homes and with representatives of the Catholic Church in Scotland.

C. Published Sources: Parliamentary Papers and Official Publications

Peterkin, W.A., Report on Pauper Children Boarded in the Island of Arran (B.P.P. 1863, Vol.XXII, App.A No.4).

Henley, J.J., Report on the Boarding Out of Pauper Children in Scotland (B.P.P. 1870, Vol.LVIII).

Doyle, A., Report as to the Emigration of Pauper Children to Canada (B.P.P. 1875, Vol.LXIII)

Peterkin, W.A., Report on the System in Scotland of Boarding Children in Private Dwellings (B.P.P 1893, Cmd.7140).

Report of the Departmental Committee into the Existing Systems for the Maintenance and Education of Children (Mundella Report) (B.P.P. 1896, Cmd.8027/8032 [evidence])

Parsons, C.T., Report on the Condition of Children who are in receipt of Various Forms of Poor Law Relief in Certain Parishes in Scotland (B.P.P. 1910, Cmd.5075).

Report by Sir Walter Monckton on the Circumstances which led to the Boarding Out of Dennis and Terence O'Neill (B.P.P. 1945, Cmd.6636).

Report of the Care of Children Committee (England and Wales) (B.P.P. 1945–6, Cmd.6922).

Report of the Committee of Homeless Children (Scotland) (B.P.P. 1946, Cmd.6911).

Annual Reports of the Board of Supervision for Scotland

Annual Reports of the Local Government Board for Scotland

Annual Reports of the Department of Health

Scottish Abstract of Statistics

Digest of Scottish Statistics

D. Newspapers & Contemporary Journals

Glasgow Herald

Scotland on Sunday

Scotsman

Stirling Observer

The Guardian

Poor Law Magazine

E. Selected Secondary Published Sources

Allen, A, & A.Morton, *This is Your Child. The Story of the National Society for the Prevention of Cruelty to Chidren* (London,1961).

Anthony, R., *Herds and Hinds. Farm Labour in Lowland Scotland 1900–1939* (East Linton, 1997).

Ariès, P., *Centuries of Childhood* (London, 1996).

Arnot, M.L. 'Infant Death, Child Care and the State: the Baby-Farming Scandal and the First Infant Life Protection Legislation of 1872', *Continuity and Change*, 9 (1994), pp.271–311.

Ashley, B., *A Stone on the Mantlepiece: a Centenary Social History of the RSSPCC* (Edinburgh, 1985).

Asquith, S.(ed), *Protecting Children. Cleveland to Orkney: More Lessons to Learn?* (Edinburgh, 1993).

Bagnall, K., *The Little Immigrants. The Orphans who came to Canada* (Toronto, 1980).

Bean, P. & J.Melville, *Lost Children of the Empire* (London, 1989).

Behlmer, G.K., *Child Abuse and Moral Reform in England 1870–1908* (Stanford, 1982).

Blaikie, A. *Illegitimacy, Sex and Society. Northeast Scotland 1750–1900* (Oxford, 1993).

Bowlby, J., *Attachment and Loss. Vol.2: Separation, Anxiety and Anger* (London, 1973).

Boyd, W., 'The Effects of Evacuaton on the Children', *British Journal of Educational Psychology*, XI (1941), pp.120–6.

Boyd, W.(ed), *Evacuation in Scotland: a Record of Events and Experiments* (London, 1944).

Brown, C.G. 'Urbanisation and Living Conditions' in R.Pope (ed), *Atlas of British Social and Economic History since c.1700* (London, 1989), pp.170–82.

Brown, C.G., '"To be Aglow with Civic Ardours": the "Godly Commonwealth" in Glasgow 1843–1914', *Records of the Scottish Church History Society*, XXVI (1996), pp.169–95.

Burlingham, D. & A.Freud, *Infants without Families: the Case for and against Residential Nurseries* (London, 1944).

Butt, J. 'Working-Class Housing in the Scottish Cities 1900–1950' in G.Gordon & B. Dicks (eds.), *Scottish Urban History* (Aberdeen, 1983), pp.233–67.

Caldwell, J.T., *Severely Dealt With: Growing Up in Belfast and Glasgow* (Bradford, 1993).

Campbell, B., *Unofficial Secrets: Child Sexual Abuse, the Cleveland Case* (London, 1988).

Checkland, O., *Philanthropy in Victorian Scotland: Social Welfare and the Voluntary Principle* (Edinburgh, 1980).

Checkland, O., 'Maternal and Child Welfare' in O.Checkland & M.Lamb (eds.), *Health Care as Social History: the Glasgow Case* (Aberdeen, 1982), pp.117–33.

Child Protection: Messages from Research (London, 1995).

Coldrey, B., '"A Charity which has Outlived its Usefulness": the Last Phase of Catholic Child Migration', *History of Education*, 25 (1996), pp.373–86.

Collins, K.E., *Second City Jewry: the Jews of Glasgow in the Age of Expansion, 1790–1919* (Glasgow, 1990).

Constantine, S., 'Empire Migration and Social Reform 1880–1950' in C.G.Pooley & I.D.Whyte (eds.), *Migrants, Emigrants and Immigrants* (London, 1991), pp.62–83.

Cowan, E., *Spring Remembered: A Scottish Jewish Childhood* (London, 1974).

Crowther, M.A., 'Poverty, Health and Welfare' in W.H.Fraser & R.J.Morris (eds.), *People and Society in Scotland Vol.II, 1830–1914* (Edinburgh, 1990), pp.265–89.

Cunningham, H., *The Children of the Poor* (London, 1991).

Cunningham, H., *Children and Childhood in Western Society since 1500* (London, 1995).

Cunnison, J & J.B.S.Gilfillan, *The Third Statistical Account of Scotland: the City of Glasgow* (Glasgow, 1958).

Davin, A., *Growing Up Poor. Home, School and Street in London 1870–1914* (London, 1996).

Devine, T.M., 'Urbanisation', in T.M.Devine & R.Mitchison (eds.), *People and Society in Scotland Vol.I, 1760–1830* (Edinburgh, 1988), pp.27–52.

Devine, T.M., 'Women on the Land' in T.M.Devine, *Exploring the Scottish Past* (East Linton, 1995), pp.213–37.

Dinnage, R. & M.L.K.Pringle, *Residential Child Care: Facts and Fallacies* (London, 1967).

Dunae, P.A., 'Waifs: the Fairbridge Society in British Columbia, 1931–1951', *Histoire Sociale/Social History*, 42 (1988), pp.224–50.

Dwork, D., *War is Good for Babies and Other Young Children. A History of the Infant and Child Welfare Movement in England 1898–1918* (London, 1987).

Evacuation: A Collection of Sources (Strathclyde Museum Education Service).

Faley, J., *Up Oor Close: Memories of Domestic Life in Glasgow Tenements, 1910–1945* (Glasgow, 1990)

Ferguson, H., 'Cleveland in History. The Abused Child and Child Protection, 1880–1914', in R.Cooter (ed), *In the Name of the Child: Health and Welfare, 1880–1940* (London, 1992), pp.146–73.

Ferguson, T., *Scottish Social Welfare 1864–1914* (Edinburgh, 1958).

Ferguson, T., *Children in Care and After* (London, 1966).

Fox-Harding, L., *Perspectives in Child Care Policy* (London, 1991).

Gillis, J.R., *A World of their Own Making. A History of Myth and Ritual in Family Life* (Oxford, 1997).

Glasser, R., *Growing Up in the Gorbals* (London, 1986)

Gordon, E. & E.Breitenbach (eds.), *The World is Ill Divided: Women's Work in Scotland in the Nineteenth and Early Twentieth Centuries* (Edinburgh, 1990).

Gordon, E. *Women and the Labour Movement in Scotland 1850–1914* (Oxford, 1991)

Gordon, L., *Heroes of their Own Lives: the Politics and History of Family Violence, Boston 1880–1960* (London, 1988).

Hadley, E., 'Natives in a Strange Land: the Philanthropic Discourse of Juvenile Emigration from Great Britain in the Nineteenth Century', *Victorian Studies* 33 (1990), pp.411–39.

Harrison, P., *The Home Children* (Winnipeg, 1979).

Harper, M., *Emigration from North-East Scotland, Volume 2: Beyond the Broad Atlantic* (Aberdeen, 1988).

Harper, M., 'The Juvenile Immigrant: Halfway to Heaven or Hell on Earth?' in C.Kerrigan (ed), *The Immigrant Experience* (Guelph, 1992), pp.165–83.

Haynes, D., *Haste Ye Back* (London, 1973).

Henderson, M., *Finding Peggy: A Glasgow Childhood* (London, 1994).

Hendrick, H., *Child Welfare: England 1872–1989* (London, 1994).

Hendrick, H., *Children, Childhood and English Society 1880–1990* (Cambridge, 1997).

Heywood, J.S., *Children in Care: the Development of the Service for the Deprived Child* (London, 1978).

Holman, B., *Putting Families First. Prevention and Child Care* (Basingstoke, 1988).

Jamieson, L. & C.Toynbee, *Country Bairns: Growing Up 1900–1930* (Edinburgh, 1992).

Jordan, T.E., '"Stay and Starve or Go and Prosper!" Juvenile Emigration from Great Britain in the Nineteenth Century', *Social Science History*, 9 (1985), pp.145–66.

Jude, Sister (Maureen McAleer), *Freedom to Grow: Sister Marie Hilda's Vision of Child Guidance* (Glasgow, 1981).

Keir, G., 'A History of Child Guidance', *British Journal of Educational Psychology*, 22 (1952), pp.5–29.

Kent, R., *Children's Safeguards Review* (Edinburgh, 1997).

Kesson, J., *The White Bird Passes* (Edinburgh, 1958).

Kydd, R. & N. Kydd (eds.), *Growing Up in Scotland: An Anthology* (Edinburgh, 1998).

Levitt, I. & C.T. Smout, *The State of the Scottish Working Class in 1843* (Edinburgh, 1979).

Levitt, I., *Government and Social Conditions in Scotland 1845–1919* (Edinburgh, 1988).

Levitt, I., *Poverty and Welfare in Scotland 1890–1948* (Edinburgh, 1988).

Lewis, J., *The Politics of Motherhood. Child and Maternal Welfare in England, 1900–1939* (London, 1980).

Littlewood, B. & L.Mahood, 'Prostitutes, Magdalenes and Wayward Girls: Dangerous Sexualities of Working-Class Women in Victorian Scotland', *Gender and History,* 3 (1991), pp.160–75.

MacCalman, D.R., 'The General Management of Maladjustment in Children' in R.G.Gordon (ed), *A Survey of Child Psychiatry* (London, 1939).

Macdonald, H., 'Boarding-Out and the Scottish Poor Law, 1845–1914', *The Scottish Historical Review*, LXXV (1996), pp.197–220.

Mackenzie, W.L. *Scottish Mothers and Children. Being a Report on the Physical Welfare of Mothers and Children. Vol.3 Scotland* (Dunfermline, 1917).

Magnusson, A., *The Village: A History of Quarrier's* (Glasgow, 1984).

Macnicol, J., 'The Evacuation of Schoolchildren', in H.L.Smith (ed), *War and Social Change* (London, 1986), pp.3–31.

Mahood, L., *Policing Gender, Class and Family: Britain, 1850–1940* (London, 1995).

McCallum, C.M., 'Child Guidance in Scotland', *British Journal of Educational Psychology*, 22 (1952), pp.79–88.

McIvor, A.J., 'Women and Work in Twentieth Century Scotland' in A.Dickson & J.H.Treble (eds.), *People and Society in Scotland, Vol.III, 1914–1990* (Edinburgh, 1992), pp.138–73.

Middleton, N., *When Family Failed. The Treatment of Children in the Care of the Community during the First Half of the Twentieth Century* (London, 1971).

Morris, R.J., 'Urbanisation and Scotland', in W.H.Fraser & R.J.Morris (eds.), *People and Society in Scotland, Vol II, 1830–1914* (Edinburgh, 1990), pp.73–102.

Parr, J., *Labouring Children. British Immigrant Apprentices to Canada, 1869–1924* (Toronto, 1994).

Parton, N., *The Politics of Child Abuse* (London, 1985).

Parton, N.(ed), *Child Protection and Family Support. Tensions, Contradictions and Possibilities* (London, 1997).

Pinchbeck I. & M.Hewitt, *Children in English Society,* 2 Volumes (London, 1974).

Pollock, L., *Forgotten Children. Parent-Child Relations from 1500 to 1900* (Cambridge, 1983).

Ralston, A.G., 'The Development of Reformatory and Industrial Schools in Scotland, 1832–1872', *Scottish Economic and Social History*, 7 (1987), pp.40–55.

Reder, P., S.Duncan & M.Gray, *Beyond Blame. Child Abuse Tragedies Revisited* (London, 1993).

Rediscovery of the Family and Other Lectures: Sister Marie Hilda Memorial Lectures 1945–73 (Aberdeen, 1981).

Reid, D.H.S., *Suffer the Little Children. The Orkney Child Abuse Scandal* (St.Andrews, 1992).

Report of the Committee of Inquiry into the Consideration Given and Steps Taken towards Securing the Welfare of Richard Clark by Perth Town Council and Other Bodies or Persons Concerned (Edinburgh, 1975).

Report of the Inquiry into the Removal of Children from Orkney in February 1991 (Edinburgh, 1992).

Roberts, E. *A Woman's Place: An Oral History of Working-Class Women 1890–1940* (Oxford, 1984).

Robertson, B.W., 'In Bondage: the Female Farm Worker in South East Scotland' in E.Gordon & E.Breitenbach (eds.), *The World is Ill-Divided* (Edinburgh, 1990), pp.117–35.

Rodger, R.(ed), *Scottish Housing in the Twentieth Century* (Leicester, 1989).

Rodger, R. *Housing in Urban Britain 1780–1914* (Cambridge, 1989).

Rooke, P.T. & R.L.Schnell, *Discarding the Asylum: From Child Rescue to the Welfare State in English Canada (1800–1950)* (London, 1983).

Rooke, P.T, & R.L.Schnell, 'Imperial Philanthropy and Colonial Response: British Juvenile Emigration to Canada, 1896–1930', *The Historian*, 46 (1983), pp.56–77.

Ross, E., *Love and Toil: Motherhood in Outcast London 1870–1918* (London, 1992).

Rountree, G., *A Govan Childhood: the Nineteen Thirties* (Edinburgh, 1993).

Sampson, O., *Child Guidance: its History, Provenance and Future* (Manchester, 1980).

Steedman, C., *Childhood, Culture and Class in Britain: Margaret McMillan 1860–1931* (London, 1990).

Stroud, J., *An Introduction to the Child Care Service* (London, 1965).

Tait, H., 'Maternity and Child Welfare' in G.McLachlan (ed), *Improving the Common Weal: Aspects of the Scottish Health Services 1900–1984* (Edinburgh, 1987), pp.411–40.

The Violence against Children Study Group (eds.), *Taking Child Abuse Seriously* (London, 1990).

Thom, D., 'Wishes, Anxiety, Play, and Gestures: Child Guidance in Inter-war England', in R.Cooter (ed), *In the Name of the Child* (London, 1982), pp.200–19.

Treble, J., 'The Characteristics of the Female Unskilled Labour Market and the Formation of the Female Casual Labour Market in Glasgow, 1891–1914', *Scottish Economic and Social History,* 6 (1986), pp.33–46.

Urquhart, J., *The Life Story of William Quarrier* (London, 1902).

Wagner, G., *Children of the Empire* (London, 1982).

Whatley, C.A., *The Industrial Revolution in Scotland* (Cambridge, 1997).

Williams of Mostyn, *Childhood Matters: Report of the National Commission of Inquiry into the Prevention of Child Abuse* (London, 1996).

Winter, K., *The Day they Took our Children Away* (Norwich, 1992).

Women's Group on Public Welfare, *The Neglected Child and His Welfare: A Study made in 1946–7* (London, 1948).

Worsdall, F., *The Glasgow Tenement: A Way of Life* (Glasgow, 1989)

F. Unpublished Theses and Papers

Collin, M.C.Y.C., 'The Treatment of Delinquent and Potentially Delinquent Children and Young Persons in Scotland from 1866 to 1937', PhD thesis, University of Strathclyde, 1992.

Dunbar, H.M., 'Philanthropy in Twentieth Century Glasgow with Special Reference to Children', MPhil thesis, University of Strathclyde, 1987.

Gough, D., 'An Analysis of Child Abuse and Child Protection Work in Scotland', PhD thesis, University of Glasgow, 1993.

Jackson, L.A., 'For the Sake of the Children: Policing Sexual Abuse in London 1870–1914', Women's History Network conference, 1996.

Macdonald, H.J., 'Children under the Care of the Scottish Poor Law, 1880–1929', PhD thesis, University of Glasgow, 1995.

McNeilly, K., 'Public Provision for the Poor in Glasgow, 1890–1914', MPhil thesis, Glasgow College (now Glasgow Caledonian University), 1986.

Sturdy, H., 'Boarding Out the Insane, 1857–1913. A Study of the Scottish System', PhD thesis, University of Glasgow, 1996.

INDEX